One Flew ~~Over~~
The Crossbar

BRIAN KENNEDY

Published by
Zesty Thorndyke Publishing

ISBN: 987-0-9553098-2-3

WARNING

This book contains bad language, sore losers and the odd bit of nudity. It also features dire defending, awful finishing and grown men crying. Readers of a delicate disposition - and Alan Hansen - should stop reading now.

CHAPTER LISTING

"OUR GREATEST GLORY CONSISTS NOT IN NEVER FALLING,
BUT IN RISING EVERY TIME WE FALL. - Confucius

19th January 2005

Was it all just a dream?
Had I actually just seen that, or had my weary eyes been playing some cruel trick on me? Did I just witness the greatest piece of skill ever seen on the hallowed St James Park turf, or was I about to wake from my sleep with a profound sense of disappointment?
Did Scott Hiley just nutmeg Ronaldo?
I rub my eyes, check I'm not dreaming and stare down at the damp crumpled ticket in my hand.
Exeter City v Manchester United. F.A. Cup - Third Round Replay.
St James' Park. Block E - Row 16.
GET ON!!!!!

CHAPTER ONE

A LOVEABLE AFFLICTION.

OCTOBER 9TH 2004

The white round object flew high into the air amid the backdrop of a cloudy sky and the billowing smoke of the terraced houses beneath.
It hung there for a while before descending on the awaiting warriors, rising majestically into the cold evening air like eager birds of prey...
then Kwame Ampadu cuts the two legs from under their number seven!
"Have some of that Hawley!" - roared the psychotic old man in the tatty raincoat.
"Get off your arse you filthy cheat!" - echoed the man in row F who seemed just literally seconds away from five simultaneous heart-attacks had the man in blue not lifted his backside off the cold wet grass.
Magic sponge. Yellow card. Free kick.
Welcome to the Conference.
Exeter City on a cold unforgiving October evening and a couple of thousand hardy souls are urging on the men in stripes to an unlikely three points. Between the Grecians and a top eight placing stands a wall of blue - more commonly known as Carlisle United.
It had been a long, tiring trip down for the Cumbrians, who reside just a stone's throw from the borders of bonny Scotland, but they were just nine minutes away from leaving the confines of South-West England with a valuable point that would keep them top of the league table.
Behind the town end, gathered together like sardines in a can and clinging to any lingering hope of warmth, are the loyal United fans, cheering their team on, hoping for a last minute winner to make that mammoth journey back north even sweeter.
I wished they were in fear of losing everything. I prayed they were saying a decade of the rosary in vain hope of even coming out of St James Park with a point. I wanted to sense their pure fear as City launched wave after wave of attacks and witness a sea of blue were throwing legs, arms and arses everywhere in order to keep out the marauding Grecians.
That was never going to happen.
Partly due to a determined display by the visitors, but mainly down to the fact we were just crap.
Nine minutes and several thousand hoarse throats later the game fizzled out to a predictable scoreless draw. On the face of things it was a good point for Steve Perryman's men, but it couldn't hide the disappointment of 2532 fans (OK, take out the thirty-two lunatics that travelled seven hours on a bus from Scotland!), as it seemed like two points dropped rather than one gained. The former Spurs legend had just been handed the temporary reigns at St. James after the departure of Eamonn Dolan. The likeable Irishman had been a regular fixture at the club for a number of years and had been forced into the limelight at the darkest time in the club's history. On the Third of May 2003, Dolan watched helplessly as Exeter City slipped out of the football league for the first time in seventy-four years. A single Steve Flack goal in front of a packed Big Bank proved to be the final act in a season that brought nothing but

failure on the field and farce off it. A season that started with the promise of a new board, Uri Geller and Michael Jackson, ended with four managers, several arrests and Darth Vader (Spielberg are you reading this?).

The final knife in the coffin however proved to be the attendance at City's last game in Division Three against Southend United.

Not a paltry crowd of die-hard fans and interested onlookers from bygone days clinging to the hope of a miracle down the road at Swansea. Not an attendance bolstered by interested media and friends and family of the board praying the eleven men in red could win their own desperate struggle, whilst hoping Peter Taylor's Hull City could hold off the onslaught of a similarly desperate Swansea City.

No. Nine thousand souls crammed into the confines of St James Park to watch Exeter City beat the seaside club 1-0 courtesy of that Flack goal. At the end, fans gathered on the pitch to console each other and wonder if this would be the last time they would ever get to set foot in the debt-ridden club. Those that had come for the 90 minutes went home having bore witness to the demise of the club, having just become part of an unwanted piece of history by seeing Exeter City slip out of the Football League.

Me? I felt bitter.

Bitter and suicidal - (it's an interesting mix. One minute you want to kill the world the next you're trying to top yourself. Try it some time, like at the end of an away day defeat to Tamworth).

Annoyed. Severely pissed off. Bad enough the club I'd taken into my heart after six credit cards, two re-mortgages, and a shattered ankle from the worst drinking session since alcohol was invented, was being relegated, but the galling aspect that 5,000 fans had suddenly sprung out of the proverbial woodwork in a ninety-minute undying devotion to the club they couldn't be arsed to watch on a cold Tuesday in November against Rochdale.

With relegation went league status and manager Gary Peters, who had almost preformed a miracle with just three defeats in the last thirteen games and then Dolan was unwittingly trust into the limelight.

And what a cushy number good old Eamo was handed! Just the trivial task of rebuilding an entire team with no money and little managerial experience! Throw in administration, ten point deductions and a club on the brink of closure, this was not exactly a walk in the park for the Irishman - who could be forgiven for thinking he felt the dark spectre of Death and his trusty sickle hovering over him everywhere he went. Let's face it, having a trim at Sweeney Todd's barber shop would be more comfortable then the seat he landed himself in at St James.

Dolan's baptism of fire started with a disappointing draw at home to Halifax and the realism that we'd hit rock bottom came two days later when Telford United - a side who went bust and now play several divisions lower than us - destroyed City in one of the most one-sided 2-0 defeats of recent years.

At this point it's worth remembering that old chestnut – 'whatever doesn't kill you makes you stronger' - which brought me back from the brink when I was in my gas-filled kitchen with a box of matches that wouldn't light. So for better or worse, we struggled on and eventually things picked up. We entered administration, avoided the dreaded 'points deduction' and managed to pay off our creditors. The gallows had been avoided and that summer the supporters trust inherited the noose passed onto them by our two departed chairmen and took over the running of the club.

Out went the media circus of Uri, bent spoons and the dark lord of the Sith and in came pride, passion and some common sense, courtesy of a board led by Ian Huxham.

Problem solved?

No that would be too easy! A boardroom struggle ensued, the Inland Revenue wouldn't sod off, and the club began to see just how much up the creek they were without the use of a paddle. A rescue mission in the shape of RED OR DEAD was launched where 1500 people were needed to find £500 in order to keep their beloved Grecians afloat. Some shaved their heads, some tattooed their arses, some even thought about waxing their legs, donning a mini-skirt and walking the docks for lusty seamen to earn the money (sorry, but I always thought I'd look dynamite as a middle-aged prostitute).

There was no rich businessman. No knight in shining armour. No last-minute saviour at the eleventh hour to say "put your money back in the pockets lads, I'm here to save the day".

Oh to win the lottery! I bet we all had our own little moments of madness where we'd dream of winning eighty-seven million and investing it all in the lads at St James Park. I had my list all made out - all my players bought, all the stands built, now all I needed was six stupid little numbers to come up at eight o' clock on a Saturday night. When they'd come up, I was off on a round trip of premiership clubs via my boss in work to give him two well chosen universally understandable words - Fuck and Off.

First stop Arsenal to convince the greatest striker in the universe he'd be better off in South Devon than the surroundings of the Emirates Stadium. When I'd convinced Mr. Henry that he's better swapping Adebayor for Ada and Toure for Todd and blackmailed him into signing for a Cornish pasty after I produced a high quality fake of him in a seductive clinch with Vanessa Feltz, I'd be off up north to tell Shay Given he's better off at the real St James. I love the passionate Geordies, but even we've won a title since their last triumph in 1969 against the almost unpronounceable (let alone unspellable) Ujpest Dozsa. It would be easy to convince my fellow Irishman his future rests in front of the worshipping masses in the Big Bank behind a back four lead by Rob Edwards.

Why? Two words.

Titus Bramble.

Whilst on the Tyne, I'd bring Michael Owen along for the ride and then pop back down to the capital where I'd buy Tottenham Hotspur. Of course I'd then set fire to White Hart Lane and sell every one of their players to Folkestone Invicta and Worksop Town, but that's just the Arsenal in me talking! (Seriously though, I'd love to see Defoe and Berbatov slogging it out on a Sunday afternoon for Stalybridge Celtic.)

The transformation would be complete when I dismember the old grandstand (before someone lets a match fall and it goes up in exactly thirty-four seconds), and replace it with a state-of-the-art 25,000 all-seater complete with bars, restaurant and porn cinema.

Boy does reality bite! The one place the creditors, Inland Revenue and F.A. could not touch us however was on the playing field. Any dark clouds and vultures circling over a corner of Devon that is forever Exeter could be temporarily lifted when eleven men in red and white ran out to a crescendo of noise every Saturday.

That was the beauty of it all. The powers that be could sit in their ivory towers and denounce from a height how the little men had done wrong whilst bungs, kick-backs and corruption is rife higher up the scale. They can sit idly by as clubs who've inherited a mess from former employers try to battle for the right just to be able to send a team out on a weekend, whilst clubs at top level hold clandestine meetings to see how many players they can poach and what agents can flog their man for the highest price.

But at three o' clock on a Saturday that meant nothing. Even if it's just ninety minutes of a release from impending doom, you still get to bathe in the time-honoured ritual of donning a scarf, rattling the turnstiles and giving your all from the stands for your team. There had been times when it looked as if every game at St James would be the last which made the experience all the more precious when the fans filed through into the old ground, but once the whistle blew it was an hour-and- a-half of roaring your heart and soul out for the cause.

And on we battled. City didn't exactly electrify the Nationwide Conference, but the team had done enough to make sure that come the spring, Exeter would have a fighting chance of promotion and the foreboding dark clouds that had threatened to engulf the landscape around Well Street disappeared and the board could concentrate on the task of finding the monies to keep the club afloat.

The British public was given their first chance of seeing the new look Grecians that season. Sky, in their infinite wisdom, decided to bring their cameras along to Edgar Street for our Boxing Day visit to Hereford. City were without top striker Sean Devine and captain Glenn Cronin was one of the walking wounded as a patched up Exeter drew 1-1 in an entertaining game which contained the greatest miss in the history of the game of football by our beloved Steve Flack. Of course he made up for it exactly six minutes later, but it made me feel a whole lot better about the seventeen open goals I've managed to miss for my local side Kilbarry Rangers.

We went close that season. A last-day win over Accrington Stanley meant nothing as Aldershot managed to grab a draw at home to Tamworth to finish one point ahead of City to grab the final play-off spot.

Bowed but not broken, Dolan carried on, until an offer from Reading came and in September of 2004, Eamonn left to take up his job at the club's academy. It had followed the hello-goodbye trend of managers at Exeter over the past few years. Since Peter Fox had left after five seasons in the hot seat, the club had gone through managers like spit through a trumpet. After Fox vacated the seat, Noel Blake came in, hired fifty-seven players, got rid of them, then hired ninety-eight more before the arrival of Steve Perryman helped the club out of what looked like certain relegation at the time.

Blake left and City employed a former favourite in John Cornforth. The Welshman at first seemed to work his magic, but with the arrival of new chairmen in the shape of Mike Lewis and John Russell, not to mention the high profile addition of a certain Uri Geller, "Corny's" fate seemed pre-destined and he went after a home defeat to York City in only the twelfth game of the season. With the overwhelming pressure to keep Exeter in league football, rash decisions came thick and fast. The board then announced that former Manchester City stalwart Neil McNab would be next in the firing line. That appointment lasted less than four months, as the Grecians managed just one win in their last thirteen games under McNab.

After Eamonn Dolan had stood in twice during managerial departures, Gary Peters became our fourth and final manager in that fateful last season in league football. His record of five wins, five draws and just three defeats would have been worthy of promotion form but his appointment came a month too late - Exeter were relegated on the final day of the season as, despite the win over Southend at home, Swansea City defeated Hull 4-2 and finished one point ahead of us.

Talk about a kick in the nuts. Not only had the fact we'd been relegated despite winning, but a side not even from England had taken our place!

Now I'm not the sharpest tool in the box, but I know my geography. Swansea are Welsh. League of Wales = Welsh clubs. Therefore Lee Trundle and the good folks at the Liberty Stadium should pack their bags and head back to the Valleys (I really hope my auntie Anna in Caerphilly isn't reading this).

And so to Alex Inglethorpe. The thirty-three year-old, who'd once been a favourite on the field for the Grecians, would eventually take over the reigns from the departed Dolan. The Epsom-born Englishman had been coaching at Leyton Orient and also had a spell with non-league Leatherhead (or Leatherface as old Uncle Arthur used to call them, which forever gives me a mental picture of eleven players running around the field of play in masks with chainsaws in tow!)

Whilst the new man would be announced under the glare of local media, director of football Steve Perryman was looking after team affairs on the pitch. This started with the home tie against high-flying Carlisle United. The Cumbrians were very comfortable outside the surroundings of Brunton Park and hadn't lost on the road as they travelled to the South West of England that afternoon. Yet another chapter in the turbulent recent history of Exeter City FC was about to begin.

Cometh the hour, cometh the nutcase. I sensed my club needed me. I sensed there was a reason for me to be there in this hour of need. I sensed there was an exciting new chapter opening in the club's history. Most of all, I sensed if I didn't get out of the country at exactly 1.43am on Thursday the 8th of October 2004 there was a better than average chance that the next time I'd visit Exeter it would be to have my ashes shattered all over St James Park.

You see, I decided in my infinite wisdom that visiting the Pink Flamingo on the night of our anniversary was actually a very smart thing to do. Why was my wife going to worry about a silly old date in the calendar when I could stay out and enjoy the night for both of us! So instead of coming home early - box of chocs, bottle of wine and in the mood for love - I decided to avail of some free passes from my Uncle Albert and head into the hottest new club in town.

It must have taken me at least twenty minutes to twig. To twig that barmen dressed in leather with dodgy moustaches singing Village People numbers is not exactly standard bartending practice. Even then I needed the re-assurance in the shape of a body-building female, dressed in a flannel and sporting more hair than Big Foot to tell me I'd landed myself in the only gay club in the entire South-East of Ireland.

Now this I should have spotted a mile away. Not on entering the club, but the fact that Uncle Albert is a fifty-seven year-old cross-dressing drag act who lives at home with an Italian construction worker named Phillipo.

Bit of a dead giveaway that one, but when you're one sandwich short of a picnic, a sense of perception doesn't come naturally.

That night was a real test of my wedding vows to my beloved. Not only had I to admit of a memory loss to the biggest date in my wife's short history, but also being paralytic and chatting up a girl called Dolores (except "Dolores" was actually Doug from the meat counter at my local Tesco).

Luckily enough, my impending trip to Devon gave Sandra time to cool down and Gary Cooper here time to get out of Dodge City before I was shot down with another hail of verbally abusive bullets.

The now monthly ritual that is my pilgrimage to the holy shrine of St James is more than second nature to me. Every trip is meticulously planned and executed with absolute precision. From timetables to tickets, Euros to underwear, nothing is left to chance. It's normally commonplace to be so meticulous that I end up checking for my passport seventeen times, then like clockwork forget where it is the moment I get to the check-in desk.

So that cold October frost-bitten morning, I took my freezing carcass down the hill to catch the 7.30 train to Dublin. Even before the engine rattles into gear and we depart in a cloud of smoke, I know we will pull into Hueston Station, Dublin at 9.55. We may have thirty-six postal strikes a year, have a health system that could kill the fittest specimen of humanity within fifty feet of a hospital but the one thing that does work in the emerald isle is our train service.

With a time frame of just five minutes, I make my way from the platform in Dublin to the bus stop where my trusty airport-link will shuttle me and a half dozen eager holidaymakers to the airport in exactly thirty-five minutes. There's always one nut-job (usually American) who waddles his fat U.S. of A. ass along at the precise moment the jam-packed bus is ready to depart. He then explains to the hapless driver how the entire transportation system outside America sucks, before lobbing on twenty-six different cases that all contain the weight of exactly seven dead bodies.

With just forty-five minutes left to spare, I arrive, check-in and briskly jog down to terminal A - gate six to take my place in line for the 11.20am flight to Exeter International Airport. It's here where I start to unwind, realise I'm just a mere fifty minutes from Devon and indulge myself with a quick brandy to steady my nerves for the upcoming flight.

Not that I should be worried. My first ever experience of flying to Exeter involved a six-seated flying death trap, complete with super-glued wings and on-board parachutes for that inevitable plummet into the Irish Sea. Things have improved ever so slightly since then and I now board a mode of transportation that had seventy seats, a competent crew and a better than fifty-fifty chance of making it to its destination.

Minutes after midday I touch down, kiss terra firma and the weekend can officially begin. It may have been a short plane ride of less than an hour, but by this stage yours truly has been on the go nearly six hours. Long it may be, torturous at times, but when the clouds clear and the sunny South-West greet me - I'm as happy as a pig in shit! It's not that I don't get out often. I've seen Las Vegas at sunset and gambled everything I had - and lost it all on black. I've stood by the majestic Niagara Falls and watched in wonder at its beauty. I've even been in Africa when my friend 'round-a-phobia' Ron actually bought me a drink, but nothing compares to wandering up Well Street, strolling into the

Centre Spot and venturing out to the Big Bank to roar myself silly in honour of the eleven men in red and white who play for my club.

Exeter City. How do I love thee? Let me count the ways. As I read my programme, check out the starting line-up and get ready to see two leviathans of the league battle it out over the next ninety minutes.

The ref checks his watch - beckons his linesmen - signals to the goalkeepers and off we go.

And that's where the perfect day ends.

Everything else seems to be downhill from here! Ninety minutes later and I'm bemoaning the defending for that corner and lamenting about the host of chances that went astray in the 1-0 defeat to Burton Albion.

So why do I and the rest of us hopeless cases keep coming back for more? Why, when we put ourselves through such mental torture, do we find the need to brainwash ourselves again a mere seven days later?

Well you see - it's a loveable affliction. A fanatical disease that cannot be shaken from the bloodstream once the virus has affected the body. A glorious drug that we need a constant hit from (well for eight months of the year anyway).

Now don't get me wrong I hate being like this. Exeter has long since taken the innocence of it all away from me. Saturday afternoons of genteel amusement and polite laughter are long since a thing of the past. Now I spend each visit to St James Park in agony. Every game became more serious, every result that bit more important, until I end up a quivering vegetable totally unrecognizable from the sane human being in row B ten minutes before kick-off.

And I wasn't a purist of the beautiful game. Not for me the flair of Brazil 1970 or the neat pass and move of the Liverpool in the '80s. Nope. 4-5-1, whack it to the target man and defend that one goal lead for your life. I can sincerely lay the blame for that depressing outlook at the door of one man.

Mr. George Graham.

I grew up supporting an Arsenal side that suppressed entertainment under Don Howe and bludgeoned it to death when George Graham came along. We got sneaky one goal wins, defended in numbers and soon I found myself being seduced by the canny Scotsman's ability to bring silverware to the marble halls of Highbury. It wasn't pretty, but it worked.

Would you rather see your team playing attractive football and losing, or as dull as ditch-water and winning? So when at Conference level you do see a game where two teams seem about as much use as a one-legged man in an arse kicking contest don't be too hard, because I'm not. It's all right for me to sit in St James and see games unfold like that because I'd been brought up on a team five divisions higher that weren't one bit pleasing on the eye, yet won six trophies in six years!

The one thing however, at Exeter that always bettered any trophy or accolade that might have been won, was the feeling of belonging. The knowing you are wanted and welcomed by a small band of followers with the same hopes and dreams with open hands. Peas in a pod sharing the same agony and despair - week in week out. From my very first visit to my adopted club to a new century that had seen more change and upheaval then most clubs have in a lifetime.

Fans that had seen the beacon of light break through the foreboding clouds above Well Street for short ecstatic moments in time. A ray of hope that manifested itself in 1977 with a promotion from Division Four. A Tony Kellow inspired cup run in '81, and that glorious Darren Rowbotham-fuelled league title of the 1989/90 season.

Chelsea we'll never be. Arsenal we ain't! But although we will never have the bulging trophy cabinet like on Merseyside or have a support to rival the good folks at Old Trafford, there's still a small fervent tightly-knit clan that care more about what happens on the hallowed turf of St James Park then they do almost everything else in life.

Even dull scoreless draws with Carlisle United.

Down but not disheartened, I joined my friends for a post match drink back at the bar. Steve Perryman was giving an interview downstairs, whilst small huddles of fans conducted their own post-mortem on the previous ninety minutes at the bar upstairs. They were one of hundreds, nay, thousands of fans who would inhabit bars, clubhouses and nightclubs the length and breath of the country nit-picking every aspect of the football match they'd just seen. Analyzing every small detail and not only convincing themselves, but the gathering masses, that they would do an infinitely better job then these high paid prima donnas.

Fresh from their shower the players file in at the bar. Though it proved a hard fought point gained against a Carlisle side that would eventually go up, it just managed to paper over the cracks on an Exeter side that had won once in seven games and were floundering in tenth place, well off the pacesetters at the top. Dolan's decision to leave, though hard, would have been made infinitely easier by this predicament. Having finished a point off the play-offs and keeping the bulk of the squad whilst bringing in new talent, hopes would have been high for a tilt at the title but the season had a disastrous start. The Grecians managed just one win in the first five games and two god-awful defeats in three days - home to Convey via a Gary Sawyer own goal and a simply unforgivable last-minute loss against relegation fodder Farnborough Town - had us fickle fans sending murmurs throughout the terraces that Eamonn would last about as long as one of our cup runs.

When the likeable Irishman did finally depart (after a lack-lustre 3-0 home defeat to Barnet, where the evil ex-Grecian Dwayne Lee scored), Steve Perryman stepped in and the managerial merry-go-round took off again.

Carlisle seemed happy. A good day at the office which started with an excruciating seven hour coach journey from the icy borders of Scotland had ended with this well-earned point. The Cumbrians were two points clear at the top and had preserved a fine unbeaten record that had held firm for the first twelve games of the season. Any superstitions the northerners had about the thirteenth game at St James Park seem to go out the window after the first half-hour when sixteen seagulls where killed by a white leather object that spent a lifetime hovering in the sky like a UFO. A game for the purists it certainly wasn't, but the end result was always the bottom line at this level. Perryman held things together whilst the board struggled on with the arduous task of putting in place their sixth manager since the turn of the century.

A week later Santos Gaia headed Exeter ahead at Gravesend before a seventy-first minute equalizer by Roy (yes, I'm the guy who scored for Wycombe in that cup shock, what in the name of Christ has happened to my career) Essandoh, meant both sides finished honours-even as a crowd of just over 1700 and manager-elect Inglethorpe watched on.

An away point against Gravesend and Northfleet was not what I pictured three seasons ago. Trips to Margate and Forest Green Rovers should have been quaint pre-season friendlies.

Still any forgettable moments and bad memories can be quickly erased by the glorious healing powers of alcohol.

City were tenth, crowds were sparse and I've just remembered chatting up a transvestite called Dolores at a gay club back home.

"Double brandy please!"

Note- I'm aware my attempts to persuade a certain Mr. Henry away from London to Exeter City FC was written before his move to that vile Spanish club. As a captain who never rolled up his sleeves and looked after the younger players at Arsenal, he'll be right at home alongside Mr. Ronaldinho at Barcelona.

Chapter Two
A SHORT LESSON IN ELECTRICUTION

To most people a Breville sandwich maker is a useful kitchen appliance. A cheap harmless snack accessory that is the godsend of students and single males everywhere.
This of course is a blatant lie.
At least this can be said in my household. For in my kitchen lies a living breathing demon. Beneath its shiny white exterior and innocent looking grill lies a device that can kill a man in less time then it takes to toast the bread and pop a cheese and ham toastie in your mouth.
My Breville is the Whore of Babylon.
Not content with cremating every sandwich it's ever made and setting off the fire alarm at least once every six hours, my Breville has now cranked it up a notch by managing to hospitalize human beings. It's surely only a matter of time before it finally takes my life and when it does set the house into a towering inferno, you can be sure the only appliance that will survive the blaze intact will be that hot-plated whore.
My run-in with the toaster from hell came after Alex Inglethorpe had just made his first mark as the new Exeter City manager by winning his first game in charge at home to Aldershot.
A crowd of just over 3,200 had filed into St James Park to watch a new saga in the recent turbulent history of the Grecians unfold.
Just the right time for Aldershot to come to town. If there was ever a collection of eleven men you'd want to line out against at St James Park, it would undoubtedly have to be the Shots. The Hampshire-based club hadn't won at Exeter since 1955 and only the biggest doom-merchant would have predicted a win for Terry Brown's men. Even my local bookie was unaware of this statistic and handed me generous odds of 7/4 on a Grecian victory that afternoon.
Money in the bank!
Alex was conservative with his team selection, the only change to the side that drew at Gravesend being Sean Devine replacing Jake Edwards in the line-up and Glenn Cronin was back on the bench after a recent injury.
For the record, the team read: RICE, HILEY, JEANNIN, GAIA, TODD, TAYLOR, AFFUL, AMPADU, CLAY, FLACK and DEVINE.
From the off there was only going to be one outcome. City attacked with vest and flair and the only surprise was that it took seventeen minutes for the deadlock to be broken and when it did it came from the talismanic Devine.
Latching onto a sweet Andy Taylor pass, the club's top marksman wrong-footed the Aldershot defence before firing an unstoppable volley past Bull in the goalmouth to give City the lead.
It was only the Irishman's (he was capped at B level, so he's one of ours!), fourth goal of the year having spent most of the season warming the sub's bench through a mixture of injury and poor form, but the twenty-five goal hit-man of the previous season would play no small part in City's eternal quest for promotion that year.
Just before half-time and the heavens opening on the lush green grass of St James Park, the home side took the lead again. This time Grecian left-back Alex Jeannin delivered a pin-point cross to former Manchester United trainee

Andy Taylor who duly dispatched his effort into the visitors' net for a two-goal lead at the interval.

Now, normally a cushion of two goals is anything but comfortable to any Exeter City side, as many a fan can bear witness to amazing comebacks, astonishing capitulations and defeat at the hands of victory. Many a half-time lead has been wiped out by a trademark "deer in the headlights" collapse at the hands of an equally stunned opposition who were more than happy to seize the opportunity to turn a 2-0 defeat into a 6-2 win!

Like the time Matt Moxey travelled with his hardy mates to a frost-bitten Abbey Stadium for his twenty-first birthday to watch City do battle with Cambridge United. Having been hearded into the tiniest enclosure ever with the tallest fences seen this side of Auschwitz, Matt and the travelling hoard of Grecians watched City race into a seemingly unassailable 2-0 half-time lead in a forty-five minutes of complete and utter dominance. By this stage poor Matty was in need of medical attention having climbed a rusty fence and placing several large gashes in his hand to celebrate City's second goal, but the sixteen stitches seemed all worth the agony at half-time.

However Matt's brother, being ever the cautionary one, ominously toned "as long as we don't concede straight away after the restart we should be ok" as they sipped their Bovril.

The rest is history...for the record Cambridge notched within thirty seconds and went on to win the match 3-2, leaving the home support elated and Matt Moxey filing out of Auschwitz with a gaping hole in his right hand.

More recent collapses included a ten-minute two-goal lead at Kidderminster under John Cornforth and a Noel Blake inspired 3-2 defeat from a winning position against Leyton Orient.

This would be my personal favourite. City had romped into a two goal lead in the first twenty minutes courtesy of Paul Read and Graeme Power - only for Orient's Carl Griffiths to take centre stage by nearly decapitating Power with a blatant elbow smack-bang in front of the officials. Decision? Throw-in and a neck brace for Power. Orient went on to win the game with a brace of a different kind from Griffiths, who celebrated by giving a v-sign to the stunned City faithful.

One word. BASTARD!

Despite these horror stories and the tendency to regularly fear the worst when we have a lead, this afternoon there was only going to be one winner and three minutes into the second half any lingering doubt was vanquished when Santos Gaia made it 3-0 from an Andy Taylor corner.

Time to relax.

Stomach rumbling. Feeling peckish. Time for a snack.

And here's where my no-good sandwich-making whore of Babylon finally managed to hospitalize me.

Being a tad hungry I make for the kitchen, grab the entire contents of the fridge, which I'm sure included a half-eaten sausage, two prunes and some out-of-date Edam, popped it on the Brev and fired that baby up.

Nothing happened.

I check the plug, feel the hot plate and scratch my head in bewilderment as I wonder how in the name of Christ my old foe has found yet another way to fuck up my afternoon up.

The answer of course was obvious. With hunger gnawing to the bone, I had rashly piled about three months food between two slices of bread and expected the Breville to close and start toasting my skyscraper of a sandwich. Now I'm no scientist and I didn't design this portable nightmare, but I'm pretty sure that plugging in this appliance will automatically get the hot plate heating. However, we weren't dealing with the average run-of-the-mill toasting machine here. This was a demonic Breville inspired by the soul of Satan. A Breville that broke one of my toes by hopping off the counter during that memorable 0-0 draw against Northampton in '94 and had caused the great kitchen fire of '87 by spontaneously combusting after a 2-1 defeat to Halifax. It now resembled a toaster from a kitchen in Kosovo, complete with charred flex and burnt enamel, but since it was a wedding present from my Aunty Anna I could hardly throw it out into a bin, even if the woman is eighty-seven and suffering from severe amnesia (she still thinks our dog Cassie is her long lost brother Cecil from New Zealand).

Determined however that I'd have something in my mouth before Exeter notched another against Aldershot, I ploughed on: finally getting the grill heating. With my cheese, coleslaw, half-eaten sausage and prune sandwich in place, I use brute force to squash the sandwich down, close the handle and get this baby started.

Ten minutes later I woke up on the floor, dog licking my face and a god-awful smell of burnt prune in the background.

In using the caveman mentality of brute force, I'd sat on the Breville, closed the handle, catching the flex and promptly electrocuted myself.

All I can remember is a shudder going through my buttocks and some choice words of profanity before passing out.

Thirty minutes later and I'm lying on a bed in hospital, shaking like mad, hair on end and suffering third degree burns to my arse.

It was only at nine o'clock that night after some painkillers and a bruised ego that I found out that Tim Sills had pulled a consolation goal back for Aldershot, but City had hung on well for a comfortable 3-1 win and three points that pushed us up to eighth in the table.

A week later Exeter started off their FA Cup campaign with a glamorous fourth qualifying round cup tie against none other than Braintree Town.

Grass roots non-league football….don't you just love it!

Because of our untimely exit from league football in 2003, it now meant that Exeter, being a Conference club, now had to play one qualifying tie in order to make the first round proper. With the club taken over by the supporters club, but still heavily in debt, the FA Cup was always a major factor in the season of small clubs like City. A run to the third round and a money-spinning away tie at a premiership club could literally set a non-league club up for years, or maybe even save them from complete ruin. It's at times like this that the eleven men on the field are solely responsible for the fate of a club. The entire financial year can be made with a last-minute winner away at Grimsby. The winding-up orders and bailiffs knocking at the door can all disappear with an injury time penalty by your thirty-eight year-old left-back, putting your club into an away tie at Anfield or the Emirates.

So to the outside world a poxy non-league fourth round tie just to enter the FA Cup proper might be laughable, but to the city faithful, or more so the club's directors, it would have been deemed as important as any Merseyside derby or Champions League final. Put simply - Exeter couldn't afford to slip up against the minnows from the Ryman League Premier.

The tie didn't exactly capture the football-loving folk of Devon and their decision to put the feet up with a cup of cocoa on a cold October afternoon seemed a very shrewd one, especially when after seventy-five minutes Exeter had failed to break down the eleven-man-wall known as Braintree Town. A replay against a club three divisions lower in their own backyard on a bleak Tuesday night was not exactly something to warm the cockles of the heart of the Grecian faithful.

Luckily enough help was on hand in the shape of Jake Edwards and it was his goal - twelve minutes from time which finally eased the tension among the 2,300 at the game. City went on to add the insurance late on with a scrappy second goal from Sean Devine to secure a 2-0 win and send the home side into the first round proper and the minnows from the lower leagues back home to Essex with a share of the gate receipts.

Within minutes, every Grecian was glued to BBC 1 as the draw for the first round proper of the greatest cup competition in the world took place. To the non-entities in the lower leagues this would be their defining moment. For clubs like Slough Town and Vauxhall Motors, who'd battled four rounds on mud-laden pitches and torrents of rain in front of handfuls of people, this would be their cup final. Their chance to mix it with the pros. And scoff as the big boys may, there's been many the league club who twitched uncomfortably at the thought of an eight-hour round-trip on a dank November afternoon to play in the cramped surroundings of Stalybridge Celtic. It's a long way back on the coach when your league team and its well-paid pros have been dumped out of the cup by a part-time painter from Hucknall Town.

All I wanted was a home draw. I sat in silence and the balls were released from the sack and placed into the drum, all the time hoping City would be first out of the hat to ease the growing tension. In hindsight, I shouldn't have been worried - since that draw, Exeter have been drawn out at home in ten of the next thirteen FA Cup or Trophy fixtures. An astonishing, if wildly fortuitous, cup statistic.

Half way through my cup-o-soup our ball was drawn.

"Number 37...Exeter City".

"Top notch, home draw" - I crow, with an air of excitement and anticipation.

"Number 82...Grimsby Town".

We'll have some of that!

A plum home tie against a relegation-threatened League Two side.

A match pitching a well-placed Conference League outfit against a team staring down the dark abyss of relegation from the football league.

Just what the doctored ordered.

Although Exeter weren't exactly setting the Nationwide Conference alight and had a Grimsby scout witnessed the excruciating 1-1 draw away at Gravesend - he wouldn't exactly be pissing himself with fear, but everybody was well aware who the pressure was firmly on.

Grimsby had made an awful start to their league campaign and needed a tie like this like a hole in the head. For the Grecian faithful however, it was something to look forward to as the battle to regain their league status continued.

However before league duties against the worryingly familiar foes like Forest Green and Farnborough could be resumed, City had another cup date in the form of the LDV Vans trophy against league one side Swindon Town.

The LDV trophy was a loveable distraction. A chance to mix it with league clubs and a feeling of belonging again, even if it's just for ninety minutes.

Alas that's what it turned out to be, as Swindon came to St James in the first week of November and left with a narrow 2-1 win.

By this stage I'd recovered from my shock, gone back to work and performed a murderous ritual on my Breville in the back garden which included a can of petrol, box of matches and one grinning owner. I administered the last rites with a bottle of holy water to exorcise the evil spirit that infested the balls of an appliance for the last twenty-three years and sent it back to hell.

I'd also put together enough money to plan a trip or two across the Irish Sea for some much needed footy. With my other love interest in Highbury doing very nicely thank you (forty-nine games unbeaten and five points clear until Wayne Rooney decided to impersonate a lifeguard from Baywatch and win himself a penalty at Old Trafford to give United victory over Arsenal) and with a November trip already planned to the hallowed St James Park, I convinced myself that an away day at Accrington was a fun way to spend a Saturday afternoon.

With my local airport becoming more cosmopolitan and offering flights to far off horizons like Luton, I booked an early morning flight to Manchester and plotted my journey to the Frazer Eagle Stadium, home to Accrington Stanley FC.

After an hour long flight, a short train journey and a taxi, my woeful sense of orienteering got me lost the minute I walked down the large slope outside the station and straight onto a roundabout in the centre of town, I finally arrived on Livingston Road, where a small flurry of Stanley fans are buying programmes and standing about outside the turnstiles.

The stadium is a picturesque setting in the heart of Lancashire, with fields and hills adorning the landscape overlooking the away Coppice Terrace End. Although now renamed after some little-known African owl (Frazer Eagle), the home of Stanley has always been known as the crown ground. On one side of the ground is the main stand, but on closer inspection it's actually two small stands with a gap between them, whilst the right-hand side is a tiny pitch length stand synonymous with classic non-league grounds. And just when you think things can't get anymore stereotyped, there's a trademark slope on the pitch. Per usual there's a housing development behind the ground which gives the interested high-rise onlookers a free ninety minutes of entertainment. All in all it looks very promising.

Ten minutes in and I don't fancy this away end. Exposed to the elements, I'm half thinking about doing a runner to the main stand, but I don't want to be seen as an away day wimp by the sizeable huddle of travelling Exeter fans.

Two minutes later however, the weather is the least of my worries. My Irish comrade and good friend Glenn Cronin is stretchered off after turning sharply on the pitch, damaging his ligaments.

It's a bitter blow for the Exeter captain having just come back from injury. We weren't to know it at the time but it marked the beginning of the end for "Keano" at City as it resulted in knee ligament damage that kept the influential young Irishman out for almost a year. What made it worse was that is was such an innocuous incident. No challenge, no incoming tackle, not even a stretch in vain to keep the ball in play. Just a simple change in direction and the twenty-two year-old's knee gave way. The stretcher confirmed our worse fears. I've chatted to Glenn many times since and the Dubliner has a very philosophical take on things, even though it cost him the biggest game of his life in January 2005. I'd have a slightly different outlook - suicide might be on the agenda.

Exeter were forced to reshuffle the pack as Stanley forced the issue. Martin Rice in the City goal had to be alert on more than one occasion and the width of a post stopped the Lancastrians from taking the lead.

The half-time whistle started a bee-line for some refreshments and yours truly tucked into what can only be described as an exceptional cheeseburger washed down with a strong cup of tea to ward off the impending cold weather. The warming glow of my cuppa swiftly wore off as the second half kicked off and in a sneaky move, which took about ten minutes to execute, I made my way into the shelter of the terraced stand to see out the rest of the game.

4.45 rolled round and three minutes of extra injury time produced the stalemate between both sides which had looked on the cards from an early stage. City defended well and came incredibly close to winning it after Gary Sawyer missed a close range header which should have at least tested the Stanley goalkeeper.

Although I wanted to linger around, chat to some Grecians and see how Glenn was, time was not on my side and, with my pre-ordered taxi waiting outside the ground; I was back at Manchester Airport just in time for my 7.45 flight back to the Emerald Isle.

By the time I sauntered back in my front door, it was if I'd never been away. Not that my wife noticed. Sandra was glad of some peace, quiet and a chance to actually get her hands on the remote control for more than fifteen minutes. It's only recently I've stopped feeling guilty about going away, as my wife is more than happy to have my sorry-ass carcass out of the house so she can catch up on five straight hours of CSI: Miami. It's only when you realise that the other option she'd have would be listening to me moaning endlessly about and away defeat to Farnborough Town that you can understand her bliss at a house free of football-related whingeing and a sports-free T.V. for the night. God bless her - love truly is blind!

The next morning whilst munching breakfast in bed (a reward from my beloved for getting out of her hair for at least a few hours the day before), I checked through the football results to see how our upcoming cup opponents Grimsby had faired.

There beneath my fried egg and half-eaten toast was the page of League Two results.

Scunthorpe United 2-0 Grimsby Town.

No goals, five bookings and an on-loan player sent off.

Sounds good to me.

I spent the rest of that Sunday the way God intended - sat on my fat ass, watched T.V. and fell asleep on the sofa. The lord said we should rest on the Sabbath day so who am I to argue with the man above?

That week in work dragged. I tried to put it down to the excitement of the FA Cup and finally seeing the Grecians do battle with a league side. But it was really just all about getting a weekend football coupon and gloating to everyone about how finally I could see my little club from Devon back on a pools coupon. Now I was fully aware my friends would rather use their nuts as a brake on a rusty blade than have to listen to me prattle on about some down-on-the-luck ex-league club from South West England, but having listened to week after week of 'Premiership this' and 'Champions League that', I felt it my duty to preach the gospel of Grecian to everyone remotely within earshot.

Thursday rolled around and with it the football coupons. I run around like a headless chicken to half a dozen betting shops to see which has the best odds on City. William Hill, Terry Rogers and Stanley's all seem the same, but on closer inspection it seems Ladbrokes have come up trumps with a tempting 9/4. Given the fact Exeter are top half in the Conference and Grimsby are struggling desperately in League Two it seems very generous, in fact, given the possible cup upset I'm slightly miffed that the BBC or Sky haven't televised the game (then again they've probably recognized the fact that the we are nothing short of deplorable whenever a camera is seen within five miles of an Exeter City game).

With the FA pumping more money into the Cup, even a first round win would be worth a nice few thousand to a small club and although City had kept the wolves from the door temporarily, there were still creditors to be paid off to the tune of half a million.

Mr. Sun came out to shine his smiley face down on me that Saturday. There's nothing like lazing in bed on a weekend, hair scattered in 6,000 directions and not a trace of that ugly four letter word - work - anywhere to be seen. The first round proper of the FA Cup. With all my bets done and mind wrecked with the many permutations the game could throw up, I relax with a hot cup of coffee and wait for the days events to unfold.

Come kick-off time just over 3,300 have filed through the turnstiles at St James Park to watch Exeter City commence their cup campaign for 2004/05. Given the fact it's the FA Cup, a league club and a potential upset on the cards, it's a disappointing crowd. Normally a cup game will prize even the most hardened couch potato out of the safe environment of his living room, but it seems the undiscovered public will need more excitement than Grimsby Town on a Saturday to get their arse warming a seat at St James Park.

The visitors arrive on the back of a woeful league run. Grimsby have gone through managers like spit through a trumpet recently and Russell Slade is the latest man to put himself in the firing line. To some Town fans, the blindfold and riflemen have already arrived on the horizon. With just two wins in sixteen games, the side third last and perilously close to dropping into the relegation zone, Slade has his work cut out. The bulk of Grimsby's problems however can't all lie at the new manager's door.

At the turn of the new millennium, Grimsby were a relatively comfortable league side that yo-yoed between the Championship and League One. The south-west of Devon would never have been a calling card for the Mariners (unless you're in Green and have Argyle in your name) as there was always at least one division separating City and Grimsby Town.

Inglethorpe set his team out to attack and right from the off City don't disappoint.

An Exeter crowd (which can be reserved at best and merciless when things go wrong) roar their side on like their lives depended on it smack bang from the kick-off. All the elements were in place for the proverbial 'cup shock'.

Within six minutes City took the lead. Coming up from his customary centre-half position, ex-Brazilian international Santos Gaia (OK, it was at under-age level but it's still an impressive stat) stabbed home an Andy Taylor cross which had evaded the head of Steve Flack and landed at the feet of the Brazilian who made no mistake from six yards. Amazingly it was Gaia's EIGHTH goal of the season from centre half!

Slade's men never really recovered. Even with less than ten minutes on the clock, it seemed there was really only ever going to be one winner. The Grecians hustled and harried Grimsby all over the park, never giving them a moment to settle.

Slade had set Grimsby up with a three-man attack but City's back four of Hiley, Gaia, Jeannin and Sawyer thwarted their every move.

Of course there was the odd hair-raising moment. Martin Rice made two fine first half stops and minutes after the restart (which you can be sure included a managerial bollocking complete with flying tea-cups from Slade) Grimsby's striker Andy Parkinson somehow contrived to blaze over from five yards out with the goal at his mercy.

Back in the isolation of my house in South-East Ireland, Sky's Soccer Saturday was my only link to the goings-on at St James Park. Normally, I'm a total and utter nervous wreck for the entire ninety minutes City are playing (waiting for a scoreline to flash on a small screen - when you have no idea what's happening on the field - can do that to a man), but today I just had that feeling it would be the Grecians' day, almost to the point of being dismissive of any chance that Grimsby had of getting back into the game (that's a mistake I've lived to regret on more that one occasion with a multitude of Arsenal games under Bruce Rioch).

There were a few frayed nerves in the last ten minutes as the visitors tried desperately to equalize and send Grimsby back to a replay in the more homely confines of their Blundell Park home, but City were looking even more dangerous on the counter attack. Local favourite Dean Moxey came on with three minutes left as City settled for what they had.

By that stage the visitors were down to ten men. Michael Reddy given his marching orders for showing a bit too much of our famous Irish temper (bless him - he's only a young fella) and, in injury time, ex-Crystal Palace man Dean Gordon fired his free-kick wide before using some not so well chosen verbals about his team's performance to a pitch side reporter.

"Basically we were shit".

City left the field to rapturous applause whilst the discontented Grimsby fans let Mr. Slade know exactly what they felt about his managerial prowess.

Twenty minutes later and Exeter City are back in the hat for the second round draw. If the match just finished against Grimsby was important, this could be deemed life or death. A good second round draw against another lower league opponent could be the catalyst for a win that would see the Grecians in the draw drum for the enormously significant third round - the stage all the big boys come in.

An away tie at Chelsea, Arsenal or Liverpool would solve Exeter's financial troubles in a millisecond. Months and months of worry could be wiped out should a giant like Manchester United be paired with Alex Inglethorpe's men.

Back home it's feet up, slippers on and a nice cup of hot chocolate as I, and several thousand fans in South West England, await our fate.

Halfway through the draw and still no City. The slim hope of drawing the last remaining non-league teams have gone. Hinckley United drew Brentford and Histon came out against Yeovil. Amazingly the two lowest ranked teams left - Slough and Yeading - draw each other!

Then the moment arrives.

"Exeter City - who beat league opposition in Grimsby today"- says FA chief David Davies in a surprised - I thought they had gone bankrupt - tone.

"Will play number 28...Doncaster Rovers".

Peachy.

Another home tie.

Another league club.

Another good pay day. And although the opposition would be a sterner test than the struggling Grimsby Town, Doncaster Rovers would certainly be beatable. With some of the tough draws handed to equally financially-stricken clubs, Exeter have come out of things smelling of roses.

For a fleeting moment I'm wondering - given the potential again for a cup shock - would BBC or SKY be mulling over a trip to South-West England, but that thought was destroyed almost immediately by the memory of Sunday afternoon, November 17th 2002 and the televised 0-0 draw v Forest Green - quite possibly the worst game of FA Cup football ever screened in the history of the BBC. I'd like to say I'm ever-so-slightly exaggerating, but when the Grecians couldn't score in ninety minutes against a Forest Green goalkeeper the size of Cornwall, you'll get the message that it was a nothing short of a suicide-inducing match.

All things said and done, not a bad day's work. Feeling chuffed with both the win and tasty tie against Rovers; I decide to reward myself and my four-legged friend with a well-earned breath of fresh air and a walk up the hills. I'm not normally a person who's at one with nature and jogging into the countryside sixteen times a week, but the fact Dingo my dog has the leash in his mouth, exposing his teeth and growling for Ireland, means he's slightly annoyed at his owner not suggesting "walkies" for a quite a few weeks.

Within a half hour, I'm roving through a sea of green fields and wooden fences and breathing in the country air. City life can be a carbon dioxide nightmare that clogs the senses and it's only when you get beyond the smoke and smog that you realize what fresh air actually is. Don't get me wrong, my home town is small, but you still can't travel to work without getting your daily intake of industrial smoke and at least seven different types of noise pollution.

I let Dingo off the leash and he takes off like a prisoner in a jail break. The last time I made that mistake resulted in the four-legged mutt going missing for four days and a subsequent pregnancy crisis in at least sixteen bitches in my estate. He was suitably punished - I put a stereo in his doghouse and made him listen to Bon Jovi for sixteen hours straight. That's enough suffering for anyone.

I survey all around me, stretch wide and take a sharp inhale of breath. Happy, contented, the feeling of life in my veins.

That lasts about four seconds...

I put my hands on a live fence and electrocute myself.

Who says lightning doesn't strike twice?

Chapter Three
AS HAPPY AS LARRY!

I wish I could kill my cat.

Seriously.

Devil, my four-legged fleabag, has an uncanny knack of being able to pry open my kitchen door, get into my fridge and devour anything that contains tuna - my favourite food.

And it's not just a fluke. I've studied the cat over the last few weeks and can safely say it's a robbery that meticulously planned and executed with the precision of a world-class thief.

The planning normally starts with the dumping of the previous week's stale tuna. I used to consider it normal that Devil was present for this, but last Sunday I was greeted by two green eyes peering at me from on top of the fridge, staring in at the exact spot the tuna lay.

On returning from my weekly shopping, I'm escorted from car to kitchen by the cunning bastard, who again jumps onto the fridge and peers into the positioning of the fresh batch of tasty tuna.

The final piece in the puzzle is put into place when my feline friend hides himself   under the sink and waits patiently for the last light to go out at night. Then within forty-five seconds it's all over. Like Linford Christie on four legs, the marauding moggie springs into action , opens the fridge, lifts the tuna and wolfs it down in one go before I've even had time to put my head on the pillow. The crime scene is sealed off in the morning for forensics to check for fingerprints, but after dusting, the unmistakable paw print of the only cat on the block is discovered leaving yours truly on a manhunt for a cat that will spend seven weeks in the solitary confinement of my shed: existing on bread and water if he's ever apprehended.

However it hasn't dampened my mood. I've just booked a flight to Exeter and will be travelling for next week's home tie against Leigh RMI.

This trip to my beloved Grecians will be slightly different as I'm bringing my best friend Ron Williams (aka – Round-a-phobia Ron) over with me.

Now I know what you're thinking. How could I have a best friend that religiously locks himself in a pub toilet the second anyone even suggests it's his turn to get the bevvies in? He'd make scrooge cringe, but by far the worst episode would undoubtedly be during last year's World Cup when on a factory night out, he was asked to buy drink for the entire table of ten watching Argentina play the Ivory Coast.

Without a hint of displeasure at having to order five pints of cider, three lagers, a rum and black and a shot of peach schnapps, Ron excused himself from the table, walked to the toilet, crawled out a two foot window over the urinals and calmly strolled home with the 34.78 Euros he'd have had to fork out safely tucked up in his back pocket.

Astonishingly, he tried to convince us he'd been robbed at knifepoint and was too embarrassed to come back out and face us. In truth, even if he had been robbed, the muggers would still be trying to find the dosh under fifteen years of cobwebs in the wallet.

He always has an excuse.

The gas bill always comes on a Saturday night.

The phone bill is issued weekly (and it's always 850 Euros)

Don't even mention the shopping.

Three weeks ago he called an emergency family meeting and announced the custard creams (a luxury item) had to be scarified as the price of Pampers had risen eight cents.

Don't get me wrong Ron's a nice guy, but if he ever falls on his wallet he'd bounce over the moon.

The only reason the tight-fisted sod was even stepping foot on a plane to Devon was because he'd bailed me out of a tight spot which involved too much drink and a website called jigglingjugs.com.

Having had a group of lads over whilst my wife was on a hen night, I was forced to trawl through the depths of depravity on the net to find some hardcore porn and choice filth by my friends (that's my story anyway and I'm sticking to it). After the guys left and seduced by twelve Southern Comforts I neglected to switch the computer off, leaving my wife to discover a giant set of silicone breasts belonging to "Dirty Delilah - who'll do anything for a fiver!"

The next morning I got the Spanish inquisition (though I could say the same of her as hen night's can be akin to swingers parties over here) and hastily blamed everything on Ron, who was the culprit who demanded to log onto the now notorious jigglingjugs.com. Three minutes later and a sneaky phone call to my tight-fisted amigo, a deal had been struck. Ron agreed to take the entire blame for the trawling of late night computer porn and I'd reluctantly agree to pay for a flight to Exeter five days later to see City play Leigh RMI.

With friends like this who needs enemies!

However I wasn't too put out. For years I'd been wanting to show my sceptical friends the wonders that this small city in Devon had to offer and finally get them to grace St James Park to watch the men in red and white in action. For years they'd been convinced it was the love of a mistress, three kids, two cats and a pet gerbil that had me flying across the Irish Sea every five weeks. Now at least I had the chance to show them it was nothing more than ninety minutes of football on a Saturday afternoon at St James Park that I was having an affair with (on second thoughts, maybe the mistress sounded more fun).

That Friday we made a two hour ride to Dublin Airport and took the brief fifty-five minute flight to land at Exeter International Airport late in the afternoon.

This was all new for Ron. As a Newcastle supporter, he'd been used to following the Magpies at the other St James' Park up on Tyneside (not that he'd ever paid to go see them play - the cheapskate). Now he was about to see a non-league side playing the likes of Margate and Morecambe, minus the 55,000 that religiously cram in to see Newcastle play each week.

Season ticket sell-outs to half empty stands. This would be a reality check for a man used to seeing sold out stadiums and thousands upon thousands every Saturday night on Match of the Day.

Leigh had arrived just seven days after the cup win against Grimsby.

The part-timers were lying rock bottom and Alex Inglethorpe's men would really only have three points on their minds today.

Although the Conference had more and more sides taking the plunge to go fully professional, Leigh couldn't afford such a luxury.

The Manchester side had possibly the worst week in the club's history. Manager Phil Starbuck had resigned after being forced to make astonishing cutbacks to the club's already miniscule budget and the Railwaymen were already adrift at the bottom with only two wins in the sixteen games to date. I'd chosen this game weeks ago, as it should have represented a handy three points, so anything but a convincing win and I'd be hearing about this game for weeks from my friends, who would naturally become Leigh RMI fans for the afternoon.

By the time we've taken our seats, Ron still thinks I'm indebted to him and sends me out for a burger before the kick-off. This I don't mind as food is a hobby of mine and I join my tight-fisted friend in his junk food binge by adding a balti pie and hot dog to the order.

It's hard to know what he made of the next ninety minutes.

He was fully aware this wasn't the Premiership, yet it was his first time seeing non-league football. The closest he'd got to this was supporting Longford Town in the League of Ireland. He'd taken a shine to them after spending a weekend there and taking in a game (he got in cheap with a student ID card - he's forty-three!) though I secretly think it's because he hated my home town club of Waterford, where he lives. Other than seeing Newcastle on SKY, that Longford Town game was the only other comparison he could make (and Christ that's an insulting comparison if you've ever seen Longford play football).

However, it would be ironic that his first ever appearance at St James Park would coincide with Exeter City's biggest ever win in the Conference to date.

A 5-1 romp which put City into their highest position of the season and continued the fine run of form under Exeter's new young manager.

It really could have been entirely different had Leigh's striker Karl Rose not missed an absolute howler from no more than a foot out after only ninety seconds. City surprisingly looked a little jittery and how Rose managed to strike the outside of the post when my eleven month-old child would have notched still confounds me.

It was a big let-off and from that Exeter never looked back and took the lead on seventeen minutes courtesy of a bullet header from our ever-willing target man Steve Flack. As bad as the visitors were, one goal was never going to be enough and Sean Devine popped up to give City a comfortable 2-0 lead at half-time.

"Don't know what to make of it yet B, but the Magpies would be at least 16-0 up now" - says Ron - stating the bleeding obvious!

"Don't be so stupid, Shearer is a poor man's Devine" - I reply.

We argue for the next fifteen minutes. Ron laughing at the fact City are playing football against a goalkeeper who has a night-shift at the local Sainsbury's after the game and me replying with the fact Ron was the only person who could peel an orange in his pocket and eat it without ever taking it out!

The next half hour proves tedious. The surface, which was dodgy before the game, has now cut up and reduced the game to a slog. Although the pitch makes Leigh feel more at home, it's still surprising the visitors get themselves back in the game completely against the run of play. With seventy-five minutes on the clock, a lapse in concentration in the home side's ranks allows RMI's Chris Simm in one-on-one and he places his effort coolly past the onrushing James Bittner. Sweet Jesus!

Now the worry starts to set in as our rock bottom visitors set about trying to take a highly unlikely point back up north.

This is typical Exeter. The Grecians have had a habit recently of placing a gun firmly at their feet and aiming when it came to playing the also-rans of this division.

For some reason City can go away and win handsomely against sides twenty points ahead of them, yet can fall apart to a pack of post office workers and construction men at the likes of Northwich Victoria.

Just when it looks as if the Grecians were going down that road again, up pops Gary Sawyer to restore that 'oh so vital' two-goal cushion. The on-loan Plymouth defender getting his head to a Gareth Sheldon free kick to make sure the visitors only had four minutes of dreaming of the draw. It proves a massive relief for the three and a half thousand fans (and heartbreak for the fifteen travelling Leigh fans - god bless 'em) and City put in a powerful last ten minutes. First Devine sets up Andy Taylor to drive home powerfully from the edge of the area on eighty-three minutes and, in injury time, Marcus Martin's run from the wing sets up Jake Edwards to rifle home a fifth for the home side.

Exeter City 5-1 Leigh RMI.

Only Exeter could win by four goals, yet still give you a bunch of nerves for at least a few minutes in the game!

The rush is on to get back to the bar (were Ron actually buys a drink - solely because there's only two of us in the round), but more importantly to check out how Arsenal and Newcastle have faired.

The look on our faces are of different contrast with a quick glance at the TV screen.

The Gunners have somehow drawn with relegation fodder West Brom at Highbury whilst Newcastle have the gall to win away at Crystal Palace with two goals in the last five minutes. Arsene Wegner's men had lost their way of recent after that record breaking forty-nine game run, whilst Newcastle, despite under-achieving in their fans eyes for the last three decades, have put together a nice run under new manager Graeme Souness who was left to fill the boots of the legendary Sir Bobby Robson.

We settle in at the bar for a few drinks whilst the City faithful do a clinical dissection of the game and the merits of our new manager. Although the scoreline was the most important thing, I'm just as chuffed my friend seems impressed by the set-up at the club. It's hard to know what he was expecting given his only foray into the unknown before today was being part of 567 people who saw Longford Town get an eighty-ninth minute own-goal winner against non-league Wayside Celtic in the second round of the FAI cup.

I'm convinced he expected a ramshackle stand and a man standing with a biscuit tin in place of turnstiles to collect the money from a crowd no more than 500 at best. So for my friend to see stands, executive boxes and two bars in the main stand must have been an astonishingly nice surprise.

The win meant Inglethorpe's men had lost just that league cup tie to Swindon under Alex and it kept Exeter in the chasing pack, all with their eyes on a play-off place.

Any hope of even attempting to catch leaders Carlisle United have long gone and even though it was City's third season in the Conference and the club yet to make the play-offs, every Grecian fan would welcome a top-five finish like a rose wishes for rain.

In an attempt to show Ron the depth of entertainment the city has to offer, I take my friend to a selection of pubs around the area.

It's here where Ron almost costs us our very lives by getting us involved with a bunch of Chelsea Headhunters.

For some reason he decides to take up an invite by seven men in the corner of the Horse and Dray Pub to join them for a couple of drinks and a chin-wag. Now when I thought about it I could see where the hungry sod was coming from. The way 'Round-a-phobia' Ron was looking at it, here were seven men, who all had to buy seven rounds of drink before he'd even be asked to put his hand in his pocket. After all we had been invited over by a burly looking guy who would stab you for a slice pan in an alley purely on the fact they'd overheard us chatting about Chelsea FC (luckily they didn't here the part about me calling them a soulless money-making corporation run by the devil incarnate from Portugal), so it wasn't our place to start shelling out for the liquid refreshment straight away.

The lads were going to Chelsea's home game against Fulham but had a "meeting" planned with some "pansy firm to do the bastards' heads in".

Charming.

What made it even stranger was the fact there was no attempt to hide the fact they were part of the most notorious hooligan firm in England (at one point we were treated to "Rodge the Nutter's" seven inch scar below his left testicle were he was stabbed by "some I.C.F. filth-bag".

By the end of the evening we knew practically every hooligan organisation in England. We found out the Inter City Firm love nothing better than a good carve-up outside White Hart Lane whilst the Blades Business Crew and the Hull City Psychos were a just a bunch of northern monkeys who had incestuous sex with each other's families!

Worryingly, Ron seemed to be warming to the conversation. Another twenty minutes and I reckon he was on the next train to London with these nut-jobs to "do some of the Fulham filth". If that happened, there'd be no turning back. The next time I'd see Ron would be in the obituaries column having being knifed to death 547 times by the Birmingham City Zulus in a Tuesday night game in the Midlands.

Luckily enough, it finally came Ron's turn to get the drinks in. Being the tight-wad he was, he'd already checked out an escape route, through a disused fire exit out the back and I didn't need his signal to tell me it was time to follow my cheapskate buddy out the back and run like the wind back to our hotel.

The next day, as we flew back home I reminded Ron, that because of his stupidity in joining in a chit-chat with a bunch of deranged would-be killers and his refusal to shake the cobwebs from his wallet and buy them a drink, meant I now had to watch over my back every time I came to Exeter or walk into a pub around the ground, knowing that I could very easily get a swift machete to the neck because of my utter dope of a friend.

With the second round cup game still a fortnight away, City had league matters still on their mind and an away day trip to Nigel Clough's Burton Albion.

This would always be a test for Inglethorpe's men so it hardly came as a surprise when the home side emerged victorious with a solitary strike by bald headed Jon Shaw just before half time.

It was a tedious game were City never got going and turned in a limp display against a side of limited ability.

Despite lots of possession, it was a woeful back-pass from Alex Jeannin which gift-wrapped the points for the home side as Shaw latched onto the resulting cross to give Burton a lead three minutes from half-time.

It didn't get much better in the second half as Bittner was called upon several more times to stop Albion completely running away with the game. One of his second half stops was made from Mark Robins - the ex-Manchester United player (or as he's known to everyone outside of Old Trafford - that little runt who saved Alex Ferguson's job). It was his goal in 1990 against Nottingham Forest that almost certainly saved the Scotsman's job and therefore launched the club into a decade of Premiership titles, cups galore, and more red-face shenanigans from the man we love to hate (mind you Mr Mourinho at Stamford Bridge has taken over that mantle long ago).

There were a few late shots in anger, mind you they came from our defenders and, by the ninety-minute mark, any euphoria from the 5-1 win against Leigh was well and truly gone, along with the stark realisation that the Grecians had a fight on their hands just to stay with the chasing pack.

People may say the fight to get into the Premiership is the toughest of all, but when you've lost your league status and are dropped into the unknown ocean that is the Nationwide Conference, you find there's equally hungry creatures there, all taking chunks out of each other, in a desperate fight to survive and eventually prevail back to the safe shores of League football.

And, although the rewards are richer, mixing it with the likes of Arsenal, United and Liverpool, the stark reality that faces clubs when relegated to non-league football or the battle for part-time sides just to survive there, is just as important as a side winning the Championship and all the rewards that come with it.

With my latest trip over and done with and Christmas just around the corner, I sensed it would be a while before I made the trip across the sea to Exeter. There was always the hope we'd beat Doncaster in the cup and go on to draw a Premier club in the third round, but right now I hadn't got the price of a packet of crisps, (which doesn't sound completely desperate - you have to splash out seventy-five cents for a packet of fucking Monster Munch over here!), let alone a plane ticket.

The following weekend comes around and so to the FA Cup again. This Saturday however, I feel really clued-in as there's radio coverage over the web on BBC Radio Devon. When you're flying blind for kick-by-kick action over here in Ireland, a radio commentary is a godsend. When you're swinging in the dark, it's nice when someone occasionally turns the lights on (don't know why I'm full of stupid clichés today). I can now get some kind of a feel for the atmosphere at St James Park as it builds before the moment of kick-off.

Doncaster arrive early. They bring an old friend with them. James Coppinger had arrived from Newcastle several seasons back and played for City in their last season of league football.

With relegation to the Conference and his star clearly rising, it seemed only a matter of time before the bright young blonde thing moved on. He did spent one productive season in non-league, but was transferred to the Belle Vue outfit in the summer of 2004. He very quickly established himself and became a regular starter under manager Dave Penney.

The Vikings, as they're known, were on the crest of a wave having won promotion the previous season and taking the 2003/04 League Two title. Penney's side had adjusted to life in a higher division like the proverbial duck to water and, although the potential for a cup upset would always lurk around the corner, Doncaster would be a tougher nut to crack than a down-on-their luck Grimsby Town.

That surprising cup win had pushed a few more souls through the turnstiles and added to the much needed coffers and, as both sides came onto the field, a crowd of just under 5,000 made a crescendo of noise to rival...well at least a top-of-the- table League One clash!

Like the round before, City were first out of the traps. Doncaster were squeezed all over the pitch and never given any time to impose themselves on the game. The work rate was phenomenal - just what I needed to hear as I'm in another country with my head pressed to a computer, screaming my nuts off like the thousand roaring voices in the Big Bank over at St James Park.

Inglethorpe employed a 4-5-1 formation like in the first round and Andy Taylor's magnificent shackling of Doncaster's danger man Michael McIndoe was a cunning masterstroke by the fledging young manager.

City hunted like a pack of wolves and the visitors just couldn't get into any rhythm at all. Sean Devine had the first effort on goal and Ampadu fired over before the veteran midfielder had to come off injured. The first quarter of an hour was all City, but the visitors were never going to come away from St James' without creating at least one clear cut chance.

In the space of a minute they created two.

Firstly, Martin Rice pulled off an outstanding save from Dave Morley, then Rovers front-man Gregg Blundell watched in total disbelief as his torpedo of a header cannoned off the underside of the bar, down onto the line, before being finally beaten away by the Exeter goalkeeper.

The nineteen year-old was only recalled after regular shot-stopper James Bittner went down with a stomach bug (if he ate at that manky Chinese chip shop down Bedford Street - I don't blame him), but he proved his worth yet again with another magnificent stop from the increasing agitated Blundell on twenty minutes.

Then, when it looked like the visitors were about to take control, the Grecians took the lead. In a blood and thunder cup tie like this, there was simply no room for hiding. And one man that relished the fight more than anyone on the park was Steve Flack.

The former boxer was as pumped up for this as any prize fighter going into the ring to trade blows with the defending champion and he landed his knockout blow just before the half hour mark.

French defender Alex Jeannin sent over a delightful free kick from the left which was met with unbelievable force by Flack, so much so he nearly went through the flapping Warrington in the Rovers goalmouth, to bullet his header into the empty net.

GET IN THERE MY SON!

Exeter City 1-0 Doncaster Rovers.

The roar could have been heard in Bangkok. The City faithful erupted as their marksman wheeled away in delight, leaving a dozen or so Doncaster players with hands on hips and demanding some answers from their defence.

Now we had a game. A good old-fashioned cup tie. Our David had cheekily attempted to slay their Goliath and the battle was now on.

Amazingly before the noise had died down, the visitors were yet again denied a goal through the brilliance of City's young number one. Rice saved smartly from Green before Blundell gave us the miss of the match when his point blank header from six yards out bounced into the ground and somehow had enough velocity to balloon up over the bar!

25

To add to the unfolding excitement, Exeter countered and right on half-time Steve Flack had his header dramatically cleared off the line by Morley, after some panic stricken Doncaster defending.

That proved to be the last action of the half.

The first forty-five minutes had produced everything a traditional cup game could ask for - and then some. For sheer entertainment it was difficult to think if there was a better game being played in England that afternoon - and I was only listening to it on the radio! As yet there was no sign of Coppinger as he'd been named on the bench, but the blonde bombshell would play his part in this cup tie shortly after the hour.

My head was full of different scenarios.

A draw was handy as a share of the gate back at the Belle Vue stadium would be welcome; however a place in the third round draw opens up all sorts of doors. But what if it landed an away day at Rochdale or an energy-sapping costly trip to Darlington or the borders of Scotland to play fellow non-leaguers Carlisle who were still in the draw? Any money made from the Doncaster gate would surely be eaten up with those nightmare journeys.

I was given the answer to these questions within four minutes of the restart. Given the ball just before the halfway line, City's Dean Moxey hadn't much on. So he jogged with the ball a bit and entered Rovers' half, then he jogged a bit more, stopped, looked up and took aim. Devine and Flack entered the area but stopped. The ball travelled past them, over the on-looking Rovers defence, travelled on, over Waddington in the goal...

4759 people stopped, stood, stared...

The round leather object finally came down and nestled in the top right hand corner of the goalkeeper's goal.

In the words of some unknown fan decades ago - pick that one out!

Exeter City 2-0 Doncaster Rovers.

The roof came off the stadium. Mr Moxey may not have been known outside the confines of Exeter City but by tonight everyone in the country would see his utterly astonishing forty-yard screamer.

Now to this day, Dean will still swear to you he meant it. People have debated this subject at length and the conclusion we like to draw is that the twenty-one year-old knew exactly what he was doing when he spotted Andy Warrington off his goal-line in the forty-ninth minute of that cup tie at the Park. To be fair to the man, he did look up before taking aim in that direction and, although he went mental after notching, the man still seemed to know this would be the outcome the second the ball left his foot.

Back home, I'd been sent into an apoplectic fit by the strike and roasted the nuts off myself with a scalding hot cup of tea.

Just past the hour mark the ex-City man Coppinger made his way onto the field. His reception was warm and friendly (though I'm sure if we were 2-0 down instead of up, there was a possibility he could have been knifed whilst taking off his tracksuit.

Now it was just a race against the clock, as the Grecians tried to break up the play and wind down the clock. Every cup shock has it bit of good fortune though and this also seemed to have something to do with the kit Exeter were wearing. City, then in their centenary year, had been granted clearance to play in an all black and gold strip to commemorate the occasion. This only applied to the FA Cup however. The first airing the new kit got was in the Grimsby match, so the lucky theory seemed to be holding up well as City were on the verge of knocking out their second league club in the second game playing in the strip.

Now nobody who supports Exeter City was expecting this to fizzle out into a run-of-the-mill two goal victory and, four minutes from time, Doncaster made sure we'd be biting what's left of our fingernails until the final whistle when Blundell finally showed he could hit a barn door from five yards and drilled home to hand his side the chance of an unlikely replay.

For the last eighty-six minutes I'd been riding a wave of emotion from the obscurity of my living room, now I'd give my right arm to be standing on the terraces with the City faithful so I'd have someone to share the heart-stopping last few moments of this tremendous cup tie.

In injury time, Exeter came agonisingly close to finishing off the game when substitute Jake Edwards scrapes the paint on the visitors' post, before three traumatic minutes of injury time where several thousands home fans are sure fire candidates for simultaneous heart attacks should Rovers manage to score. Finally - at 5.54 pm - when it seems like every other result the entire length and breath of Britain has been decided and every team has hit the showers - the man in black, Mr Andy Penn puts the whistle to his mouth and brings to an end a barnstorming cup tie in which the Grecians have eventually triumphed.

The relief is audible. A sheer wave of elation replaces the past hour-and-a-half of pent-up anxiety. Every fan endures this rollercoaster of emotion literally once a week, be it on the terraces of their home ground or the far away environment of an away end, miles upon miles from home.

That night Dean Moxey's cheesy grin can be seen adorning Match of the Day. The Exeter man has put himself into the limelight with his forty-yard screamer and is a contender for goal of the month. Speaking on the show the winger says he's "happy as Larry" and automatically launches a money-spinning t-shirt business which sees hundreds of fans walking around the town in white t-shirts with Deano's arms aloft and the slogan "Happy as Larry" emblazoned across the front. The goal eventually wins Moxey the "player of the round" award and with it hospitality tickets to that season's cup final courtesy of the FA.

With the all-important third round draw not until the next day, I allow myself to dream of the potential multi-million pound clubs the Grecians could draw whilst enjoying a night on the tiles with my friends.

They all watched the wonder goal and I'm convinced the only two things that can be seen from space tonight are the Great Wall of China and Dean Moxey's smile.

Having not been out for a while, I overdose on my friend Jim Beam and end up talking to a doner kebab on the sidewalk for forty-five minutes before my wife comes to rescue my carcass.

The next morning I wake up with a mouth like Gandhi's flip-flop and several thousand hammers banging on my noggin.

It could be worse.

Round-a-phobia Ron ended up shelling out 200 Euros after the lads caught him trying to climb out the window of the ladies toilet.

They helped him down, took his money and promptly beat the crap out of him. Needless to say the drinks were on Ron for the night.

Chapter Four

NUMBER 64

The second Sunday of December greets my tired eyes with a cold grey sky and the promise of at least six hours of rain.

Hopefully there will be sunshine emanating from the television at precisely 3.20pm when Exeter City's ball goes into the third round draw drum. Until then I hide my time scoffing some toast whilst tuning in to what the goggle-box has to offer.

Reality TV does have a lot to answer for.

There really is no form of degradation to low to stoop in the so-called named of "entertainment".

Everything from pubic hair sandwiches to celebrity enema's have graced our screen and unless Channel 4 are going to start showing male cockfighting - and I do mean naked men fighting each other with their genitalia- then there's not many taboo's left to be broken.

What's next? Live sheep-shagging from the Outer Hebrides? I'm pretty sure you'd find at least one ex-Big Brother contestant willing to have sex with an animal in Scotland in order to get on television.

This morning proves no different. I'm watching a reality TV show based on the daily events on the London Underground.

Tom is a 57 year old counter clerk who faces a 16 hour shift and a multitude of eager tourists all wanting to know the way to Madame Tussauds. His job is made tougher with the threat of a lightning strike at midnight and the closure of the Bakerloo line. To cap it all off, Tom's forgotten his lunch.

Are you kidding me with this!

When the last bastion of entertainment is classed as a manically depressed tube worker telling a bunch of Chinese pensioners the train to Marble Arch is closed we are really up shit creek.

I can take the biggest waste of human life living in a house for three months for everyone to see. I can even stomach a complete non-entity of a woman pleasuring a pig while the whole of Britain watch in horror. But when I'm reduced to a 50-something civil servant getting excited because a strike been diverted on the Circle and District line, it's time to get the sleeping pills and go for the overdose.

Celebrity Detox, Celebrity Circus, Celebrity Cardboard box sleepover!

Have people just turned into gerbils?

Are things gone that bad that grown adults are now rushing home and tuning into the latest bowel movement of a Z-list star in a 24 hour toilet-thon where the winner is the quickest one to clear entire his digestive system of the pooh! And there's seemingly no end to it. No limit to the amount of sad, deluded individuals, ready and willing to humiliate themselves in the hope of a centre page spread and 15 minutes of fame before the fickle public erase them from their memory for all eternity.

As bad as the "celebrity" status that is bestowed upon these people for however short a time, there's nothing worse than a Z-lister who actually thinks they have talent and try to convince the entire universe that their witty charm or a fake set of tits are unbelievable talents that the outside world just have to see.

Then again can you blame them? For every idiot out there willing to do almost anything to get on screen, there's another pathetic production company who think filming holiday rep's drinking, vomiting and contracting a doze of gonorrhoea is a sure fire ratings winner.

All you need is to be able to drink for six weeks straight and have the morals of an alley cat. And it doesn't matter if you're paid nothing, come casting, there will still be a line as long as Hadrian's Wall outside the studio.

Cockroaches have a higher standing on this earth then these people.

With the FA cup draw drawing ever nearer it's time to switch from reality television nightmare to some live footy to get me in the mood.

That afternoon BBC 1 televise a live second round clash whilst at half-time I go on a mission to find the exact number Exeter City are in the draw.

By the time little Hinckley United have held Brentford to a scoreless draw (top notch entertainment folks!), I've discovered the number to watch out for in the draw drum is 64. With sixty-seven other teams going in the same drum - there's still some replays to sort - City have a good chance of drawing a decent team. Considering that 20 Premier teams and 24 Championship sides come into the draw for the first time, the Grecians just needed to avoid trips like an away day at Northampton or a home tie with Rochdale to be in the money.

And make no mistake about it; this is what it was all about at this stage for the cash-strapped Grecians.

Come on number 64!

Now with luck playing the all important part in this ten minute drama I turn to the man above for some devine inspiration. As I've mentioned on many an occasion I get on fabulously with the lord almighty. We have this understanding. I pray every morning and night for health happiness and 17 straight wins in a row for City, and God obliges by making sure the Grecians don't get beaten by a injury time winner off the fat arse of a Kidderminster Harriers defender.

At times I've questioned my faith (when Nayim scored that winner from the half way line for Zaragoza we weren't on speaking terms for at least a month), but we always end up making up (Arsenal's three FA cups in a row saw to that). You may think I slightly psychotic, but I'm convinced Arsenal's unbeaten 2004 title season was down to me saying three decades of the rosary at least once every hour. Henry's goals, Viera's midfield play-making and Campbell's defending had nothing to do with it! If I hadn't made a pact with the man upstairs to go to mass every night and repent my ass off , the Gunners would still be struggling in mid table obscurity!.

Given the fact I'd prayed Arsenal to the title, and got them to last years Champions League final (I neglected to go to confession that evening and I know it cost them the cup), I thought it was time to call in another favour.

I asked him to draw Arsene Wegner's majestic men in red and white and promised to recite three hail Marys, two Our Fathers and try keeping the profanity to a minimum over the next seven days.

Now all I can do is wait.

Finally the time comes. It's our first entry into the third round bag since the club went to Charlton in our relegation season of 2003 and gave Athletic a real shock - for ten minutes anyway- before the Londoners eventually won the game 3-1.

It was at this point that, arguably, one single man saved Exeter City Football Club. Step forward ex- Irish international and former Millwall, Aston Villa,

Chelsea, Celtic (and that's just the British clubs) player Mr Tony Cascarino.

The giant target man from Orpington, Kent was unknowingly about to write himself into Grecian folklore.

With the Centre Spot bar at the club thronged, Alex Inglethorpe & Steve Perryman watching at home, and yours truly kneeling with a crucifix and reciting the gospel according to St John, the stage was set for the big man to become a star in the eyes of every Exeter fan worldwide .

The magic moment arrived shortly before the midway point of the draw.

With everybody from Arsenal to Aldershot still a possibility to be paired against and everyone praying for a home draw, out come United.

That's United of Manchester United Football Club.

With his long lanky arm in reaches Big Cas into the draw drum.

"COME ON NUMBER 64" - roared the Centre Spot.

"COME ON NUMBER 64" - roared Alex and Steve.

"COME ON NUMBER 64" - roared the United fans!

Cascarino runs his hand around the black shiny numbered balls and takes one out. "Now I wonder if he picked out......"

He looks up. Clears his throat. Announces the number.

"64".

My brand new Homer Simpson mug hits the floor.

OH SWEET LAMB OF GOD!

SIXTY FOUR.

64!! 64!!! 64!!!!

GIMME A SIX. GIMME A FOUR. WHAT'VE YOU GOT?

64 - THAT'S F****** WHAT!!!!!!

Queue absolute pandemonium.

A sea of fists, scarf's and several hundred pounds worth of drink fly into the air in unison. A roar that would shatter a thousand glasses and measure ten on the Richter Scale (if we were in Los Angelus and it was an earthquake!).

Exeter City had drawn Manchester United.

The 1999 Champions League Winners.

The club that won seven of the last ten Premier titles. The side that dominated the... (OK that's enough of that; I'm a Gooner for Christ sake!).

Away...at Old Trafford.

The Theatre Of Dreams.

It takes three hours celebrating, and a multitude of phone-calls to everyone who knows me on the entire planet later for the penny to drop. To come to terms with the fact we'd actually drawn them. To actually believe in this massive stroke of luck, and the realisation that in less than a month this non-league club from South West England will kick off in front of a possible capacity 65,000 fans.

At this point life just simply could not get any sweeter. A sky high level in personal inner fulfilment and happiness. This is where I peaked. It felt like no matter what comes after this in my lifetime, nothing could possibly top this singular moment in time.

How wrong that would prove!

The next week saw me strut around the factory, chest out, head up and positively beaming with pride. Sure it presented United with, what looked on paper, a safe passage into the next round, but for me it meant much more than a tilt at the Red Devils and current cup holders. That little black ball with the number 64 on it would guarantee the survival of Exeter City Football Club.

All of a sudden the club who produced Uri Geller, Darth Vadar and the fraud squad were the team on every hack and sports editor from Topsham to the Thames. Television rights, match tickets and interviews. That Monday morning was a wee bit busier for the mild-mannered Andy Gillard at the club's commercial department. Twenty-four hours ago he'd been concentrating on mascots and match ball sponsors for a home game against Scarborough, now he was dealing with press the length and breath of Britain. For the first time ever they'd be queues at St James Park. Queues of fans all wanting to get their hands on tickets to the game at Old Trafford.

Seeing an opening in the merchandize market, the club needed no second invitation to capitalize on the Manchester United game. Scarf's, shirts, cups, hats, everything that you could print on was available to the discerning punter, as the club started the first stage of making a million quid to finally see off the creditors.

After some haggling and debate Exeter were eventually allocated 9,000 tickets to the United game at Old Trafford which would take place on January 8th 2005. This may seem a large amount for a side who barely scrape over 3,000 every other Saturday, but put a trip north to the Theatre Of Dreams and a multi-million pound Alex Ferguson led side, and you find an astonishing outbreak of renewed interest in Exeter City Football Club.

People who hadn't been to St James Park in years, or decades, suddenly realise how they missed the pure unadulterated joy of City winning 1-0 against Aldershot on a god-forsaken rain drench Tuesday night.

Not that the club cared. And rightly so. Although the hardened folk on Exeter's big bank might have shunned such glory-hunters, the directors of the club were more than happy to see every Tom, Dick and Harry stump up the dosh and buy their tickets to the Old Trafford Odyssey.

Me, I was sitting pretty. With tickets being guaranteed to season ticket holders, Red Or Dead pledgers, and Trust members, yours truly was one man already booked onto a flight to Manchester.

Best of all I wouldn't have to queue. No standing in line for my fat ass. That particular nightmare would go to Stuart - my soon to be standing in the pissing rain for four hours to get two tickets - best friend in the entire universe. The fact I could relax at home whilst my season-ticket holding pal was lining up with the trench coat brigade on a cold weekday morning, made the whole experience a little sweeter (though I did phone him as he queued and promised to mail him some hot soup - as he'd still be in line by the time it arrived!)

In all the pandemonium and press interest it was very easy to forget that two days after Cascarino had drawn number 64 from the drum, Alex Inglethorpe had to prepare his team to travel for a crucial midweek game against Dagenham and Redbridge.

Exciting times for City and their little band of hardened travel-weary supporters who made yet another midweek pilgrimage to the big city lights of London to take on the Daggers on their home turf of the Victoria ground.

With the delightful turmoil of a mere 48 hours ago, Alex's men could have been forgiven for letting their minds wonder to Old Trafford, a team of internationals and 65,000 screaming fans, but rather then distract Inglethorpe's men it inspired them, so much so within 15 minutes City had a comfortable two goal lead courtesy of Gareth Sheldon and our goal machine centre half Santos Gaia!

Have some of that Dagenham!

Unfortunately our hosts got a little annoyed at this and decided to try and spoil our little party by having the bare faced cheek of making a game of it! Just before the half hour mark Craig Mackail-Smith pulled one back for John Still's men and the home side completed the comeback on 57 minutes when Chris Moore done a fantastic re-enactment of the assassination of JFK by falling back in a heap after an imaginary sniper in the away end terrace shot him in the head.

With a patched up Exeter side having thrown away a two goal cushion and the home side now looking to snatch all three points, the men from Devon were up against it. Things somehow managed to get progressively worse and with twenty minutes left City's young goalkeeper Martin Rice was sent off for bringing down Chris Moore, who was actually fouled this time (though I'm sure he had William Defoe's death in Platoon in his locker had Ricey not touched him).

Exit one teenage goalkeeper only to be replaced by another. 19 year old Paul Jones replaced Ricey between the sticks and became a instant three second hero by turning away Moore's penalty and keeping Exeter in the game. The young Maidstone-born shot-stopper had worked under Inglethorpe at Leyton Orient and this would serve as an appetizer for further heroics down the line.

With nine minutes to go the under-strength Grecians were hanging on for the point when the travelling fans were presented with one of football's most satisfying pleasures - a goal completely against the run of play. On-loan Wayne O' Sullivan, who had replaced the ineffective Les Afful on 65 minutes, received a pass, found   some space, and rifled home from the edge of the area past big fat Tony Roberts in the Dagenham goal.

Queue bedlam courtesy of 350 red-and-white-scarfed nutcases crammed into an away end terrace and stunned silence from a severally ticked off home crowd. Trust me there's nothing as sweet as a goal completely out of the blue and utterly against the run of play when your sides being battered for most of the match and hanging on for dear life. What makes that moment even sweeter is if it's an unbelievably poxy goal. Not for me a 40 yard stunner which rips the entire net off the goal, or a Thierry Henry type run from midfield, beating 27 players before calmly placing the ball past a mesmerized goalkeeper.

Nope I want a twenty-man scramble in a muddy goalmouth and a deflected shot from our 44 year-old, 999-game playing defender whose hoofed effort goes in off the arse of the home sides top goalscorer who shouldn't have been back in the goalmouth in the first place.

Typically, it knocks the stuffing out of John Still's men and Wayne O' Sullivan's first goal of the season proves to be the winner in a game that had everything - five goals, two penalties and a sending off.

The real shame however, was that there was just over 1000 people at the Victoria Ground to witness the game. Just another depressing statistic of life in the Conference. A match that had everything any Premiership game could want was attended by a tiny crowd who at least had some great entertainment. Although there would have been less than 800 home fans roaring on their side, it was hard to point the finger at the home side's failure to entice more fans from their homes. Take in the midweek fixture, monopoly of Sky, and the fact Dagenham are a London club based in the heart of the country's capital, it was understandable that the club's directors were fighting a losing battle. Unless the Daggers were top of the league knocking on the door of league status, or had the money-spinning tie that Exeter had just been handed, it's really a case of cutting your cloth and watching the pennies for not only the London based non-league sides but every team in the Conference.

That unlikely win moved Alex's men up to seventh and within three points of the play-offs. The initial feel good factor that a new manager seems to generate at a football club was still apparent and the mid-table misgivings of some pessimists had given way to a general optimism that Exeter could finally make the play-offs at the end of April for the third time of asking.

I was cock-a-hoop that weekend when I lined up for a Saturday morning match with my Junior League side Kilbarry Rangers.

Now to understand this English equivalent of a Sunday League side, one needs a brief introduction to my club.

Kilbarry lie in the fourth division of Waterford Junior League football. It's a position that hasn't changed in nearly twenty years of the game and not likely to this season either.

Put bluntly, Rangers are the East Stirling of league football.

Each season they plod along turning one goal leads into 6-1 hammerings and several years of annihilation outside of their home ground have landed the team in the Guinness Book of Records for the least amount of points away from home in the history of Irish football - 3 points in 11 years (and that was only because the other team didn't show up). That 1997 walkover against Seaview Celtic is still talked about with great pride in the Shotgun Arms - we're the club went to drink after games.

A curious choice of pub, the Shotgun got its name in the '60s when old Fred Tinkle - on finding out his 55 year-old wife had been having an affair with the pub's owner Sacky Malone - loaded up his trusty double-barrel, marched into town, found the pub and blasted the living shit out of Sacky before ordering a double whisky and walking out.

The pub (originally named The Seaman's Tavern) was then sold and re-opened in the 90's as a theme pub - complete with Fred Tinkle's shotgun on the wall and the straight jacket he wore until his death at the age of 98 last Spring.

The 2004/05 season had begun the same as the last two decades for Davy Quilty, manager of Kilbarry and scorer of the quickest two own goals in football history. Somehow in a derby game against St Saviours in the late '90s he managed to turn a 1-0 lead on 45 minutes into a 2-1 half time deficit courtesy of two own goals in 55 seconds of injury time.

Now as a defender you can be unlucky to concede an own goal once in 90 minutes, but when you've drove past your own 'keeper from 35 yards then turn the opponents cross into your own net with the speed of a bullet a mere 50 seconds later, you really have to question what the fuck you're doing on the field.

This morning we played top of the table Piltown and the chances of getting something from the game are slim to none.

90 minutes and five second half goals later and nothings changed.

Kilbarry did manage to go in level at half-time thanks to two missed Piltown penalties and a five yard miss than even Stevie Wonder would have notched. But as we continued with our slightly defensive 9-1-1 line up, we finally fell behind just two minutes into the second half when the visitors scored a highly controversial opener. Controversial because at least five of our players tried their best to maim the Piltown forward before he netted.

Now I'm no ref, but if three men try to snap a player's leg off and a 20 stone centre half almost separates his head from his shoulders, you should really blow for a free before the man loses his life on the field of play.

Everything else was downhill from there. Three more goals followed before we finally made some headway - we gained a throw just by their corner flag.

In injury time the visitors scored their fifth but not before we made the inspired substitution of yours truly for Tosser Riordan - our regular playmaker and local jailbird. The only reason he'd got some action was because our manager felt sorry for him.

"Ah leave him on B; he's just got out after four months inside for breaking and entering!"

He'd broken into an electronics warehouse and stole an expensive plasma screen television but was caught when he went back in for the remote.

Tosser by name - tosser by nature.

With another 90 minutes of misery ended for another week, I head home, giving my team-mates and the Shotgun Arms a miss, and head to the bookies to do my coupon for this afternoon's football.

Despite the recent good form, Exeter still have a lot of work to do in order to pry their way into that all important top five play-off position. With at least ten teams chasing league leaders Carlisle and the all important Christmas period a mere two weeks away, City would have to keep maintaining solid results just to stay among the pacesetters.

This push would continue that afternoon with another trip east to play Stevenage Borough (or as they'll loveably know by Grecian fans SATAN-age!).

The Hertfordshire men haven't been on many clubs Christmas cards lists for many a year. They'd always been seen as a Conference cheque book club but this title owes more to the appointment of former Farnborough Town manager Graham Westley.

Back in 2003 Mr. Westley was manager of the little non-league club when they captured the nations hearts by putting up a spirited display against Arsenal at Highbury, even scoring before eventually losing out 5-1 to the then cup holders in the third round of the FA cup. Little did the Conference side know that, as they walked off to a standing ovation that afternoon, Westley would walk out on the side 8 months later for Stevenage and take half the team with him, a fact that condemned the little Hampshire based side to eventual relegation.

As for relations between Exeter and the Hertfordshire club? Let's just say there was more hope of Elvis making a comeback then both teams finding a new found respect for each other.

This would undoubtedly be put down to the 2003 meeting at Stevenage's Broadhall Way ground where the dust-up included accusations of cheating, flying missiles and a boardroom bust up - and that was just off the field!

Stevenage's chairman Phil Wallace started the controversy by denouncing Exeter for trying to slash their debts and avoid a possible 10 point deduction. On the field the game ended all square but not before City manager Eamonn Dolan had a missile fired at him and an ensuing boardroom argument broke out after Stevenage had accused the Devon men of blatant cheating.

With this in mind it wasn't a surprise that today's meeting between both clubs would produce an equally fiery encounter that started with a deranged Graham Westley touchline dance, and ended with a mass brawl at the final whistle.

From the start the loveable Mr Westley had employed intimation tactics by ranting and raving at any decision given against his side by the referee. After one particular offside decision he catapulted out of his seat, screaming like some kind of demented exotic bird at the officials, complete with waving arms like a mental patient on day release .

He need not have bothered. Exeter seemed to be self-inflicting all the damage and by the 45 minute mark the Grecians were lucky to be just one behind. Anthony Elding (who has been forever linked to Exeter in recent years) put the home side ahead with a magnificent header past the helpless Jones. Borough had plenty of chances to double that lead but the City back four - again changed due to an increasing long injury list - managed to get several body parts in the way to stop the net bulging again.

Inglethorpe's men looked strangely nervous and out of sorts. Just when the City bench were praying for the half-time whistle, Steve Flack decided it would be fun to score two goals in a minute and give us the lead!

With the stadium announcer stating there'd be two minutes injury time, Flackie latched onto Gareth Sheldon's parried shot to level the scores. And before you could say "get in there my son!" the striker astonishingly notched again. This time a cross from Marcus Martin was toe-poked past the disbelieving Andy Woodman to confound everyone in the ground and give Exeter an amazing 2-1 half time lead.

A body blow like that should have completely taken the wind out of the home sides sails but credit where its due, Westley's half-time team talk seemed to rejuvenate the home side and by the hour mark they were level .

With the game locked at 2-2, Inglethorpe would have been happy to settle for a share of the spoils, but Stevenage still sensed all the points were there for the taking.

Borough pinned the visitors back in their half for the final 15 minutes and Paul Jones made some outstanding saves just to keep the Grecians in the match. The Broadhall crowd roared the home side on and it wasn't really a surprise when six minutes from time Dino Maamria latched onto a dangerous Danny Bulman cross and scored a spectacular over-head kick.

The 1400 strong home fans went wild (not that they could be heard in the Ferrett and Donkey boozer at the end of the road) as Stevenage took a 3-2 lead which had looked on the cards for a while.

City tried to muster a late rally to finish the game level and make it a six goal thriller but the only attack launched was from City's young midfielder Marcus Martin who tried his best to separate Borough's Simon Weatherstone's torso from the rest of his body - amazing escaping a red card.

The bad feeling lingered until the final whistle when a mass brawl erupted between the teams as tempers boiled over.

The loveable Mr Westley came out after the game announcing his delight with the result and the pleasure of putting one over on the Devon side.

In truth you couldn't argue with the man. Despite the surprise of two first half injury time Exeter goals, Stevenage were by far the better side and only the fine form of Paul Jones had stopped it from being a more convincing scoreline for the home team.

The result dented City's promotion hopes but with two home games over the Christmas period to come, our heroes in red & white still had a chance to close the gap on the chasing pack.

Given two away trips to London against both Dagenham and Borough, a return of three points was acceptable enough. City could have drawn twice and came back from the capital undefeated, but they'd have returned with a point less then the 47 currently on the board. Exeter's fledging boss was also lamenting on a long injury list and small squad, not to mention the club's tiny budget. Not saying the club was broke but there's hobo's drinking wine and living in cardboard boxes with more money than Exeter City had. The club had a great youth policy but it's hard to throw in a young YTS lad up front when the opponents' centre-half is an eighteen stone 6'4" brick shithouse called Chopper. It brought to end an eventful week in the recent history of Exeter City Football Club.

A seven day period which started with City knocking out classy league opposition in Doncaster and ending it with a ten man no holds barred brawl with a mid-table Conference side. A week which started with the club's directors worrying were the next pound was coming from and ended with a possible million pound windfall.

I wondered to myself what United made of all this. Was it possible they'd have a scout at our home game at Scarborough. Were they aware of the goal-scoring prowess of Sean Devine, the majestic midfield play of Kwame Ampadu and the ex-boxer-cum -powerhouse target-man Steve Flack?

Would it be of concern that City had a free-scoring centre half in Santos Gaia and a potential leg breaker in Marcus Martin, or was it all just a laugh up north in the pubs and clubs around Old Trafford.

Either way the clubs directors and supporters were all going to enjoy their day out when the Grecians travelled up the M6 to Manchester in the first week of 2005.

Of course I'd had my fun with it in work, and on the football field. It felt great annoying my team-mates at Kilbarry Rangers, who all supported the Red Devils. This became very annoying in the 90's when Ferguson's men where winning all around them and I had to hear about it every weekend. (I feigned injury for the whole of May '99 when the dirty sods won the Champions League.)

Apart from myself there were only three other guys who didn't support the Old Trafford outfit.

There was Curly Power (Liverpool), Nelchy O'Mara (West Ham) and Chris Gillespie who supported Stenhousemuir after spending a weekend their in 1987 (mind you he hadn't a choice as his divorced alcho of a dad had kidnapped the child from his mother and ran away with him).

I'm not about to do a runner with my wife's kids anytime soon, but if I did I'd think I'd bring young Callum to a more exotic location the a depressing industrial town in northern Scotland.

It was the topic of conversation yet again the following Tuesday when we travelled to play Mullinivat Academicals in the preliminary round of the fourth division cup.

Although we lost 7-2, our manager Davy Quilty cleverly diverted the blame from his players in the local newspapers and blamed the hammering on the fact his team had their minds fixed on the upcoming basement battle with AFC Stradbally.

That and the fact his back four had been the victim of seven horrendous offside decisions.

Poor Davy.

He just hasn't a clue.

Chapter Five

FOOTBALL, FLU AND THE NAIL GUN MASSACRE.

I'm not a found lover of the word - work. It's only because I have two hungry mouths to support and a hefty credit card bill to pay off (mind you I'm about one day away from several large men with baseball bats paying me a visit) that I pull my weary body out of a lovely warm bed at 6 am to join the masses in our prison of choice for thirty-nine hours a week.

Don't get me wrong I'm not lazy and when you get over the fact you can't spend the rest of your life in a coma underneath the bed-sheets, I'm a pretty good worker. It's just that I'd rather not!

With a measly two floating days to play with for the whole year and an electricity bill for the entire country of Iceland, any time off from the daily grind is welcomed like a bacon double cheeseburger to a junk food addict.

As it so happens, yours truly has been laid low by a timely doze of the flu and will be spending the next five days away from the insane asylum I call work.

This came about from a weekend game with my beloved Kilbarry Rangers. The worst team in Division Four of the Waterford District and Junior League had come away from an away day league game against mid-table Woodstown Wanderers with a highly creditable 0-0 draw.

It was a barnstorming display by Quilty's no-hopers which saw us heroically defend for almost all the game, yet almost throw it away with a ninety-seventh minute penalty for the home side.

The game had been held up after our goalkeeper Morris Fitzgibbon knocked himself unconscious after a collision with his post and had to be resuscitated by a large bucket of water over his head. No such thing as smelling salts and physios at this level, just a magic sponge and a bucket of ice cold water. Once in a while you'll get lucky and receive some fancy spray to your groin for the challenge by that madman on the wing, but mainly there's a grin and bear it mentality at Sunday league level.

The heavens had opened after Morris's injury just after kick-off and rather then hinder the man between the sticks, it inspired our forty-two year-old goalkeeper who began to bring off a series of stunning first half saves to keep the score level. This gave our manager the idea of thumping Morris with a metal bar before every game, a practice which had to stop after Morris reported him to the police for aggravated assault.

With no dressing room, the half-time break was spent sucking on an orange in the safety of Curly Power's van before we returned to the field of play like drowned rats in skin tight jerseys.

Again we faced a barrage from the home side, occasionally breaking the play with the odd corner and a free kick from just outside the visitors' area after Jimmy Lynch made the most insane dive in the history of football. Although that free kick didn't produce a goal, it did result in Wanderers going down to ten men after Tommy's resulting free kick was driven straight into the genitals of their centre-half. With the home side having already used their substitutes, it gave us a one-man advantage which we exploited by putting one of our ten defenders into midfield - a brave move by our adventurous manager.

"It was a massive gamble but it paid off," announced Quilty after the game.

Just when it looked like we'd snatched a hard-earned point, the idiot of a ref announced he'd forgotten to put the added time from our goalkeeper's injury in

the first half and was now adding it on - in the ninetieth minute of the game!
For seven long agonizing minutes in a monsoon and hailstones that could break
a car window, Kilbarry hung on for dear life until a hand ball from our dope of
a player-manager gave Woodstown the chance to steal all three points.
We all tried our best to put the home side's striker off, everything from
staying in the penalty area, arguing with the ref and shouting obscenities about
the striker's fondness for sexual relations with farm animals, but in the end it
came down to two men against each other.
It was at this precise moment Morris re-enacted the ending sequence from
Escape to Victory.
With all the odds against him, our forty-two year-old slightly concussed shot-
stopper threw himself to the right, just like Sly Stallone, to save the penalty
with both hands and start a mass celebration among the Rangers' players.
Elation, joy, and spontaneous male bonding erupted. All we needed was Pele,
Bobby Moore and a thousand allied fans covering us in coats and breaking down
the gates as Max von Sydow and the German army watched on.
The price of this magnificent scoreless draw however was a hefty chest cold
and a doze of the flu which saw me bedridden and a slave to several packets of
Lemsip for the next seven days.
This came at a perfect time. With Christmas just a week away it gave me time
to root out the decorations, hang up the ten year-old lights and tell Santa I
needed nine points over the festive season for the Grecians.
That had started on Saturday when Exeter got back to winning ways with a
weekend victory against Scarborough.
The Stevenage game had seen a depleted City side stretched even more with
niggling injuries to Andy Taylor and Scott Hiley, but hopes would still have been
high against a Scarborough side who, although above Exeter, had struggled on
their travels.
Like my weekend drenching for Kilbarry, St James Park was also bathed in
God's tears from heaven, but for once this didn't seem to matter.
With this being Exeter's first home game since the Manchester United draw,
a thousand more interested locals had got out their maps and orienteered their
way to St James Park to swell the coffers for the cash-stricken club.
A crowd of over 4,500 - the highest league attendance of the season - popped
along to watch the men in red and white do battle with the Seasiders.
It was also a return home for a prodigal son. Paul Buckle had been a Grecian in
two previous spells in 1995 and 1999 and the thirty-four year-old midfielder,
whose career started in the '80s as a trainee at Brentford, had accepted an
SOS from Alex Inglethorpe to help out his injury-ravaged midfield. City had
already lost Kwame Ampadu, Marcus Martin, Barry McConnell and Glenn Cronin
from midfield plus injuries to Wayne O'Sullivan and the influential Chris Todd
meant that Exeter were struggling to even get three substitutes for the
bench.
The disjointed team started poorly and was forced on the back foot in the
opening minutes.
Struggling to get to terms with the game on an equally dodgy pitch, it wasn't
really a surprise when the Grecians finally went behind just before the half-
hour mark. However, the goal-scorer was a bit more of a shock.
Forty year-old Scarborough midfielder Neil Redfearn had cost over two million
in transfer fees throughout his career and had more clubs than Tiger Woods.

But that didn't stop the former Bolton, Charlton, Watford, Bradford (OK, you get the drift, there's eight more clubs in there!) from scoring a laser-guided free kick past Jones after a foul on one of the visitors.

You could here the groans all the way to the Duke of York pub. After attracting a thousand plus punters to a mid-table league game, City were yet again aiming the gun firmly at their feet and taking aim.

It was a common reoccurrence in the recent history of the cash-strapped club. Just when the team had gained interest from the armchair brigade and finally got them into the ground, Exeter produce ninety minutes of dross that quickly sends them running to the safety of an armchair, fire and the comfort of Sky Sports.

Exeter spent the rest of the half chasing shadows and the seaside outfit went in one good to the break.

With the regulars disgruntled and the newcomers wondering how in the name of Christ Exeter had beaten Doncaster Rovers - a side two divisions higher - City finally got their act together and a barn-storming second half saw the Grecians collect all three points.

Fifty-six minutes were on the clock when a hesitant Scarborough defence let Dean Moxey in to head City level. It took only five more minutes for the home side to complete the turnaround when Sean Devine played in Steve Flack and the big man stuck his drive sweetly past Walker in the visitors' goal.

The six-minute salvo completely took the wind out of Scarborough's sails. Having controlled the game for the first fifty-five minutes, the visitors where now looking to salvage a point when three had looked on the cards.

Boro manager Nick Henry put three up front and, late on, Paul Jones was called into action to deal with two long range efforts. But the points were made safe when City were awarded a penalty in the dying moments of the game. Scott Hiley's cross was headed down by Flack and struck Scarborough's Paul Foot on the arm. It was left to City's new captain Sean Devine to confidently strike past Leigh Walker to finally put the result beyond doubt.

All's well that ends well.

The result moved Alex Inglethorpe's men to within three points of the play-offs and made sure City's only home defeat since the new manager's arrival was still just that low key Vans Trophy loss to Swindon Town.

This made for interesting times as Exeter and the other twenty-one Conference sides entered the Christmas period with various expectations and hopes. For a side like the Grecians, nothing but a play-off place come the end of the season would be acceptable. That's not a cocky assumption, more a fact based on the fan base, full-time professionals and the status as one of the few ex-league teams in this division. And although Alex had hit the ground running with his tenure as Exeter manager, he knew that to keep the current love-in he had with the Grecian faithful – especially as he was seen as the man solely responsible for getting Exeter City back into the Football League. That fact could prove a millstone around any manager at a club with passionate fans and high expectations. Only time would really tell if Mr Inglethorpe was the man to lead us back into the Promised Land.

With a glorious week off work to look forward to, my five days of fun began with a Monday's leisurely stroll with my dog. Not that I could go outside with him so I tied him on the treadmill, set the timer to sixty minutes and gave him five miles in my own living room.

Tuesday, I became a bit more domesticated, folding some ironing and attempting spaghetti bolognese which gave both myself and the wife a two-hour appointment with the toilet bowl that night (it's times like this you remember those two words – 'best before' - are on the pack for a reason).

Wednesday however, saw me indulge in some entertainment and with it, I finally managed to see something that utterly defied belief - an eighty-minute piece of filmmaking that words just simply couldn't describe. I've been around thirty-seven years and have seen some woeful films in my time, but today changed history forever.

That's because I watched NAIL GUN MASSACRE.

THE worst film in cinematic history.

I'd managed to stumble across this nightmare when I rented it from Michael Myers - the video van man.

I've always found it amusing that a fifty-seven year-old divorcee who drove around a luminous green van selling DVDs could share the same name as the most notorious serial killer in horror film history.

When you think about it, Michael Myers is a pretty common name; it's just when you're named after the mass murderer in the Halloween film series, people don't know what to expect when you pull up at their door trying to flog a pirate copy of the latest Tom Cruise blockbuster.

Michael Myers hadn't much on offer today. Since he'd taken over the business from Tony Two Blues (he'd got that name from two notorious pornographic movies that everyone always rented), business was slow - which might have had something to do with the fact Tony Two Blues had been arrested for those exact two movies and was now spending eight months inside for flogging illegal porn to the whole of Waterford City.

However, he did have a special on a little "massacre collection" he had in a tatty brown box in the corner of his van.

He may have had the latest cinema releases on pirate, but for some strange reason Michael had put together an original collection of every movie ever made with the name "massacre" in the title.

Slumber Party Massacre. Sorority House Massacre. Cheerleader Massacre. Drive-In Movie Massacre (and that's only a few titles) - the list seemed endless.

With the pickings very slim on the new releases and the quality of the pirate copy being as visible as an Arab in a sandstorm, I thought I'd try my luck.

There, nestled between Microwave Massacre and Mountain Top Motel Massacre, lay the 1985 classic (and I use that word VERY loosely) Nail Gun Massacre.

Now I love my horror movies and consider myself somewhat of a film buff on the genre, but for some reason which is still a mystery to me, I decided that a mega-cheap '80s slasher flick about some deranged lunatic going around the backwoods of Alabama shooting people with a pneumatic nail gun was a great way to spend a Wednesday afternoon.

From the opening reel, I knew this film was going to go down in history for all the wrong reasons.

To summarize; the film starts with a group of rugged redneck builders taking advantage of an unfortunate brunette. Cut to the very next scene and we see the killer in army camouflage, complete with yellow oxygen tank on back, nailing one of the workmen to the floor of his own house courtesy of a pneumatic nail gun.

The fact the black helmet-wearing assassin is 52", built like a woman and has long brunette hair sticking out at the back, gives the killer's identity away in reel two of the film.

I watch in horror for the next seventy-eight minutes as the killer manages to track down and murder every one of the redneck builders before finally disappearing into the distance leaving the viewers with the assumption that the director had the bare-faced cheek to plan a sequel.

Now I'm no film director, but there are certain rules needed to make a film creditable and poor Terry Lawton - the sap responsible for this tripe - manages to break every single one of them. I present a few typical examples.

A) If you dress in standard issue army camouflage, you will be invisible to human eyes, even if you're standing three feet from someone with a big yellow oxygen tank strapped to your back.

B) Apparently, if you're a rampaging psycho killer it is possible to adjust your height by nearly two feet between murders (or even during the same murder).

C) Alabama has officially one sheriff and his badge can magically switch from one side of his uniform to the other - seemingly at will.

D) If you leave a lovemaking session with your unbelievably hot girlfriend with the greatest breasts in living history so you can go "chop wood" with your best buddy, you are clearly gay.

E) When a series of brutal slayings occur in your town, the local sheriff should not call the state patrol, FBI , or anyone for help because that would be too easy.

F) If your boyfriend is executed on the hood of your car, by all means run defencelessly towards the killer – topless - instead of the other way to safety.

G) Two construction workers who spend their free time having live nail gun fights with each other should probably be fired...or killed for the safety of those working with them.

H) Apparently a nail gun has the power to pin a man's hands to an Alabama highway with such force that the man can't free himself.

I) When killing off local rednecks, make sure to make savage wisecracks about their deaths right before they snuff it. That way, if the nails fail to kill him, the jokes will.

And finally...

J) When the murders have been solved, you can walk off into the sunset with a young woman you've just met, for no apparent reason, in the middle of nowhere and in the opposite direction from where your car is parked.

For all the God awful mistakes and monumental cock-ups in Mr Lawton's film, I laughed harder than any comedy I'd ever seen in my life. Trust me, if you're feeling done and need some cheering up, spend a few hours online trying to track down the last lunatic in the world who still has a copy of Nail Gun Massacre (probably Terry Lawton) and have yourself a fun night in.

Christmas came along and with it a bumper week of festive football. Exeter had gone into the festive season with that rousing 3-1 win against Scarborough and three crucial games in six days saw City turn the heat up on the chasing pack and finally get Exeter City into a play-off position.

On St.Stephen's Day (or Boxing Day, depending on your country) Graham

Turner's high-flying Hereford United were the visitors to an ice-cold St James Park.

The West Midlands outfit had been lingering about in the Conference ever since their heart-breaking relegation from League Two on the last day of the 1996/97 season.

A final-day victory was needed at Edgar Street, but a 1-1 draw against second-bottom Brighton managed to relegate the Herefordshire Club.

Guess who finished third-last that season?

Since then Turner's men had flirted with promotion from the Conference almost every year and this season was proving no different. Although both clubs hadn't met this season, by the time Christmas was over they'd be sick of the sight of one another. Apart from this game at St James Park, the club would reverse the fixture just six days later with a New Year's Day meeting at Edgar Street.

This would also be a chance for the City supporters to renew acquaintances with United's manager Graham Turner. As the Grecians fought administration and a ten- point deduction in their first Conference season, good ole Graham was extremely vocal about Exeter City's dilemma. The Hereford boss made it known he wanted the Devon club to face the firing squad and if they needed a rifleman to shoot first, the loveable Bulls' boss would be first in line to take aim.

So when Turner walked out with his team for the midday kick-off, he was about as popular as dose of piles.

Lucky enough for Exeter, their players played like they had a dose of them too. The rout began in the tenth minute when Hereford goalkeeper Craig Mawson got his bearings all wrong and punched the ball into his own net. It was to be the first of two own goals in the game for the hapless visitors.

City doubled the lead in first half injury time when Dean Moxey scored to put daylight between both sides at the interval.

Again the Grecians drew a 4,000 plus crowd to the Park, as the growing excitement about the impending Manchester game continued. With the Old Trafford tie now just two weeks away, the club was keen to keep the momentum building and three more points this afternoon in front of a sizeable crowd would keep the vultures at bay for another week.

Spirits were high and there must have been a child-like giddiness in the boardroom at the thought of exactly how much money could be made from the cup tie.

The second half was a mirror image of the first. Another own goal and another strike from a popular Exeter player.

Within just five minutes of the restart, Gareth Sheldon played in Sean Devine and the City number ten put the game beyond any doubt.

Fist aloft, kiss of the crest and a smile you could see from space, he turned to the fans on the big bank who adored him.

SEAN DEVINE, DEVINE
HE WEARS NUMBER 10 NOT 9
AND SCORES ALL THE FUCKING TIME
SEAN DEVINE, DEVINE

The former Wycombe striker and record buy for the Grecians may have been on good money, had a goal bonus and been the subject of much debate at the cash-strapped club, but when you have a man who could consistently hit the back of the onion bag and get you out of awful away day scrapes at Tamworth and Halifax, a player like that can be worth his weight in gold.

Not content with a three-goal deficit, Herford defender Tony James said he'd give us a belated Christmas present with a calamitous own goal on the hour mark.

Thanks Tony for remembering the spirit of Christmas and thumping the ball past your own goalkeeper to give us a four-goal lead.

Mr Graham Turner was not amused.

The Hereford boss sat in his dug-out and hoped the last half-hour didn't cause any more embarrassment for his promotion chasing team.

Twenty feet away, City manager Alex Inglethorpe cut a different figure. Out barking orders in his technical area, the young City boss knew how important this victory was. Exeter had been plodding along nicely of late, but this was a hammering dished out to one of the title chasing favourites. Three points that not only moved the Grecians into seventh, it started a few murmurs among the stands that maybe; just maybe, this could be City's year.

Christmas in the Kennedy household was the usual affair. Turkey overdose, hospital visit for broken toe after Lego accident and alcoholic Uncle Norm clearing the drinks cabinet out of your last four bottles of whiskey.

It's funny how the festive season is the one of the two times you meet your relatives (funerals are the other). Uncle Norm was one of those annual torments. It was the only time a year we saw him. I didn't want to be cynical and put this down to the fact the pubs were closed, but when the bars of Ireland shut on Good Friday he can normally be found cleaning his mum out of vodka in Cleethorpes.

Despite Norm's whiskey-swigging visit, calling my kids the wrong names and cursing the Catholic Church to high heaven, it couldn't detract from the real spirit of Christmas...three games in six days for Exeter.

With a multitude of football fixtures being played over the festive season, it also gave me time to catch up on the goings-on in a corner of North London that is forever Highbury.

Since their forty-nine game unbeaten run came to an end, Arsenal had struggled to gain momentum and had fallen off the pace, five points behind the Russian-owned corporation in West London (Chelsea) - though a 2-2 home draw against Roman's men at Highbury had helped steady the ship somewhat. Chelsea, under Jose Mourinho, had become the league leaders and the runaway train everybody was trying to catch.

The festive season was kind to the Gunners as well. A Robert Pires-inspired 2-0 win against Fulham on Boxing Day coupled with a single goal victory against Newcastle at the other St James Park kept Arsene Wegner's men in the title hunt.

Although I'd been planning a trip to London to see the Gunners play, any monies I had in the Credit Union account would be strictly going towards a trip to Devon and making sure I don't get knee-capped by paying off my credit cards. Back in the unofficial Fourth Division (my preferred choice of title for the Conference), it was all change at the top.

West London side Barnet had taken over at the top and put some distance between Carlisle, Hereford and the chasing pack. Since November, Paul Fairclough's side had gone on a run that put a nine-point gap over second placed

Carlisle. Although the Cumbrians had only lost three of the twenty-two league games to date, it was the amount of draws, coupled with the Londoners' amazing run, that had seen the gap develop.

City were in seventh place, just three points off the play-offs when they travelled west two days later to take on Staffordshire side Tamworth. This meant another trip to The Lamb - Tamworth's compact little home ground.

I used to think The Lamb was a strange name for a football ground until I found out Tamworth used to play at the Jolly Sailor! In doing some further research on the team, I've found out they acquired their floodlights on the cheap from Scarborough in the late '60s and when you visit The Lamb it's the very same pylons you'll see in place.

Exeter brought their usual few hundred to that afternoon's game as yours truly tuned into Sky Sports to watch the drama unfold via Soccer Special with Jeff Sterling and the boys.

I didn't have to wait long for some good news. Whilst munching on some leftover turkey and cursing Leyton Orient for letting my docket down after only nine minutes (they're 3-0 down at home to Chesterfield already) the name of Kesie Ibe flashes up on the screen.

A pumped fist is raised into the air, as I knock half my turkey and cheese sandwich to the ground (actually it doesn't even make the floor as the cats have caught it mid-air and ran off into the garden). The name isn't familiar, as Ibe has just been signed on a month's loan from Yeovil and was starting his first match for his new club. City hung onto the lead until half-time, but from the match stats and the grainy radio report, I could scarcely hear on the web, you just always felt that Alex's men needed the second goal to kill off the tie.

With just three minutes left, I was ready to settle for the tried and trusted George Graham '1-0 to the Arsenal' method when up popped Taylor to piss all over that theory.

With injury time fast approaching and three points on the horizon, the thirty-nine year-old ex-Premiership veteran (I'll not even mentioning the amount of clubs he's signed for - let's just leave it at Bolton!) stroked home from a corner to bring the home side level.

Luckily for Devil the cat, he was out of kicking distance when the scoreline flashed up on screen - (the dirty sod was still chomping on my turkey sandwich outside).

Per usual the air is turned blue, I curse the heavens above and pour scorn on little Tamworth for have the audacity to draw level with the mighty Grecians.

Just when it looked like City were having a great Christmas.

Just when it seemed Exeter were beating everyone in front of them.

Just when we've finally put together a decent...

Strike that!

Goal update!

TAMWORTH 1 - 2 EXETER CITY (Jake Edwards – eighty-nine minutes!)

Glory, Glory Hallelujah! His truth is marching on (as Elvis Presley once said!)

It proves to be the winning goal.

Another game, another three points. My Christmas wish of nine points from three games is just ninety minutes away from fulfillment.

Come on Santa don't let me down now!

The Boxing Day results are kind to the Grecians and a win away on New Years Day would put us into the play-offs. There's even a possibility of going third if results again go Exeter's way.

Easier said then done of course as the opponents, for the second time in a week, will be Hereford United.

New Year's Eve is possibly the worst night of the year. There's no point going out (unless you want to spend five hours grabbling with complete strangers to get to the bar). The nightclubs decide to rip everyone off and charge you fifty euros to get in (and that's only the price of checking your coat!). And if you order a taxi after midnight, you're lucky if it comes by the end of the month.

So the last day of 2004 is spent in quiet reflection back in the Kennedy household by yours truly and my beloved.

It wasn't a bad year. We re-mortgaged again (the last time to date - thank Christ). I cleared, cut up and burned two very troublesome credit cards. And a few more grey hairs set in, as I approached my mid-thirties with my mind at least still someway intact.

On the football front, Arsenal won the league, going through the entire season unbeaten and again proving that if you want value for money from a team playing the beautiful game right, then Highbury was the place to be.

It was the year of EURO 2004. Ireland flattered to deceive in the qualifiers. England did the same in the finals. And astonishingly Greece went on to upset hosts Portugal in the final.

As for Exeter...there was really only one talking point. Tony Cascarino plunging into a draw drum and picking out number sixty-four. All the problems with Cava's, creditors and possible closure had automatically erased with that away tie against Manchester United.

For the first time in the club's history, it felt liked they'd already won without even kicking a ball. Normally I couldn't give a fiddler's nancy what went on at Old Trafford. Now I was looking at recent attendances and hoping every United fan would pack the Theatre of Dreams to the rafters, just so Exeter could have a bumper share of the gate. There was no question the Devon club were never going to use their allocation and by New Years' Eve the club knew there would be over 9,000 Grecians travelling up north to watch Exeter do battle with the Premier giants.

The first day of 2005 started with a bang. That bang was my arse off the bathroom floor after slipping on a fresh batch of soap, which was promptly sent hurling out the bathroom window (several of my neighbours reported a strange looking object hurtling through the sky to the police at 9.37 that morning).

Despite being in pain that morning, by the afternoon Exeter had softened the blow considerably.

Although I would have been more than happy with a point from the visit to Hereford, Exeter put up another outstanding display against Graham Turner's men to beat the Bulls for the second time in a week.

With United well placed in the table, and Turner wanting revenge for the Boxing Day mauling at St James Park, it really wouldn't have been a surprise to see City slip up at Edgar Street, but Alex Inglethorpe seemed to have installed some real grit and tenacity into his men.

Still it's nice when the opposition start you off with an own goal!

As with the previous meeting at St James, Hereford seemed to have a fondness for putting the ball into their own net. After twenty-one minutes they were at it again when Adam Stansfield (now a Grecian) miscued and fired past the unfortunate Craig Mawson in the home goal. Poor old Craig was getting a tad annoyed with his defence, as by this stage it was the fifth time he'd walked into his net to pick the ball out.

The predictable onslaught from the home side ensued and City managed to hold out until just after the hour. Having put through his own net in the first half, Adam Stansfield made amends by collecting a pass from Jamie Pitman and coolly slotting past Martin Rice.

The scene was set for the home side to go on exact sweet revenge by winning the game. The crowd of almost 4,000 roared Hereford on to score that clinching goal and take three points from the visitors.

A twenty-minute period of utter dominance was surely the game plan now and a resulting victory for Graham Turner's men.

Andy Taylor didn't think so.

With the odds stacked against them, the ex-Manchester United trainee decided there wasn't enough misery heaped on Graham Turner yet, so just to annoy the Hereford manager even more, he popped up to score the winner.

Just when it looked like the travelling Grecians would have to endure a nerve-wracking last quarter of the game, Taylor managed to drive home from the tightest of angles to put Exeter ahead within five minutes of Hereford getting back into the game.

Sweet Jesus. This was too good to be true! Surely I'd been in some type of coma for the last month and the four straight wins and Manchester United tie where all just a wonderful dream which would be shattered the moment I woke up.

Exeter managed to see out the remaining minutes of the game and finally, for the first time this season, had forced themselves into the play-offs.

A Christmas period, which saw the Grecians win all four festive games and put Alex Inglethorpe in serious danger of winning the dreaded Manager of the Month, had pushed City smack bang into the title race and if any club had momentum at the moment it was the men in red and white at St James Park.

What a nice way to start the New Year. I could have done without the bathroom incident which nearly led to a hip replacement forty years early, but when all is said and done, I'm not paralyzed. Fifteen straight days of rain has stopped and I'm off to see my non-league team play Manchester United in the cup next week.

Thanks Santa.

I owe you one.

Chapter Six
CHAMPIONS LEAGUE? YOU'RE HAVING A LAUGH!

Whilst sitting down munching on my wife's lasagne and watching my hero Homer Simpson struggle against the tide of life, I get a two-word text from my pal Stuart in Exeter.

"Billericay Town"

Billericay Town? "What the hell are you on about?" - I swiftly text back.

"Can't talk. Doing ninety down the M5. Took wrong turn at Tewkesbury".

Thanks Stuart - you just managed to complicate things even more. Not only do I not know what Billericay Town is about, I'm now worried my pal will be arrested for shattering the speed limit after taking a wrong turn in a town I've never heard of until this summer: when Noah's Ark rode into town during the astonishing floods which submerged Tewkesbury and half of Gloucestershire.

Three hours later and after evading arrest, my pal clears up the whole story.

It seems Exeter have been drawn away to Ryman League club Billericay Town in the third round of the FA Trophy. With all the focus on Old Trafford at the end of the week, I'd completely forgotten about the draw for this competition. The FA Trophy is basically the FA Cup for non-league teams. With City dropping into the Conference in 2003, last season was the first taste the Grecians had of this tournament.

From automatic first round entry in the FA Cup, Exeter were now faced with long haul journeys to clubs like Braintree Town and Nuneaton Borough. Having graced the fields of league clubs week-in week-out, City were now coming up against the best of what the Ryman, Northern and Isthmian Leagues could throw at them.

Not exactly the stuff of dreams, but there would be a morbid fascination among some City fans to seek out these tiny ramshackle grounds and cheer their men in red and white on.

It's the adventurer in the away fan. The thrill of the hunt, the fun in the chase, the battle to get to the smallest location in a town you've never heard of, just so you're there to add a voice to the dedicated few who've also made the same mad trip as you to the middle of nowhere.

In their first season in the Trophy, Exeter safely negotiated three rounds (beating Hereford, Kings Lynn and Arlesey) before going out to fellow Conference side Aldershot 2-1 in a highly controversial game where City had a perfectly good goal ruled out by the referee's assistant.

Four words.

She is a woman.

Billericay were a Ryman League side from Essex, and managed by former Spurs stalwart Justin Edinburgh. Because of City's upcoming cup tie with Manchester United, Billericay would now have their own big day out against Exeter, and the fact it was the very next game after Old Trafford, had spiced things up for the Ryman League club. City may be overwhelming outsiders when they kick-off against United, but the tables would turn when Exeter had to travel to Town's New Lodge ground and the 68,000 Old Trafford capacity would be replaced by a humble Essex arena that topped its capacity at 3,000.

The week in work seemed to drag endlessly. Per usual I had to put up with United fans ribbing me over the fact Exeter where destined to concede at least fifteen goals in the first half and the embarrassment I'd face on my return from Old Trafford.

To counter that however there was an abundance of Liverpool, Chelsea and Arsenal fans more than happy to wish the little Grecians all the luck in the world when we took on United.

Hatred runs deep folks - no matter who United are playing!

With an early morning flight from Dublin to Manchester sorted, I decide to travel from Waterford Friday night and stay over in a plush Dublin hotel to start the weekend off on the right note.

Excited beyond all comprehension, I set off shortly after five that evening but need a stiff drink by the time we reach our capital thanks to three hours in the company of Yodelling Andy - the passenger from hell.

I was made aware of my loveable friend within seconds of departing from Plunkett Station in Waterford. Andy was a middle aged businessman with a passion for yodelling. He longed to break free from the chains of oppression and release his hidden talent on an unsuspecting world. His lifelong dream (which was explained to me at great length whilst he furiously munched a homemade pickled onion sandwich) was to sell out Carnegie Hall in New York to a yodelling-loving public who'd made him a star.

I loved the guy's enthusiasm, but I felt he had too many obstacles to overcome. The first one was being able to yodel.

Because...well, he couldn't.

As much as I wanted to here something that sounded remotely like yodelling, I'm pretty sure the excruciating noise that emanated from his throat was certainly not. It was only after the third rendition of The Blacks Hills of Dakota that Andy finally realised there was a better than average chance of him being kicked to death by the passengers, the second he stepped onto the platform in Dublin.

Even then he wanted to give an impromptu performance on the platform for the passers-by. I told him he'd be better saving his best yodelling for his real fans who would pack Carnegie Hall to the rafters the moment they heard he'd step foot in New York.

Luckily enough he agreed, and saved his vocals chords for his imaginary fans (and avoided a public stoning in the process.)

And off he went on his merry way. Our paths probably never destined to meet again, unless he phones me from Carnegie Hall, though I'm probably more likely to read about him being checked into the nearest mental institution.

Still God loves a trier.

That night is spent relaxing in a bar and making a pig of myself over a taco chip and doner kebab.

The next morning I'm up at the crack of dawn; wipe the salad cream and taco chip residue from my face and a stone cold shower later I'm out at Dublin airport.

A quick flick through the sports pages sees several articles on the David and Goliath clash today at Old Trafford.

How great was this. Here I am, standing in Dublin, wearing my best City jersey and bursting with pride. And I wasn't even on the plane yet!

By this afternoon, I'd be shoulder to shoulder with 9,000 other Grecian supporters, as I watch Exeter City stride out side by side with Premiership giants Manchester United. It would be an emotional moment for lots of people at the club, though the enormity of the moment was yet to hit me.

Since I was travelling alone, I'd arranged to meet up with Stuart, Bob and his son Crazy Greg at the hotel. Greg was a spur of the moment type of guy who could wake up tomorrow in a B&B in Lewisham and by sunset by snorkelling with turtles in Goa, or doing an Aboriginal dance with the locals out in the Bush.

The plan goes to a tee and by one o'clock we're all standing in the reception of the Britannia Hotel. A ton of familiar faces renew acquaintances and continue the chat they'd last had on the terraces of St James Park. It's like a Grecian reunion up north and everyone in red and white stripes is invited.

There was the North Devon Grecians from Bristol. The Exeter Exiles from London and even the Norwegian Exeter City Supporter's Club (I kid you not) were represented.

Fans from Germany, Canada and the good old US of A had travelled to be part of this piece of history. Even as far away as Australia you could find a Grecian willing to travel, as one amazing soul did. A hallowed congregation indeed.

By 2 pm the Grecian army is on the march!

A twenty-minute train journey from the hotel leads us to the Greater Manchester Borough of Trafford and a short walk to the ground itself.

Although the surrounding area seems very sterile, the same cannot be said of Old Trafford Stadium. From the towering three-tiered North Stand to the spectacularly redeveloped East stand with trademark glass front were thousands flock, all under the watchful eye of Sir Matt Busby.

Old Trafford's sheer size makes it a bewildering sight. A modern day monolith against the Mancunian skyline.

However, this is not my first visit to the home of Manchester United. As a young ten year-old in 1979 I was brought abroad for the first time in my life by my uncles - the Butlers.

Why my mother thought I'd be safe with a crowd of free range lunatics like her brothers I'll never know.

These were the guys who wrote the book on insanity. From sharing girlfriends to impersonating football managers (which Uncle Ray did when instead of paying through the turnstiles at a QPR match, he walked out the tunnel with the team instead).

That afternoon we were brought to Old Trafford to watch a scoreless draw between United and Derby (I still don't know what the hell I was doing there!), before hopping back on the ferry back home.

Although the surrounding area hadn't changed much, the theatre of dreams was now a pristine 68,000 all-seater stadium. Within its walls many a glorious tale could be regaled throughout the years. By 4.45 pm today a small team from South-West England was hoping to have made some memories of their own.

The first port of call is one of the many Ladbrokes betting shops inside the ground to place a bet on today's game. The lucky recipient of my £10 will be Exeter's captain Sean Devine. At odds of 20/1 for the first goal, I could be pocketing a juicy 200 smackers before the day is out.

A quick drink later and I'm off to my seat. For a man who teeters on the brink of a nervous breakdown every Saturday afternoon, I'm strangely calm. For the first time in my life the result isn't the most important thing. If this was a home game against Halifax or an away trip to Morecambe, I'd be pensively waiting for City to break the deadlock or praying to heaven above for that last minute, twenty-two-man goal mouth scramble to be cleared and the final whistle blown.

I sit down and take in the atmosphere for a few moments. To their credit, United will have close to a full house today which can either inspire or destroy visiting teams. That's a daunting thought for any league side, but when you happen to be a small squad of Conference players playing in front of the biggest crowd in their life you couldn't help but wonder which path City where going to go down today.

Five minutes to go...

Stuart's reading the programme, Bob's in a state of expectant frenzy and Crazy Greg is wondering where the best strip club in Manchester is.

"It's all about the titties B. All about the tits".

Then the teams emerge to a resounding crescendo of noise. Little Exeter City, the non-league club from South-West England , striding out toe to toe with Manchester United - possibly the most famous club on this planet.

It's an emotional moment from thousands of Exeter fans.

For some it's too much.

All around me are grown men with lumps in their throats, holding the tears back, chests stuck out with enormous pride. A pride that seemed to have been lost in the wilderness years of relegations, administrations and managerial merry go-rounds. A pride that blossomed with a glorious cup run in '81 and a majestic league title at the end of that decade.

To my left I see young fans, not even born when Tony Kellow was the darling of City's Cowshed stand, faces painted and waving their scarf's around in wild delirium. To my right, the weather-beaten face of an old man sitting down, perplexed, tears streaming at will from his face. A veteran of many a City game who's been deprived of this moment for far too long. A dedicated soul who's waited decade after decade to see his beloved City play in such a stadium to a crowd of this magnitude.

He just sits there in silence, nodding, capturing the moment and hoping it lasts for an eternity. Pride. Bursting with pride. Finally he wipes away the tears, looks up into the cold Manchester sky and a glowing smile is etched upon his face as if to say - thanks Lord. Thanks.

That was the moment it hit me - the sheer enormity of it all - to come from within minutes of extinction to walking out alongside former Champions League winners in the space of eighteen months.

For some, the world could have blown up at that precise moment and there still would have been thousands of Exeter fans who could die happy, safe in the knowledge they'd been here to spend their last moments on earth watching the team they love.

After all the hype, all the build up, Tony Cascarino's lucky dip and the clamber for tickets, the moment was finally upon us.

9,000 Exeter City fans prepared themselves to start ninety minutes of constant, non-stop, lung-bursting screaming in support of their team.

Exeter City, captained by Sean Devine (he's Irish remember!), lined up in front of a crowd of 67,551 as follows;

JONES, HILEY, SAWYER, GAIA, JEANNIN, MARTIN, CLAY, TAYLOR, MOXEY, DEVINE and FLACK.

United line up as expected with Alex Ferguson leaving out most of his major stars, but still putting out a competent Manchester side which should be well capable of dealing with the non-league minnows.

The team reads; HOWARD, NEVILLE, BROWN, PIQUE, SPECTOR, EAGLES,

DJEMBA-DJEMBA, JONES, MILLER, BELLION and RICHARDSON.

Even though Fergie gave youth a chance, he also included six full internationals with over 100 caps between them.

Phil Dowd - the man in black, signalled to each goalkeeper, checked his watch and shrilled his whistle into the air.

Here we go!

Now although Alex Inglethorpe would have had his troops well drilled, motivated and ready to lock horns with the Red Devils, I had my own plan in mind for the Grecians.

I'd broken the game up into seven different segments with its own little target.

0-15 minutes - Get through this without conceding and the chances of a 16-0 massacre could be really slim!

15-30 minutes - Still defending, but gain at least one corner by this stage.

30-45 minutes - Highly important. Throw everyone behind the ball and kick every United player in sight - thus not going behind to a jammy first half injury-time goal and hear United being booed off the pitch.

45-60 minutes - After the hair-dryer treatment from Fergie - United swarm all over us, but Paul Jones will make the first of fifty-seven important second half saves.

60-75 minutes - Still scoreless, we create our first chance, prompting Ferguson to throw on his "big-guns" to finally kill off the pesky Grecians.

75-90 minutes - City build an eleven-man human wall in the six yard area and defend the goalmouth like their whole life depends on it.

95 minutes and 34 seconds - Exeter win a free kick. Andy Taylor floats in a ball, causing panic in the United penalty area. In a massive scramble, Phil Neville attempts to clear the ball, drives it off the head of Wes Brown, knocking him unconscious. The ball rolls past Tim Howard, who in an attempt to save it has been blinded by mud from Neville's boot, and lands at the feet of Sean Devine who knocks the ball in from two yards out.

Great...now all they have to do is the simple task of carrying that out!

Exeter cope brilliantly with the all important opening exchanges. As expected every City player hassles and harries their illustrious opponents, not giving the hosts a minute to dwell on the ball. What's more impressive however, is the fact it's done without the standard lower league, slightly mistimed, crunching tackles that would have been expected (there's not a single booking in the entire ninety minutes).

Nearly twenty minutes pass before Liam Miler's tame header is comfortably saved by Paul Jones, who follows that up soon after by smartly turning away Chris Eagles free kick. Amazingly, Exeter might have had a penalty moments later when Dean Moxey's run into the United penalty area ended with the ball striking Phil Neville's arm.

A cry of unison up from 9,000 Grecians at the opposite end of the stadium.

"PENALTY!"

But referee Phil Dowd dismissed the claim with a wave of his arms.

"Bottled it!" - cried one fan.

"Typical" - roared another.

"When's the last time you've seen a penalty given against them here? I tell you there's no fucking justice for the little teams...NONE!" - said a slightly deranged fan on the verge of spontaneously combusting two rows away from me.

It didn't matter to us that we were at the opposite end of the stadium, miles away from the action, and referee Dowd was no more than ten feet away from the incident.

If we were to lose now the fans, press, and public would conveniently have a scapegoat.

In truth it was a lame shout: more in hope that would have been extremely harsh on United's stand-in captain.

The heavens then opened and 67,000 people were greeted with a thunderstorm of pelting rain and hailstones which could have killed a man had he been running back to his seat with two hot dogs and a balti pie for his mates.

Then Andy Taylor nearly gave us a heart-attack by almost scoring. A route one punt by Paul Jones was not dealt properly by ex-Barcelona player Gerard Pique and the ball landed at Taylor's feet who struck a stinging drive at Tim Howard who had to be alert to fist the ball back out.

Just when the United faithful had got over that shock, Andy had the bare-faced cheek to go even closer minutes later!

Marcus Martin, who covered every blade of grass on the Old Trafford pitch, passed to Dean Moxey who was crudely tore down by the increasing shaky Pique before he could access his options.

The scene was set for Andy. Taylor, who'd been frozen out as a Manchester United trainee just three years earlier, lined up the free lick on the edge of the area.

Wearing number seven, it echoed a similar scene to another ex-United player of the same numbered shirt who used to thrill the Stretford End with his mesmerizing free kicks. However Mr. Beckham had since departed for sunnier climates and now the Exeter midfielder was trying to replicate the former darling with one of his trademark free kicks.

Taylor jogged up, struck it sweetly and the net bulged.

To a man 9,000 Grecians jumped up in unison and an almighty roar shook the rafters of the East Stand.

Greg turned to me, grabbed my throat, ecstatically hopping up and down, shouting like a deranged lunatic.

"One Andy Taylor...there's only one Andy Taylor".

However I wasn't sharing his enthusiasm.

Although City had technically hit the net, it soon became apparent to me that it was the outside of it that had been struck with the ball.

I searched for a sentiment of incredibly bad luck to describe Andy's effort but "BOLLOCKS!" just about summed it all up.

The joyous scenes were abruptly cut short when instead of bringing the ball to the centre circle, United's 'keeper Tim Howard put it down for a goal kick.

There was some light hearted ribbing from the United fans as we realise our mistake and the scores stay 0-0. That moment, just before half time when every Grecian heart missed a beat, proved to be the closest Exeter would come to scoring all game.

City continued to hold their own until half-time (Moxey even had a half-chance) and left the field to a rousing reception from the travelling Grecians and a mocking joke at the host's expense.

"Champions League? You're having a laugh!"
"Champions League? You're having a laugh!"
Half Time; Manchester United 0-0 Exeter City.

The first half plan had worked brilliantly.

To get into the dressing room scoreless at half-time was a massive achievement. Now all the lads had to do was carry out the second half of my plan - defend for their lives - and score the winner in the fifth minute of injury time!

A scoreless first half would have been part of the plan for City manager Alex Inglethorpe as well. His troops had run themselves to a standstill in the first forty-five minutes, tracking United everywhere and closing off any avenue for Fergie's young starlets to exploit.

They'd imposed themselves of United and created the best chances of the first half, twice through ex-Manchester man Andy Taylor.

They'd been the better side in the half.

Now they had to do it all over again.

By the hour mark I was dreaming.

Thinking the unthinkable.

Allowing myself a moment of madness and imagining IF Exeter City could actually get something from the game.

My reasoning for this seemingly absurd thought came from what was unfolding right before my very eyes. Because with an hour gone at Old Trafford, Exeter City were, arguably, still comfortably holding Manchester United in their own backyard. Sure the red devils had possession and players that could turn a game with the flick on a boot, but other than Paul Jones being called on to catch routine balls and divert a first half free kick, Exeter could be more than happy with their hours work.

But that had to change...surely?

At some point United would have to start turning the screw, forcing the issue, and if need be, bringing on their big guns to finally put this increasingly irritating pesky little non-league club to bed.

United's starlets finally managed to beat Paul Jones soon after, but the evergreen Scott Hiley was on his line to drive away the David Jones effort. City began to sit a little deeper and the nerves began to twitch in the East Stand as we willed the seconds to pass like minutes.

Finally, on sixty-four minutes Ferguson had enough and conceded he'd need the help of two English internationals and a Portuguese sensation to get rid of this annoying little team who were actually threatening to take this to an almost unthinkable reply.

The Mancunian crowd breathed a sigh of relief as Paul Scholes and Cristano Ronaldo came on and Alan Smith was warmed up for further involvement should he be needed.

Now, thought the home crowd, this should be put to rest once and for all.

Although there was a collective groan from the Grecian contingent, I didn't mind the sight of a wafer-thin Portuguese teenager and the foul ginger hair of an English international one bit.

They way I saw it - Alex Ferguson had sent out the cream of his young talent, who had failed miserably to see off a side four divisions and ninety-four places below them, and had been humiliated into bring on his big guns to see Exeter City off.

Seventy minutes in.

Twenty minutes left - and still the travelling Grecian army is in full voice. Roaring, singing, willing their heroes in their lucky centenary black on for possibly the most nerve-wrecking, gut wrenching, heart-attack inducing twenty minutes of their life.

"Shall we sing a song for you?"

"Cider...Cider...Cider...Cider!"

"Are you Torquay in disguise?"

Even Bob - an argent United fan all his life - was giving it socks!

"You filthy little cheat Ronaldo!"

"You ginger tosser Scholes! Piss off home you fat lump of shit!"

"You dirty northern bastards!" - And that's some of his cleaner insults!

He may have followed the old Trafford outfit all his life- but they were a poor second to his beloved home town.

Football was his religion, and he worshipped at the altar of everything Grecian.

Alongside him Stuart was his pessimistic self.

"They're going to score, they're going to score. Don't know when, don't know how, but there's one thing for sure..."

"Jesus Stuart stop... for the love of Christ... It's hard enough watching this without you being the merchant of fucking doom for the last twenty minutes. "

United pile on the pressure.

Ronaldo jinks done the right hand flank, cuts inside Jeannin and unleashes a fierce drive at Exeter's goal, but eighteen year-old Paul Jones is equal to it.

Danny Clay is replaced by Kwame Ampadu. The equally young nineteen year-old has run himself to a standstill and makes way for ex-Arsenal midfielder Ampadu.

The hair bristles on the back of my neck.

Kwame's Irish.

How proud am I.

United counter that with Alan Smith for the woeful Bellion.

The blond striker strides onto the pitch.

"Who are ya? Who are ya?" - roar 9,000 Grecians.

Inglethorpe goes to the subs bench again.

Afful for Flack. City's veteran striker has seen enough of the Old Trafford grass to last him a lifetime and is replaced by a young twenty year-old Liverpudlian.

Surely the fairytale couldn't include a goal from a man born on the soil of United's most hated enemy?

Eighty minutes – ten minutes left.

I'm getting weak at the knees. Hoarse in the lungs. Heart in my mouth.

Ampadu sits in front of the back four and tries to break up everything United are throwing at them. Gaia and Sawyer attack every lofted ball into their area like it's a Plymouth supporter - and kick the living daylights out of it straight back up the park. Jeannin continues to knock heads with Ronaldo but sticks to him like a fly on a cow's arse. Scott Hiley continues to be inspired. Even the lord above wouldn't interrupt the thirty-seven year-old in the greatest game of his life.

Eighty-five minutes - five torturous minutes left at the theatre of dreams.

By now I've lost the feeling on my right hand side and I'm probably a few seconds from a stroke.

Christ this is unbearable.

I've travelled from another country to put myself on the verge of being hospitalized over a game of football. I've been on my feet for almost ninety minutes, my larynx is shattered, vocal chords shredded and I'm praying to heaven that this fucking match would end.

And this was supposed to be entertainment?

By this stage any notion Exeter had of pulling off the greatest shock in the history of the modern game has gone out the window and anything that came in City's half was just volleyed back into United's with interest. Only Sean Devine stands out of City's penalty area - and he's not even on the half way line. Despite this, Exeter's work-rate is phenomenal. With just minutes before the final whistle every single man is running, hassling, harrying, as fervently as they did from the moment Phil Dowd blew his whistle at three o' clock.

4.45 pm - The fourth official raises his electronic board.

9,000 heads turn left to the man on the sideline.

The tannoy announcer clears his throat.

"There will be three minutes of injury time ...Three minutes. "

The Grecian faithful defiantly raise the roof from the East Stand.

"WE LOVE YOU CITY, WE DO

WE LOVE YOU CITY, WE DO

WE LOVE YOU CITY, WE DO

OHHH CITY WE LOVE YOU!"

It's a hair-raising moment. Every single voice that travelled from Devon to Australia are on their feet - singing in unison. A crescendo of noise aimed to give the eleven men on the pitch the strength to make that extra tackle, run that extra mile, chase every single United player until every ounce of strength has evaporated from their body.

Another attack. Neville races down the line and sends over a cross. Smith chests it down, turns, but fires wide. A collective breath is sighed.

4.48 PM - ONE MINUTE OF INJURY TIME LEFT.

Having passed out two minutes ago when the fourth official raised his board (a fact I put down to thinking the board flashed up 8 minutes instead of 3), I come too only to find out the nightmare isn't over.

"Sweet lamb of Devine Christ I can't take this!" - I roar.

"Smith you twat! You cheat! You dirty Leeds reject!" - screams Bob.

"I just know their going to score. I just know their going to score!" - moans Stuart.

"Are we going clubbing tonight?" - ponders Greg.

Manchester United, realising the gig is almost up, launch one final attack. Although there is little more than seconds left, everyone in the stadium is well aware THIS is the time when United are so routinely lethal.

How many times down through the years have Fergie's men won games with virtually the last kick of the game? How many times has a 0-0 draw been transformed into a one goal victory be it from the boot of Ryan Giggs or the head of Gary Pallister (remember Steve Bruce's header against Sheffield Wednesday - SEVEN MINUTES into injury time some years back and the victory dance of Ferguson and the embarrassing Brian Kidd?)

So, not one of the travelling Grecians or the Stretford End faithful were counting the proverbial chickens before the final whistle has sounded.

One last time United get the ball. City pull back. It's now or never.

The ball comes to Kieran Richardson who bursts into the area. Scott Hiley moves out and blocks the midfielder, but the ball rolls to Paul Scholes from no more than ten feet out.

55

Stuart turns away.
Bob closes his eyes.
I'm now clinically dead.
He shoots...

Chapter Seven

IS THIS WAY TO BILLERICAY?

....the ball rolls past Paul Jones...and rolls...and rolls...and rolls inches wide of City's left-hand post.

9.000 souls in the East Stand collectively get up off their knees. The biggest novena ever offered up inside a football ground has been answered by our saviour Jesus Christ's intervention as the ball rolls wide and out of play.

Call it divine intervention. Call it Paul Scholes' crap left foot. Call it what you like and even though the game wasn't over, everyone knew THAT was the trademark last gasp chance that United seemed to put away so consistently over the years. We all knew they'd be ONE glorious United chance. We prayed it wouldn't come in the third minute of injury time with the game still scoreless, but we knew as great as City had been, there'd be one chance carved out that United should put away.

Jones drove the ball out...United returned it back deep into the left-hand corner where Richardson chased, but fouled Scott Hiley.

Relief was quickly turning to anger at the man in the middle. Where was the full time whistle?

United won a throw...

Suddenly I relaxed. 8,999 other Exeter City fans were moments away from storming the field and throttling the ref, but for the first time in ninety-three long, drawn out, agonising minutes, I had my hands in the air.

Whilst everyone around me seemed to focus on the throw, I'd noticed Phil Dowd, check the watch and put his whistle to mouth and...

1.4 seconds later...

Y E S S S S S S S S S S S S S!!!!!!! S W E E T   J E S U S   L O R D   O F   C H R I S T ... Y E S S S S S!!!!!!!!!!!!!!!!!!!!

4.49 PM - Manchester United 0 - 0 Exeter City FC

Whatever was left of the East Stand roof had been systematically blown away into the Manchester skyline by the sheer ferocity of the roar from underneath it!

Agony had turned to ecstasy. A massive love-in began with thousands of strangers embracing each other. Flags waved, fists raised, scarves twirled, men cried. A spontaneous outburst of sheer immense pride and joy whose warmth would heat up the Antarctic on its coldest day.

The players hugged and ran to salute their fans - every single one of them a hero. The United players left the field, heads down in collective shame and sought refuge among the safety of the dressing room (until Mr Ferguson came in that was). Their fans bemused, annoyed and angry at the fact that a non-league club had come to fortress Old Trafford and made away with a rather comfortable scoreless draw.

On the touchline Alex Inglethorpe shook hands with his gracious counterpart and pondered the press conference of his life.

It was almost too much joy at one time to handle. Anyone not embracing was on the phone to their favourite Manchester United-supporting uncle or aunt and laughing at them from the safety of their mobile. I've no idea how many people were giving or receiving abuse that moment, but I'm sure Vodafone made a small fortune from a corner of Old Trafford that evening. And boy were we enjoying it! The game might have been over ten minutes ago, but nobody was leaving this stadium. For a club whose cup history could be defined by a quarter-final in 1981 and another similar run over seventy-four years ago, there was now a new chapter to etch into the annals of the club's history. A story that would be regaled to their children and their offspring in thirty years time.

Only the FA Cup can produce this kind of magic. Only this tournament can seem to script a storyline like this when two sides, a world apart historically and financially, can be levelled on a playing field on a cold Manchester evening in January.

Finally, after what seems like an age of celebrating, we file out of the Theatre of Dreams, past the shell-shocked United fans, vendors and hot-dog stands and onto the train back to a hotel that will be rocking until the early hours of Sunday morning.

The twenty-minute ride back to the city centre proves to be an absolute joy to behold.

The train is so monstrously packed with elated Exeter fans, that it would put an Indian train to Calcutta to shame. There's not even standing room. Somehow 9,000 or so Exeter fans have squashed into seven tiny carriages. If there are 7,000 inside, I'm pretty sure the other 2,000 are on the roof or hanging out of the doors.

In between this bedlam stands the only man in the entire city of Manchester to get on the train. George Bartram – a sixty-four year-old pensioner who needs to get out three stops before the entire train falls out onto the platform back in the city centre.

"Get out of my way you young pups!" - he growls.

"Back in my day I could ride the tram for a crown and have a seat, without you ruffians jumping around with your flags and your knuckledusters!"

I'm not kidding - the man was priceless.

Needless to say there was as much chance of George being able to get out as a black man at a Ku Klux Klan convention. The only way grumpy Mr Bartram could get off was to punch a hole in the roof with his walking stick and hop out (even then he'd have killed about 500 Grecians on the roof).

Several minutes later, the train doors open and the entire population of Exeter spills out onto the platform.

Everyone has just one thought on their mind and it involves copious amounts of alcohol.

Business is over. Now it's time for pleasure.

Bob gets to the bar first and orders three bottles of champagne.

I'm glad I brought the Visa. This is going to prove as pricey as a three-week holiday in Barbados. I'm glad my friend Round-a-phobia Ron isn't here. He may get away with a round of lager for four people, but when you're asked to buy champers for eleven thirsty Englishman you will be kicked to death for trying to get out the window in the ladies toilet.

The feeling of euphoria was still evident at 2 am as eleven drunken Englishman and one alcoholic Irishman, attempted something that looked vaguely like dancing on the dance-floor of the Britannia Hotel's nightclub.

Even nine hours after the match, everyone's still doing their own little post-mortem and blow-by-blow re-enactment of a game that will go down in Exeter City history.

The drinks have been flowing like Niagara Falls and my credit cards going to spontaneously combust any second. In fact, the only time alcohol hasn't touched our mouths was between 10.45 pm and 11.30 pm when we all left the nightclub to huddle around the biggest TV we could find to watch Match of the Day.

Now the rest of Britain could see how a little non-league Club from Devon had went twelve rounds with the mighty Manchester United and scored a decisive points victory. Looking at the camera's scan over the sea of Exeter fans, seeing Andy Taylor's free kick, watching Alex Inglethorpe's interview (not to mention Fergie's red face!), and the glowing tributes praised by the pundits made it finally sink in what had actually been achieved by 4.49 pm on January 8th 2005. Pride isn't big enough a word.

I'd also managed to chat to Glenn Cronin - my injured Irish friend.

Although it had been gut-wrenching to have missed the biggest game of his life through that early season injury, he was still proud to have been part of a side that will be long remembered after this game.

Back at the nightclub, the dance floor has been taken over by different groups of celebrating Grecians intent of living the moment to the very max. Although there was a precession of buses and cars heading back down the M5 with portable parties taking place in each one, I was glad the option of staying over was taken up as, being Irish, I was going to get annihilated with alcohol whatever the scoreline.

If we got an absolute tonking - drink to erase the memory.

If we lost to a dodgy injury-time penalty - drink to console myself.

If we won or drew - well...drink to celebrate a monumental achievement.

Either way, I was getting baked out of my head! The perfect win-win scenario.

By now the triumphant City had arrived back in Exeter Airport to be greeted by a sea of red and white. Those unlucky enough not to get their hands on the tickets had arrived at the airport armed with flags, scarves and banners to welcome back a side that would be remembered around the city for decades to come.

The fact Alex Inglethorpe's men would be subjects of bar-room debate and stories regaled over firesides long after they'd hung up their boots was something none of them could even contemplate or come to terms with yet.

Taking thirty-somethings Sean Devine, Steve Flack and Scott Hiley out of the equation, Exeter's starting line up would be an average age of twenty. Players like Marcus Martin, Danny Clay, Gary Sawyer and Dean Moxey hadn't even celebrated twenty-one years alive and goalkeeper Paul Jones had just turned eighteen. Yet throw them into the biggest game of their short lives, against one of the giants in world football and a crowd of 67,000 watching on - they turn in a performance that completely belies their age.

This fact, more than the result itself, would prove to be completely astounding. Playing in front of sparsely attended stadiums against part-time teams, the only time these youngsters got a peek at the other side of the fence was in pre-season games against classier league opposition. Even the pressure of running out at St James Park in front of an expectant home crowd can be harrowing if things aren't going right and the home support particularly unforgiving.

So the mere fact none of these young men - many in their first year as a professional - didn't freeze in the face of such a monumental task and went on to produce an adrenalin-fuelled performance to stun a team of internationals and the British public, would make it a landmark moment in not only their lives, but the history of an entire club.

5 am - We're still partying like it's 1999 (only six years later). By this stage we've gone through the entire week's alcohol consumption of Germany and given our hotel enough money to buy the barman a Bentley. The party has dwindled, however, since around 3.15 am (lightweights!) and it's just myself, Greg and a handful of other Exeter City fans who arrived separately, but are brothers-in-arms tonight.

"Just think...in two hours time the morning papers back pages will all be about one football team - Exeter City" - says Greg (who's spent the entire annual budget of Romania tonight)

"How good a feeling is that?"

And how right my Visa-waving, slightly bankrupt friend was.

In a few shorts hours every coffee table in England and beyond would tell the story of a little club in Devon who humbled the mighty Manchester United in their own backyard.

Finally, at 5.37 am, my body shuts down and I pass out on the floor of my room. I awake to the annoying sound of incessant rapping on my room door.

"Get up you dirty alcoholic - you've got some explaining to do" - laughs Stuart.

A shower, shave and three packets of Panadol later, I'm munching away on a nice fry-up and scratching my noggin.

Apparently I've been accused of chatting up a sixty-three year-old divorcee from Cleethorpes who was particularly enamoured with me and my accent.

A flashback to a ten-minute chat with a mature lady, whose leg I nearly broke on the dance floor is, according to my friends, grounds for promiscuity and a possible extra-martial affair these days!

Now don't get me wrong. I'd flirt with a barn-door, but I draw the line at chatting up women who draw a pension and the contents of their mouth are left in a glass by the bedside each night.

The morning papers sprout headlines that are an absolute joy to the human eye.

EXETER GRITTY - say The Star

DEVON CREAM - crow The Mirror

EX-FACTOR - write the News of the World.

Oh God it felt good to be alive!

On landing back in Waterford, every newspaper shop is pillaged and there's not one publication in both countries that yours truly hadn't got by midday that Sunday. Shattered tired, but living on adrenalin, I manage to stay awake for two hours reading every piece of print on the Grecians before falling into a coma just as Bolton versus Blackburn kick-off on Sky (good thing I fell asleep).

By Thursday I managed to just about piss off every living and breathing Manchester United fan who'd come within five miles of me. As if it wasn't bad enough that the side they worshipped had been humiliated by a team four divisions below them, they now had to here a blow-by-blow account of it from the one man they knew who had been at the game.

That weekend I risked being hanged from the rafters of the Kilbarry Rangers dressing room as I goaded my Red Devil-loving team-mates before we went out on the pitch and threatened to play with the passion and fire of Exeter at Old Trafford seven short days ago. We attacked with renewed vigour and forced a corner after only twelve seconds. Unfortunately, that's as good as it got. Eighty-nine minutes and three sending-offs later, a routine 5-0 defeat to Southend Celtic ensued. Fortunately, our relegation rivals AFC Stradbally were also beaten, after only six of the squad turned up, annihilated 15-2 before the ref blew up - forty minutes early!

To be truthful, my United mates took the Grecian goading in good spirits. They were more annoyed that the rising cream of talent at Old Trafford had failed to put away a side who this week was taking on Billericay Town in the FA Trophy.

With the cash signs still dilating in the club's directors eyes and the realization that Exeter would make almost one million pounds from Old Trafford and the impending St James' replay, City had to come back over the other side of the fence again and prepare for a third round clash in the FA Trophy against Billericay.

The Essex club, currently playing in the Ryman League, had built up their own little media storm with the tie and now everyone wanted to beat the side that held the mighty Manchester United. Five days ago, everyone outside Greater Manchester wanted to see the Grecians put one over on Fergie's men, but by the time Exeter arrived at Billericay's New Lodge Ground, it was the Conference side that would be the greatest notch on the belt of Justin Edinburgh's Ryman League side.

Saturday afternoon brought a fine brisk day to the little Essex town of Billericay.

City arrived without fanfare, ready to begin life back in the real world after the fairytale of last weekend.

As always there would be a noticeable City support present (for exiles living in London it was a short forty-minute minute train journey), but despite what many may have thought New Lodge was a very pleasant Ryman League ground.

Situated just outside the town and surrounded by fields and woodland, it proves to be a most attractive setting. Manager Justin Edinburgh had urged locals to turn out and support Town and the rallying cry made sure there was a crowd six times the regular Saturday attendance come kick-off.

An hour later and City had been brought crashing back to planet Earth with an almighty thud.

Despite fielding a capable side, Alex's men were 2-0 behind and facing a slightly embarrassing early exit from the 2005 FA Trophy.

And City could have absolutely no complaints. Goals from Trott (38) and Forbes (46) had stunned the Grecians and the crowd of over 1300 would - in the words of Kevin Keegan - "love it, just love it" if they put one over on a side United couldn't even hit one against!

Now you'd think at this point Alex Inglethorpe would break a few tea-cups, bollock his players and tell them to get a grip and go out and win the game 3-2 wouldn't you? Surely to Christ that would work?

Well, not really!

City again struggled badly in the second half to break down their hosts and with just five minutes left, Billericay were already celebrating a highly impressive win over a side three divisions higher in the non-league footballing pyramid.

Then finally a glimmer of light. Captain Sean Devine managed to find space on eighty-five minutes and fire past Town's goalkeeper to, at long last, give the travelling Grecians something to cheer about. Amazingly within the space of sixty seconds Billericay had totally fallen apart. All the good work carved out in the first eighty-six minutes was completely undone literally seconds later when Jake Edwards brought Exeter City level at 2-2!

Astonishingly, that five-minute burst out of the blue almost even gave City a winner, with Devine again going close. You couldn't help but feel a tad sorry for the home team (even if their manager was an ex-Spurs player), as that could have so easily have been our story in Old Trafford. City could have played the proverbial blinder for the same eighty-six minutes, but could have been cruelly denied their reward with a couple of quick-fire, heartbreaking goals in the final moments of the game.

Billericay Town 2-2 Exeter City. And a replay at St James Park that had looked highly unlikely four minutes ago. Consolation for the Essex side came in the form of a bumper home crowd and a share of the gate in the replay.

By this stage, City had slipped out of the play-offs and the backlogged fixture list would mean Inglethorpe's men would have to play catch up.

Meanwhile the FA Cup fourth round draw had been made. Although it was still highly unlikely the Grecians would actually put United to the sword at St James (though try telling that to the whole of Exeter after Old Trafford), it was still interesting to see that a home tie against another Premiership side would be the reward.

Mid-table Middlesbrough would be the opposition should Sean Devine notch a routine hat-trick and dump the Red Devils out of the cup 3-0 (well lets say 3-2, as I think Rooney might manage to notch at least one!)

Before that however, there had been another insane clamour for tickets for the replay against Alex Ferguson's men. Again it was simply a delight to be living across in the Emerald Isle on the day Stuart was forced to stand in line for several painstaking hours to secure my ticket.

After four hours in the car park freezing his nuts off, my weather-beaten friend called to say he was a trifle tired by the days exploits - or as he put it - "I'm pissed off queuing for your tickets Kennedy!"

Given the fact he'd put in six hours of the harshest wind and rain the Devon skies could throw at him when collecting my Old Trafford ticket, the forty-something (he'll love that!) season ticket holder had been on his feet over TEN HOURS in order to secure a couple of tickets to a football game.

Bless him.

The question of IF I was travelling across the water to the replay was never in question (well maybe for about twenty minutes when I got the credit card bill). The chance to see City lock horns again with United was far too good an opportunity to miss out on. Competitive games like this, against world class opposition, in such an historic competition, just don't come round each week. And yes it would cost a small fortune again and yes I may be a sad individual, but I was an individual who was at Old Trafford to see Exeter hold United scoreless.

Sad? I beg to differ.

Sacrifices had to be made however and the weekend before the replay I was forced to stay in and watch the goggle box. Not that this is a chore as I love nothing more than stuffing my face with a pizza and kicking back to scour every single channel in search of the slightest bit of nudity.

My night's entertainment strangely started with a film I'd seen at least 627 times since its release. The Karate Kid is possibly the cheesiest film ever made, but that still won't deter me from watching the story of Daniel LaRusso - the lonely kid from New Jersey - overcoming bullies, bad hair days and the worst actor in Hollywood history to win the Hill Valley under-eighteen karate championship.

Poor old Danny, played by Ralph Macchio - who was probably about forty at the time, but for some reason always looked seventeen (he now looks nineteen - so I reckon he's about sixty-two in real life) - has been forced to move to California by his attractive, but slightly dim mom (she's moved to the other side of America to take up a job as a waitress in a Chinese restaurant) and spends the first few weeks of his life getting the crap kicked out of him by the local ham-acting teens.

Cue Mr. Miyagi -the only seventy-eight year old pensioner who can take on a bunch of punks sixty years younger than him and kick them to death quicker than you can microwave a chicken chow mien.

Together Daniel and his mentor take on the karate-kicking upstarts and their evil mentor, played by a 6'4" walking block of cheese called Martin Kove.

Poor old Marty. Whatever school of acting he graduated from his teacher should be hung, drawn and quartered (which no doubt happened the moment this film was released). He plays the role of the merciless sensei John Kreese so awfully that it's one of the best comedic performances in cinematic history. God blast the Academy for not nominating him for Best Supporting Actor in '85 (that pesky Haing S. Ngor won instead for The Killing Fields, though if you ask me Marty just about shaded it because of his mullet).

With the help of his teacher, Daniel masters the art of karate though painting houses and waxing cars for about fifty-seven weeks straight. Strange you may think, but I paid my brother to paint the garage for four days last summer and he's now a black belt. So the next time you leave some wax the car or paint the house watch out - by the time they've finished they'll probably be skilled in every martial art without even taking a single class.

Another thing The Karate Kid teaches is that you really don't need fancy moves and roundhouse kicks to the head in order to defeat your opponent. No. When facing defeat from an adversary who's beaten you fifty shades of black for the last half hour use the Miyagi crane technique by standing on one leg and make the shape of a deranged praying mantis. Your opponent will be so confused, he'll let his guard down, allowing you to deliver a swift kick to the head and render him unconscious for the best part of three weeks.

In the end, Daniel beats the bullies, wins the tournament and professes his undying love for Mr Miyagi, who's managed to get two houses painted and five cars waxed in the process.

I'm so pumped-up from Danny's dramatic one-legged praying mantis victory that I follow this up with Chuck Norris in Good Guys Wear Black...and here's where things start to go horribly wrong.

I only manage twelve minutes of the film before the poor man's Bruce Lee has me changing to The Shopping Channel to watch someone flogging BY-GUM!, the latest in denture adhesive.

Martin Kove probably knew he couldn't act. Chuck REALLY thinks he can. Starring in a film made by a man who couldn't direct a hosepipe, let alone a movie, Chuck tries to come across as Robert De Niro whilst roundhouse kicking his enemies into the middle of next week.

Even if Chuck is tied up, paralyzed from the neck down and faced with the entire continent of Asia, he'll still manage to kick their asses whilst delivering a line he thinks Al Pacino would be proud of.

This is after all the man who starred in INVASION USA. The story of a bearded redneck who finds out America is being invaded by those nasty communists, gets an Uzi, hops in his truck and manages to slaughter Brezhnev, the KGB, and three quarters of the entire population of Russia.

When film producers finally copped on to Mr Norris - Chuck had to reinvent himself on TV - which unfortunately he did with Walker Texas Ranger (he's so tough he evens sings the theme tune). Chuck can now been seen on the nearest shopping channel to you flogging his own line of gym equipment.

Please stick to that Chuck - not that I'd tell him that to his face.

Three days later and yet again I'm 20,000 feet over the Irish Sea full of hopes and dreams. If there was a frequent-flier scheme with the airline I'd surely qualify for at least a return flight to Skegness by now. (At this point I'd have loved to have mentioned the airline I use, but considering they're tighter than two coats of paint and only look after soulless corporate businessmen; I'll be passing on the free advertisement for them).

For the first time in years St James Park is buzzing. The prospect of Manchester United arriving tonight and a full house to boot has the club, supporters and the entire town abuzz in expectation.

An expectation that was no more than a crazy pipedream when City kicked off up north in Old Trafford. Back then, United versus City was to be one of several routine victories for the Premiership big-guns on their way to the next round. Just a three minute Match of the Day segment to an unsurprised audience.

Now the entire English press and media had descended on the south-west of England to bring the full story of our little club to the entire world.

Now the trails and tribulations of Exeter City Football Club would be regaled to all and sundry and a few misconstrued points could be put to rest.

Before this, everyone outside Devon thought Uri Geller was the spoon-bending psychic saviour of Exeter City and money was plentiful at St James Park. Why else would players like Lee Sharpe and Don Goodman hop on the Grecian gravy train unless the dosh was being handsomely doled out.

Now the club could tell the nation how relegation and administration had almost crippled the club in its centenary year and that Uri wasn't even a director. How the police had arrested City's two colourful chairmen and brought charges of fraud against them and the subsequent millions the club were in debt.

How City seemed destined to become another depressing football fatality.

An Accrington, Maidstone or Telford.

A statistic. Until the people who matter most, stood up and made themselves count for something. By setting up a trust, fighting prejudice, points deductions and agreeing terms to pay off their creditors, Exeter City were saved by their fans.

Not Uri Geller, Mike Lewis or John Russell.

Not even Michael Jackson, David Blaine or Darth Vader.

And with the Cascarino-inspired number sixty-four ball, the British media now had their ready made happy ending. Their story would have the feel-good factor that real fans of real football clubs love to here. The United games and the probable windfall of one million pounds had saved Exeter City and by 9.55 pm tonight the British public would have seen the transformation complete of the Devon club and could go to sleep knowing that dreams actually do sometimes come true.

Of course we wanted more!

We wanted to win and play Middlesboro in the next round!

I popped up to the Centre Spot bar. It's only 4 pm and the bar is doing a brisk trade downstairs. By six, the place will be heaving. BBC have arrived. ITV are wandering about. Reports are reporting.

Outside a marquee is being erected in the club car-park for visiting Manchester officials, whilst the makeshift television gantries and studio for Messrs Lineker, Lawrenson and Hansen is being fastidiously set up.

For the pundits who've convscated over Brazil, Argentina and the world's greatest footballing nations, tonight a non-league side from South-West England would be the focus of their attention.

They knew of Rooney and Ronaldo. Now they had to brush up on Sawyer and Sheldon.

Amazingly the first two people I've met since arriving in Exeter are ex-football players!

Former Middlesboro, Norwich and Irish international Keith O'Neill was a pleasant surprise next-seat passenger on the short fifty minute flight from Dublin.

The midfielder had just called time on his all too brief career and was doing some pundit work for Sky and Soccer AM. He was also on the bum for a ticket! "I think Roy Keane said he'd sort me for a ticket tonight, so I'm hoping to get that sorted...otherwise it's a TV and a bar buddy".

Being a fellow Irishman I was sympathetic to his plight.

"Go way out of it ya cheapskate!"

Keith shrugged his shoulders, grinned and wished City all the best before I dragged him back for the obligatory snap for the photo album.

No sooner had I walked into the Centre Spot than I was chatting to Mickey Thomas. The former Manchester United favourite-cum-pundit was in town for the night and buying a few drinks - minus the doggy fivers - at the bar. Being an Arsenal fan all my life, I finally got the chance to playfully abuse him for scoring that brilliant free kick for the Wrexham side that knocked the Gunners out of the 1992 FA Cup (which is still a travesty as we had two perfectly good goals disallowed!).

Outside the ground some ticketless fans are making enquires. Not only was a seat at tonight's game the hottest ticket in town, but some people are prepared to pay almost anything for one.

"I'll give you £350 for it" - said the bifocaled man in grey suit as I wondered around outside to sample the atmosphere.

I could sell my grandmother for that, but tonight was never an option.

With an hour to go Stuart and Bob arrive. They're closely followed by Crazy Greg who's made it along for the replay (luckily enough I've managed to re-mortgage my house in order to be able to spend a night on the tiles with him again).

Also trailing along is a familiar face in Peter Skinner - aka: "Kiss the Seat Pete". At the end of each home game Pete has a quick chat with his seat, gives it a kiss and waves his plastic-moulded friend goodbye for another week. His bond with the posterior-cuddling friend runs deep and each end of season game is an emotional moment for Mr Skinner as the realization he won't see his season-ticketed seat again until pre-season, can result in a mini-mental breakdown.

Thank goodness he has an emotional crutch in wife Sandy, who has become an expert councillor during those almost unbearable long summer weekends.

Crazy? - Well not really. It may seem like the ramblings of a deluded middle-aged lunatic to the opposite sex, but the hardened dyed-in-wool footy fan would embrace this behaviour as completely natural. In a world of prawn sandwiches and corporate clients, it's refreshing to know there are fans like Pete around. And he'll continue to chat to his silent friend about the sunny Saturday against Burton or that miserable Tuesday night when Crawley came to town long after the crowds have dispersed and the floodlights have gone out.

Shine on you crazy diamond - shine on.

Glenn pops in before kick-off to say hello. I can see his impish grin from miles away as he walks towards me. Seems he's had an interesting day.

Whilst sitting at home his phone rang. The voice on the other end of the receiver was a certain Mr Roy Keane. Apparently the United captain got wind of the Irishman's knee ligament injury that's ruled him out for the season and phoned to offer some sympathy and tips on training schedules for when he returned to the fray.

At first it took Cronin at least five minutes to actually believe it was United's captain on the other end of the line, but when the penny finally dropped, Glenn was happy to chat at length about the injury and his determination to get back into the engine room of the Grecian's midfield.

The Ballyfermot man was made up. Keane was his hero and to receive a phone call from him at his lowest ebb done wonders for the Exeter man who himself was lovingly labelled "Keano" by the City faithful in the stands and seats at St James Park.

Although I might not see eye to eye with some of the Corkman's views, (I still rate Vieira a better ball player) it was a real touch of class from a man who demands respect and doesn't suffer fools gladly.

With five minutes to go, I take my seat among a full house. 9033 people are packed into the Park. The last time this happened, City were heading out of the league and possible extinction.

Tonight there'd be nothing but celebration regardless of the scoreline.

That scoreline, however, was of massive importance to Mr Ferguson. United had travelled with a full squad and Sir Alex would not be attempting further humiliation by playing the same eleven that started twelve days ago in Old Trafford.

Ryan Giggs, Paul Scholes and Wayne Rooney would all start the replay and United's back four would include O'Shea, Fortune and both the Neville brothers.

Oh and there was also the small matter of Cristiano Ronaldo.

A team sheet to frighten many a side. The thought of facing both teenage sensations could scare even the hardest of centre-halfs and petrify a hesitant defence.

City hadn't time to think about that.

They had a replay to win.

Bring it on.

Chapter Eight

KING OF THE NUTMEGS

The eyes of England, nay the world, are firmly focused on a small club in Devon and round two of David versus Goliath.

When 9,000 Grecians left Old Trafford twelve days ago, the football fraternity would only get to read about City's achievement through newspapers and a smattering of BBC highlights. Now the entire country and millions further afield would get to see the Nationwide Conference club that almost created one of the biggest upsets in the recorded history of the game.

Again, Alex Inglethorpe's starting eleven would become part of football folklore even before they'd kick-off tonight.

Exeter showed just one change from the scoreless draw in Manchester - veteran midfielder Kwame Ampadu being recalled at the expense of Marcus Martin.

United's line-up was every so slightly different!

Out went the likes of Eagles, Pique, Spector, Bellion and Richardson.

In came Giggs, Scholes, Neville, O'Shea, Fortune, Rooney and Ronaldo.

Methinks it's safe to say Mr Ferguson wasn't exactly pleased with his international bright young things after the first ninety minutes.

Fergie can be psychotic with his players after away draws at Chelsea and Liverpool and berate his million-pound strikers after a 1-0 home win against Premiership giants like Arsenal.

Can you imagine what he was like after a 0-0 draw with Exeter City?

The infamous hair-dryer effect would have been so vicious that afternoon; none of the players would have needed a towel after a shower. Fergie would have blown every single one of them dry with one lash of his mouth.

Love him or loathe him, the man brought up in Govan, one of the toughest parts of his native Scotland, always commanded respect and ruled his dressing room with an iron fist.

From the start United take the game to City. There's urgency about Ferguson's men and the intention to show the world the scoreless ninety minutes in Old Trafford was an astonishing fluke, never likely to be repeated.

The main instigator would be Cristiano Ronaldo.

The Portuguese man may be as annoying as a doze of piles and go down quicker than a Thai hooker, but his genius was never in question.

He served notice of this after only three minutes when the nineteen year-old flashed a low drive across the penalty area which the on-rushing John O'Shea just failed to connect with (though some might say had he actually connected the ball would be halfway to Jupiter by now anyway).

Exeter replied by stringing together some passes and trying to force United back into their penalty area. Devine revelled in his captaincy. Flack determined to out-muscle every player in red. Moxey running himself to a standstill against the team he idolized. With a full house and a fiercely partisan crowd, United would need to silence the Grecian faithful soon. The longer this went on, the more expectant the crowd, the more edgy the visitors. The more time City went without conceding: the amazing likelihood that the Grecians would become so adventurous that they might have a go at actually win this game!

Ten seconds later Ronaldo changed everything.

Picking up possession on City's left flank, the nineteen year-old drove menacingly onwards, exchanged passes with Paul Scholes and drove his shot low and hard through Paul Jones legs in Exeter's goal.

Exeter City 0-1 Manchester United.

Finally, after almost 100 minutes of deadlock with a non-league team, Alex Ferguson's multi-million pound outfit had the lead.

Eight minutes in. A goal down. Just the start the Grecians were dreading.

In the makeshift studio, Messrs Lineker and Hansen frowned, whilst an audience of a million armchair critics reached for the remote.

"Game over - what's on ITV love?"- went the cry in households the length of Britain.

"Long night in store for Exeter now." - sighed a disappointed Mark Lawrenson.

"Christ this looks bad." - said Stuart rather predictably.

And who could blame them.

Exeter had been punished after less than ten minutes for having the bare-faced cheek of embarrassing United on their home turf twelve days ago and now it was payback time.

Or so we all thought.

Predictably United continued to dominate and play with their usual swagger, but City managed to just about keep them at bay. Gary Sawyer and Santos Gaia had their hands full with United's teenager tearaway Rooney and it seemed Scott Hiley had Ronaldo, O'Shea and Quentin Fortune attacking him on the left hand flank.

Although the visitors looked menacing at every attack, Ryan Giggs seemed to be having the proverbial 'mare'. The Welshman had fired in the direction of City's goalmouth on three occasions in the opening fifteen minutes, but only succeeded in hospitalizing eighty-seven year-old Mavis Watts who was struck by one of his efforts while walking home down Sidwell Street.

I found it quiet funny. As soon as Mr Giggs trudged back to the right hand flank, where yours truly was within earshot, I let him have it!

"If you played a few more times for your country you might have notched that one!"

Good healthy banter my friends. The Welshman is used to foul-mouthed tirades in giant stadia every Saturday from opposing fans, so an unknown voice in the crowd in rural Devon wasn't going to bother the United winger.

Unfortunately, it bothered some of the Manchester directors sitting three rows behind me. Within a minute I was politely asked to refrain from the Welsh team wisecracks and lay off insulting the Red Devils.

I agreed.

2.5 seconds later...

"Ryan Giggs' a Homo-sexual!"

Anything to make them feel uncomfortable.

Twenty minutes in, and the Grecians are still clinging onto the coat tails of their guests. Liam Miller sets up Rooney whose rasping drive is brilliantly dealt with by Paul Jones who does well to stay on his feet. Scholes tries to fashion an effort, but is blocked by the marauding duo of Sawyer and Gaia. Giggs again attempts to kill someone who's walking home from the pub three miles away.

Then on twenty-four minutes, the single moment of brilliance that seemed to define the tie. A second of disbelieving delight that astounded the public. A moment of individual artistry, cunningly planned an executed by one of the greatest players to grace this playing field of St. James Park.

Scott Hiley nutmegs Ronaldo.

Coming out of his own area, the veteran defender is closed down by United's young Portuguese international. Not one to panic, Hiley calmly stops, stands on the ball, and with his right leg strokes it between the nineteen year-old's legs and strides out to mass delirium from the home support.

"Scott Hiley will dine out on that one for the rest of his life!" - chuckles John Motson.

And how we loved it!

To United, and their thousand-strong travelling support, a mere fluke from an anonymous ageing left-back.

To the Grecians and millions of fire-side football fans – priceless!

Spurred on by Scotty's brilliance, City pushed forward and just before the half-hour mark create their first meaningful attempt on United's goal.

French defender Alex Jeannin passed the halfway line and unleashed a high ball into the visitors' goalmouth. Devils' goalkeeper Tim Howard race from his line to retrieve the routine long ball, but inexplicably flapped at the last moment allowing Steve Flack to beat him to the ball. Unfortunately Flackie's header was about as weak a eunuch's jockstrap and just about reached the six-yard box before being easily dealt with by Gary Neville.

United countered and win a corner on the right. Giggs lofts it into the danger area, but Rooney balloons his effort.

The Big Bank erupts and onslaughts of insults are hurled at young Wayne.

"You fat bastard! "

"Where's your granny gone?"

"You're Shrek...and you know you are!"

Moments later - another chorus about Rooney's portliness and weakness for middle-aged prostitutes are sung into the Devon night air after the Manchester striker blocks down an attempted clearance by Paul Jones, but uses his elbow and is flagged offside anyway.

Exeter's youngsters, despite being outplayed in midfield, are still sticking to their task with typical youthful exuberance. Willing to go in where it hurts, win every header and chase every lost cause. Danny Clay typifies this, as does Dean Moxey, whereas the older Andy Taylor looks for that killer pass and Kwame Ampadu tries to protect his overworked defence and break up anything coming from midfield.

And the defence was paramount. If City were to get anything from the game, it required its back-four (which was a back-ten at times during the tie), to snuff out anything their multi-million pound counterparts could throw at them. On-loan Gary Sawyer had filled in superbly for the missing and influential Chris Todd, whilst the swashbuckling Santos Gaia had thrown his body full length at anything that attempted to past him. Leg, chest, arse, there was nothing getting past Gaia unless it had laid him out flat first. Exeter's left-back Jeannin had been curtailed from his usual forays into the opponents' half, but had still managed to stand toe-to-toe with whoever came down his flank (which at any one time could be at least half the United side).

And then there was Scott Hiley. Still running, still tracking, still tackling and above all, still smiling.

Nutmegging Ronaldo can do that sometimes.

With the teams entering injury time in this enthralling first half, Exeter attempted to blow the roof clean off the Ivor Doble stand by going agonisingly close to scoring on the stroke of half-time.

Ampadu found Jeannin in space on the left wing and the Frenchman drove a cross into the visitors' area. The on-rushing Devine flicked the ball towards goal from just outside the six-yard box, but the effort went across the face of goal and narrowly wide. Had he missed by more, either one of the onrushing Flack or Taylor could have so easily poked it home.

Injury-time elapsed. Ref puts whistle to mouth. Half-time.

Exeter City 0-1 Manchester United.

9,033 people are allowed catch their breath. After over two hours of football between two teams four divisions apart, still only one goal separates them.

I'd been so caught up in the ensuing drama that I'd neglected my injury time jaunt to the burger stand for a double cheeseburger and lashings of hot Bovril. I'm not saying there was a queue at the burger stall, but I'd have caught a flight home, ordered a chicken burger from Greasy Ned's Takeaway, scoffed it down and still be back in time for the second half before I'd get to be served here.

Back in the studio, the pundits reflected on the first forty-five minutes. A game that seemed all over after just eight minutes was now giving Alan Hansen renewed hope.

"When there's the one goal in it, ye cannae write off the home team." - said Alan in his distinctive Scottish dialect. How the former darling of Anfield would have loved City to hammer one past United and strike a blow for every Liverpool, A.B.U and neutral fan worldwide.

In the land of armchair theatre, the slender one-goal margin would be ample reason to kick back, lash the kettle on and reheat the leftover Christmas mince pies.

Nobody was going anywhere just yet!

My mobile rang incessantly during the break. Thoughts of my friends in the Emerald Isle on the unfolding drama.

"They're panicking, Rooney's bollocksed, and he couldn't hit a barn door from five yards!"

"Drive that Portuguese stick insect into the back of the fucking stand!"

"That Steve Flack wouldn't score in a brothel with £200 in his pocket!"

"If United lose, I'm taking my life - just wanted my blood to be on your hands!"

However insane the text messages were, it still made me glow with inner pride that they'd taken time out to watch the game and text me their thoughts.

Before long both sides stride back out and the battle recommences.

City managed to string together some neat passages of play and a sustained period of five minutes of pressure ensues.

This results in both John Motson and henchman Lawrenson ignoring the play and cracking some more of the lamest witticisms ever heard on TV. Motson has created a new world record for saying "David versus Goliath" in the space of three minutes, whilst Lawrenson seems intent on letting the watching public know how upset he is at Liverpool's cup defeat to Burnley the night before - a fault he lies firmly at the door of the wonderfully inept Djimi Traore.

A strong wind has picked up and favours Exeter - still playing in their lucky, if unfamiliar, black centenary kit. Despite this advantage the Grecians are still chasing shadows, though the work-rate is still phenomenal.

Rooney - still the figure of hatred for the partisan home crowd - drives a shot which deflects off Paul Scholes, beats Paul Jones, rolls goalwards and with

Speilberg ready to shoot the next frame, gets stuck in the mud about six inches from the line.

Glorious, filthy mud - how I do love thee.

Jones recovers to smother the ball, but not before the United midfielder slides in and repeatedly tries to kick the ball from Jones hand.

"Get out of it you minging ginger bastard!" - roars the wonderfully psychotic Bob.

Whilst he roared abuse at his boyhood team in Old Trafford, there was always the tendency that, at the sight of a bad challenge from Scholes, Bob could make his way pitch-side and grab a fistful of ginger. There was something about the United man that triggered off an Incredible Hulk-style metamorphosis in Bob. Just the sight of the feisty flamed hair footballer gave this middle-aged man a rush of the Lou Ferrignos and unleashes a hulking green giant ready to decapitate the United midfielder at will.

Moments later Rooney plays a lovely through ball. Scholes sprints from the halfway line, takes possession, looks up and is penalised for offside.

I grab Bob before he changes from Dr Bruce Banner to a raging green psychopath.

"Premiership? You're having a laugh!" - comes the latest insult from the Grecians.

On the hour, Sean Devine gets another sniff of goal. Peeling off Gary Neville, he tries to volley home a cross from the left to the far post. Not sure whether to blast or place it, he ends up doing neither. Wide.

United look happy to leave Exeter have the ball, as for the Grecians, despite little spells of pressure; they still look pretty toothless in attack. Speaking of toothless, Liam Miller is withdrawn just after the hour, bringing to an end a night where the Irishman has been marginally the worst player on the field - just pipping Mr Giggs to the accolade.

Astonishingly there'd still been no booking in both games, a fact that Kwame Ampadu felt needed addressing. After all, what good, honest, blood-and-thunder cup tie would be worth its salt without the obligatory rush-of-blood suicidal hack by a lower league player?

So in keeping with that stereotype, Kwame decided someone needed pole-axing. Step forward victim number one - Eric Djemba-Djemba, who was almost making funeral arrangements from his deathbed after Mr Ampadu cut him in half on sixty-five minutes.

Not wanting to inform Eric's next of kin about his untimely death at the hands of a dreadlocked Dubliner, Ferguson ran out off his bench and demanded retribution from referee Phil Dowd. Fists waving, teeth clenched and glowing an unhealthy shade of purple, the fiery Scotsman was about ten seconds from becoming the first manager to spontaneously combust in front of a live audience.

The Exeter crowd didn't need to be prompted.

"One Arsene Wegner! - there's only one Arsene Wegner!"

A mass show of unity had just broken out in South-West England for Arsenal's French aristocrat and number one nemesis of Mr Ferguson.

By the time I'd got back from my sixteenth toilet break (a weak bladder and Siberian weather conditions aren't great bedfellows folks!), there was just over fifteen minutes left.

In keeping with my fantastically predictable knack of missing a key moment in a game whilst I'm empty the contents of my inflated bladder, I've just missed Andy Taylor sting the palms of Tim Howard with a well-taken free kick and Bob's lost his false teeth after spitting them out in rage when Scholes attempted to feign injury.

"Get up you filthy poof and put your stilettos back on!"

Then - a sight even the most cynical City fan thought they'd never witness - A moment that justified the most wide-eyed, blindly optimistic among us and sent the rose-tinted specs brigade into a new plateau of ecstasy.

Exeter City scoring against Manchester United.

Alex Jeannin's effort from outside the box falls to Sean Devine and the most expensive signing in City's history (£80,000) drives the ball past a static Tim Howard.

At that moment an earthquake measuring 5.7 on the Richter scale had just been recorded in South-West England. At 9.16 pm, nineteen days into 2005, a little corner of Devon has been hit by a tremor that would take out fifty Los Angeles apartment blocks and rattle San Francisco's Golden Gate Bridge.

It didn't matter it wasn't the winner. It didn't matter it wasn't even the equalizer. In fact, it didn't matter Devine was at least sixteen miles offside and the linesman had raised his flag long before he'd even touched the ball.

We'd seen Exeter City score. And even though most of us knew before the ball hit the back of the onion bag and the dead giveaway of United's players with hands on hips, we had, just for a moment, given St James Park, England and practically every Manchester United hating armchair individual in television land, a moment of sheer unbridled joy.

That was the moment. I sat back in my seat, look to the heavens and gave the man above a smile that could be seen from Saturn. There's many a Russian astronaut who's wondered what that strange glowing object coming from Western Europe was on the night of 19th January 2005. A satellite picture would have confirmed it was my cheesy smile- along with the Great Wall of China.

As much as I wanted City to actually go on and record a legitimate goal and bring this pulsating match level, I secretly felt that was our moment of glory. I think we all did. Sure it raised the roof and got pulses roaring into overdrive, but it acted as a frightening catalyst for Ferguson's men.

Maybe the Red Devils had thought the one goal was always a very comfortable cushion and that Fergie's men could pick off little City at any given moment. Maybe they'd gambled on a multitude of glaring defensive lapses by the home side, or convinced themselves Exeter would fold under persistent pressure. Up until seventy-five minutes on the clock United had looked solid if not spectacular, but the sight of a ball nesting in their net and 8,000 lunatics in the stands going ballistic, was still an embarrassment and a reminder that, after almost three hours of football, United STILL hadn't killed off this pesky little non-league side.

United step up the pressure. Paul Jones saves brilliantly from Ronaldo. A goalmouth scramble is cleared, and Wayne Rooney drives one straight into the bread basket of City's number one.

Exeter counter and two more missiles are launched into the visitors goalmouth causing United fans a serious case of the heebie-jeebies.

Ferguson is going nuclear on the sideline.

Jesus this is great.

72

Finally on eighty-eight minutes the game is put to rest. Predictably it comes from the boot of England's finest. With the match approaching injury-time, Wayne Rooney breaks free, rounds Paul Jones and delights the 1,000 strong Mancunians behind the Well Street road end by rolling the ball into an empty net.

Exeter City 0-2 Manchester United.

At long last and to the eternally grateful Manchester masses, the Premiership giants managed to quench the persistent fire in the house of Grecian.

178 minutes into the tie, Alex Inglethorpe's men have been finally killed off and United can plan for the visit of Middlesbrough.

In truth this scenario was beyond our most optimistic expectations. Not one soul who travelled North to Manchester twelve days ago could really have expected the tie to finally be settled just 120 seconds from the end of a replay at St James Park.

The final whistle shrills into the Devon air moments later. A game has been lost, but friends made worldwide by an audience who witnessed the pride, passion and unbreakable spirit of a club who many had not heard of.

No miss-match. No massacre. Just the magic of this glorious competition restored by a side that were almost defunct a year before. The money - the glorious money - that Exeter would make was certain to top one million pounds and insure that nice guys don't always finish last.

The standing ovation is worth the entry fee alone. Players walk to all four sides of St James, applauding their fans and receiving it back ten-fold. It's a moment of sincerity between both that's genuinely heartfelt.

The players know what we've done for them. We know what they've done for us. If there's a place for a happy defeat in football, it's been displayed tonight.

A battle on the pitch had been lost, but the war off of it won.

There's no time for gin and regret at the bar. Again the drink is following and the bank balance dwindling. Someone ordered champagne - I stuck with cider. The bubbly will be kept for our triumphant return to league football.

We might need a lot of ice.

As I clocked up my air miles the next morning and a multitude of headaches made their way back to the shop, factory and office, the same thought was filtering through our minds….could the Grecians kick on from here and win promotion?

Three days later Barnet revelled in the role of party-poopers by putting the first nail in that coffin with a 1-0 win at Underhill and, despite wins against Forest Green and Tamworth, Exeter would have a disastrous February losing four of their next five games.

Their single solitary win in that time came away at a woefully inept Leigh RMI who where doing their level best to enter the annuals of football history as the team with the worst points total in over a century of English football.

The Lancashire club was just eight weeks from the Conference finishing line, yet with just twenty-six games played was staring into the dark abyss of almost certain relegation from the division.

By the time Exeter came calling in late February, Leigh had managed just ONE win in all of those twenty-six games (that came back in AUGUST against Forest Green, whose manager has been living underground in a man-made shelter ever since).

RMI had managed just five more draws and an astonishing twenty defeats, leaving them with just eight points and a goal difference of minus forty-two! I'm not saying the outlook was gloomy for Leigh, but even East Stirling wanted a challenge game to boost their morale.

Although Manager Geoff Lutley had just resigned from the hot seat, I found this surprising.

Why you ask? Simple.

Geoff Lutley should have had the safest job in English football.

Many a rival manager most have woken in a cold sweat in the middle of the night before a fixture against Leigh RMI, imagining their fate if the seemingly unthinkable happened and they managed to lose to the worst side in England. As bad as RMI were, you just knew the inevitable was going to happen at some stage and with it the distinct possibility of the opposing manager being executed by way of balti pies and half-eaten hot dogs before he even got to the dressing room.

Lutley's three month winless run and job ended with a routine 3-0 defeat against York in front of a sizeable 701 fans (when your crowd of 252 against Gravesend is bulked up by eighteen travelling fans and a Manchester bound stag party you count 701 as scintillating progress).

Exeter's game - attended by 451 - wasn't deemed as top priority as York's visit; however RMI had made progress since Lutley's departure.

The board had taken poor Geoff out of his misery and replaced him with Steve Bleasdale (of Big Ron Manger fame) and the Liverpudlian had taken a point in his first game away to Forest Green Rovers.

The Grecians had slipped to tenth and, although the cup run had left Inglethorpe's men with games in hand, points in the bag are what really counted. And goals would be expected at Hilton Park that afternoon.

Leigh had three strikers with a deflected free kick between them.

Exeter has Sean Devine.

And it would be the talismanic Londoner with Irish blood that kept City in the promotion hunt with a goal on the half-hour mark. That nightmare scenario that saw the Grecians succumbing to the Lancashire part-timers almost became reality in the very first attack of the game when Gary Sawyer made a last-ditch challenge to stop RMI's debutant Chris Clarke scoring.

City, however, stuck to their task and Devine's scuffed shot rather fortuitously beat Mann in the home goal to give the Grecians a lead which they never looked like relinquishing.

City took the points, 451 people plodded home and Leigh manager Bleasdale would soon be seen on SKY ONE wanting to kill Ron Atkinson at Peterborough United.

The win had pushed Exeter back to seventh, but a home loss to York and a bad-tempered away defeat at Aldershot meant Inglethorpe's men would enter March in tenth place - four points of the last promotion spot.

However, the silver lining to this particular dreary February cloud came in the form of the FA Trophy where, having safely negotiated Billericay (2-0 in the subsequent replay), Tamworth and an outrageously poxy single-goal victory away to Stamford, City were drawn away to Conference South side Grays Athletic.

The Londoners were romping away with their league and were near certainties to be locking horns with the best the Conference had to offer in 2005/06.

This was due in no small part to the financial backing of millionaire Chairman

Micky Woodward. A self made man through his company West View Rail, Woodward had brought his money and business acumen to the London club and made Athletic a full-time professional side - unheard of outside the Conference.

Despite an average home crowd that rarely topped 1500, Woodward seemed determined to finance the club to a final resting place of league football - the holy grail of non-league clubs.

Exeter travelled east to the capital as favourites and with few Conference clubs left in the last eight, the Grecians could be forgiven for dreaming of cup glory in a competition they'd only just familiarized themselves with. Given the London-based Grecian Exiles would be out in force, it would also help spur on a City side that needed this timely distraction away from recent poor league form.

That sunny March afternoon 1800 walked through the turnstiles at the Recreation Ground to watch both sides do battle.

Unfortunately, only one team managed to actually show up. And it sure wasn't the west-country outfit.

Exeter were torn apart like a Kleenex at a snot party. From the opening minute, City seemed destined to play the entire ninety minutes in their own penalty area. Twenty-two minutes in, Gary Hooper headed the Conference South side ahead and three minutes later the lanky Dennis Oli doubled the home side's lead. The chortling locals and depressing skyline of high-rise buildings encapsulating the Recreation Ground did nothing to improve the slightly embarrassed (and highly agitated) visiting support.

Stuart and Bob had travelled for the game. Bang on half-time I receive the text.

"Two down. Need to change things. Uphill struggle. - Stuart"

Bob was briefer in his prognosis.

"Fucking abysmal."

His mood wasn't about to change anytime soon. Grays continued to press the issue after the break and, on fifty-six minutes, put any lingering doubt about the scoreline to bed when Oli raced through to make it 3-0. The striker - reported to be on a figure close to £2,000 a week - terrorized City's defence all afternoon, a defence he'd get familiar with in the coming season.

At 4.35 pm - whilst shaving six weeks of growth from my chin - the phone buzzes again.

It's another text from my loveable contacts at the Recreation Ground.

"Three down. Four hours on the A30 for this. Depressed. So depressed. Stuart"

Again Bob summed up the mood of the City support in two words.

"Utter bollocks".

With two minutes to go, the by now bewildered City support got a moment of celebration when Gareth Sheldon made it 3-1.

A text arrives.

"3-1. Might come back".

This was close followed thirty-four seconds later by another.

"Nope. 4-1."

The Grays Athletic defeat hurt. Not the fact Exeter had been well-beaten by a side a division lower and a financial status higher, but it seemed since the Old Trafford moment a mere six weeks ago, City had gone into reverse and were killing off any chance of league and cup glory.

With ten games left and City in tenth, Inglethorpe needed to get the good train Grecian back on track and pelting full steam ahead for the promised land of League football over that faraway distant horizon.

That would start with a chilly Tuesday in Devon against Burton Albion.

It would also clash with Kilbarry Rangers most important game of the season - the all important relegation clash with Stradbally FC. A massive six-pointer which both clubs would view with the reverence of a World Cup Final.

It also proves the worst possible time for Kilbarry's new Tourette's-suffering goalkeeper Danny Albion to make his debut.

Away day at The Shay - home of Halifax Town.

Callum Ryan Exeter Kennedy - he's just heard we're 1-0 up at Stafford.

First leg of play-offs against Oxford. We were crap that night.

City Till We're Dry! - The unbelieveable soaking at St.Albans.

GET IN THERE!! - Super Lee Phillips puts us 1-0 ahead against Morecambe in the play-off final.

Hero despite defeat - Paul Jones at Wembley.

High drama at the Kassam - the penalty shoot out v Oxford.

How we wanted it to stay this way - Wembley after 11 minutes play.

Lee Elam - scoring a hat-trick on his debut against former club Weymouth.

Alex Inglethorpe - Ex-City manager on the day Exeter held United at the Theatre Of Dreams.

Ian Tarr, Sandy Ample Charms and Kiss-the-seat Pete.

Mickey Thomas buys us all a drink (with a rubber £5 note).

Not a bad seat in the house. My view from block 140 at Wembley.

Oh the pain of it all! Chris Todd sits devastated on the wembley turf, Richard Logan looks on and some Morecambe player tries to console Adam Stansfield.

82

Out of nowhere, City find 26,000 new fans!
The 30,000 strong Grecian army at Wembley.

City's manager appaulds the Exeter faithful -
most of who are on the verge of suicide.

Paul Tisdale telling his team to claw their way
back into the game whilst impersonating a jungle lion.

Santa at Weymouth - (Rudolph is at the burger bar getting a balti pie).

Tamworth - home of City's first defeat of 06-07. Dick Turpin must have played up front - that's the only way to explain the daylight robbery.

The FA Cup replay against United at St James. I'm about to get cautioned for abusing Ryan (I'm having a nightmare) Giggs.

The FA CUP - possibly the greatest cup competition in the world! AFC Wimbeldon bring some colour to St James. They had the cheek to give us a good game!

The memorable return leg at Oxford -
a night we actually won a game on Tv - at the 15th attempt.

The picture says it all.

The teams line up at Wembley.

This picture captured the exact moment 37 seconds of fine weather broke out at St Albans.

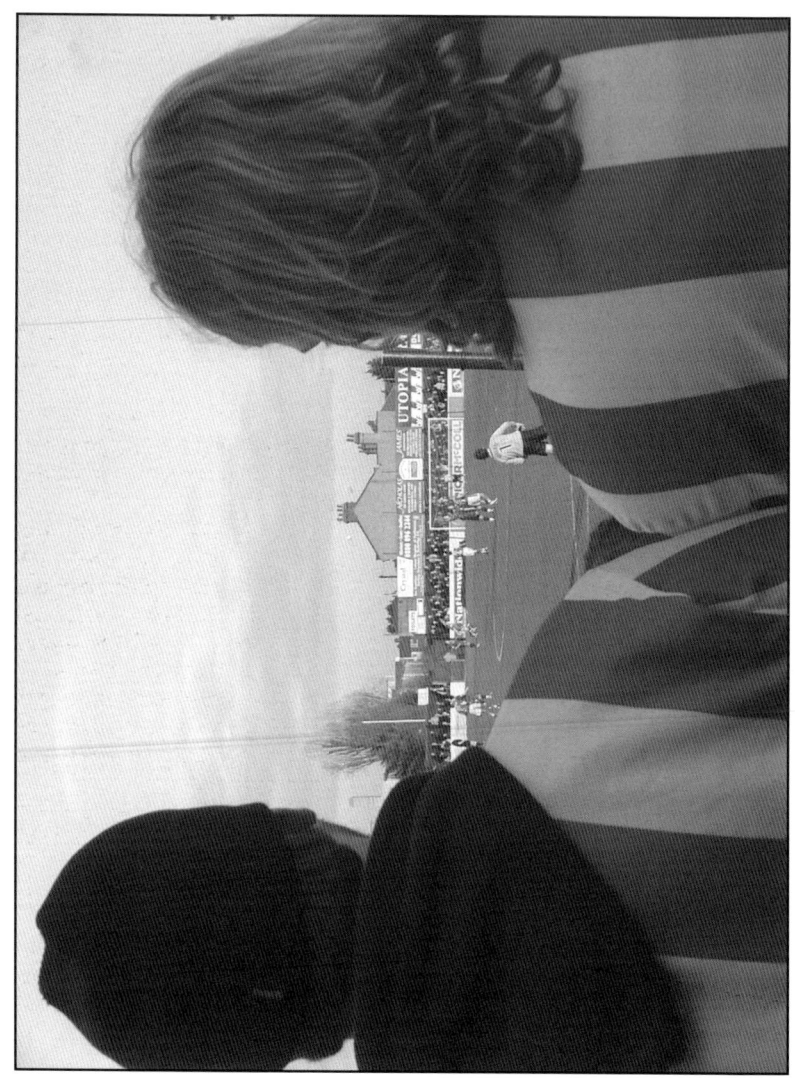

We Love You City - We Do. Away at Dagenham & Redbridge.

Chapter Nine
TEN CHIPS, THREE FISH AND A RIBSTEAK.

Tuesday night in Stradbally and the air is tinged with raw fear - a fear that threatens to engulf twenty-two young men about to do battle for the title of the second-worst team in Waterford.

For the last seven months, both Kilbarry and Stradbally had matched each other's results. Side by side, maintaining an astonishing winless run and failing gloriously over ninety minutes each weekend. For all the inept defending and woeful strike rates, both sides knew something had to give today. Three points for either side this evening and the Patsy McGuire Butchers Division Four League wooden spoon would surely be avoided. The league table made grim, but morbidly fascinating reading;

	P	W	D	L	F	A	PTS
KILBARRY RANGERS	16	1	2	13	11	47	5
AFC STRADBALLY	16	1	2	13	9	51	5

Both sides would have just one game after tonight. Stradbally would be at champions elect Mooncoin Celtic, whilst Rangers would travel to mid-table Tramore.

With both clubs expecting a routine slaying in those final outings, tonight would be a titanic clash of epic proportions. And although other clubs could scoff at Rangers line-up to pulverise our overworked defence and smirk as our strikers hit corner flags from the penalty spot, none of us cared.

We were enjoying ourselves. Turning up every weekend like thousands the length and breath of the country and giving our all for the cause. Sure we took the odd pulverising. Sure our goalkeeper had arthritis from picking the ball out of our net and sure the opposition didn't always needed eleven men to beat us, but it didn't matter. We were a ramshackle side of teenagers and tearaways enjoying life in Division Four of the Waterford Junior and District League.

Tonight's cliffhanger would prove a baptism of fire for Ranger's new goalkeeper Danny Albion. The Scotsman had arrived alone at training one evening with our centre-half Terry McGrath and dislodged Maurice Fitzgibbon between the sticks much to the annoyance of the twenty-one year-old student.

"Three years of broken teeth and concussions and you replace me with a five foot Scottish midget. Go fuck yourself from a height Quilty" - or words to that effect.

Danny may have been small, but what he lacked in height he made up for in agility and soon earned himself the nickname - The Cat.

Unfortunately, Danny had a handicap. Normally that was the ten men in front of him, but it soon became aware that our Scottish shot-stopper suffered from Tourette's Syndrome - meaning Danny couldn't control the volley of profanity that uncontrollably flew from his mouth.

"Danny sprint to the centre circle and back son."

"Bollocks!"

"Danny let Chris Gillespie take some goal-kicks on you."

"Bastard."

"Danny make sure you get the defence out early after we clear a corner."

"Wank. Balls. Cocknobs".

A sympathetic ref would be needed tonight, but instead we'd be handed Joey

Johnson - the tough-nut Barrack Street Undertaker, or as he's more commonly known - that Bastard in the Black.

Tonight would prove especially taxing on me as well. Bad enough I would have to play the lone striker in a 6-3-1 formation, but my nerves would also be shred as I couldn't park myself near a radio for a blow-by-blow account of Exeter's crunch home tie against Burton Albion. With my mobile confined to the sideline, I would have to devise a strategic system in order to check my texts from St James Park every few minutes.

The first of my checks-ins came on eleven minutes when I ran fifty yards in order to take a throw-in from the opposite end of the field.

"Christ he's up for it tonight!" - beamed our manager Davy Quilty.

The text made for grim reading.

"1-0 down. Goal scored by Simpkins. Typical"

And it was. In time-honored fashion an ex-City player had returned to the Park and put one over on his former club. Former Cardiff defender Michael Simpkins may have only played five times in a loan spell for the Grecians, but it was his header after only two minutes that had given Nigel Clough's Burton Albion an early lead at St James Park.

"That's just fucking peachy!" - I howled out sarcastically. I'd just busted a gut to break the Irish national 100 meters record, only to find out City had gone behind to an ex-Grecian who's just scored his first career goal (to date it's still the only time he's notched in almost 100 league appearances).

Somehow the hatred-filled anger I felt towards Clough's side, metamorphosed my performance and within five minutes I'd played my part in giving Kilbarry a priceless lead in the battle of the basement clubs.

Danny "The Cat" Albion's long hoof had deceived the Stradbally back-seven and allowed me to steal in behind the defence and chip the ball goalward over their advancing goalkeeper. Every player froze as the ball travelled in slow motion towards its resting place in the back of Stradbally's net.

Everyone that is except Curly Power. Seeing a chance for personal glory, Rangers centre-half sprinted seventy meters in four seconds, threw a wiry outstretched leg and made the minimal of contacts with the ball a millisecond before it crossed the goal line. He celebrated like his wife had just given birth. Despite his greed and blatant disregard for team camaraderie, I was still happy we'd taken the lead in this extremely crucial game.

If he cost me the top goalscorer award, I'll tear his eyes out with a can-opener.

By half-time both Kilbarry and Burton share identical scorelines. City have struggled and that ever elusive play-off ship is sailing away from shore without Alex Inglethorpe's crew. City just hadn't got into gear and even a draw at this stage was of no real benefit to the Grecians. An important team-talk for City was now needed.

A hundred miles away in a different country, a team-talk of more colourful adjectives, but of equal importance, is taking place. Kilbarry Rangers boss Davy Quilty is happy his side is leading (thanks apparently to Curly Power's vision!), but is nervous of a second half collapse to our fellow relegation strugglers. With three massive points and his reputation on the line, Davy lets everyone know they've still a job to do.

"Chrissy - keep it tight at the back. Nothing fancy. When in doubt - hoof it out!"

"Tosser - you're a streak of paralyzed piss and smell like a fucking brewery."

"Terry - If you've had another all-nighter in Burger King, I'll blind you with Mace".

"Ned - you're a waste of fucking space."

"Kennedy - That dormant organ in your head is called a brain - fucking use it!"

"And Cat - make sure you drive those kick-outs low. We're against the breeze now."

Now this type of constructive criticism might work in the lower leagues of English football, but when a manager, on a record forty-eight away match losing run, abuses you for carrying out his tactics, the insults will come back at twice the speed of sound.

"Davy, go fuck yourself!" - came the reply from eleven men in unison.

Despite the verbal abuse Davy got back for the rest of the break, his warning about playing into a fierce breeze was not heeded and within forty-five seconds of the restart Stradbally were level.

With his very first kick-out and driving into a gale force wind, Davy The Cat launched a thunderbolt into the air which was immediately caught in mid-flight by the howling wind and returned at lightning speed into the back of his own net. Having beaten himself from almost thirty yards, The Cat seemed hell-bent on repeating the trick at every opportunity. His spooned clearances seemed to catch the wind at just the right velocity and were sent flying back into his goalmouth. The Cat had become his own shot-stopper.

By this stage my phone had two texts illuminating the front display. Feigning injury and hobbling off the field for medical attention (and by medical attention I mean mouldy wet sponge to groin); I find out - thankfully- that Andy Taylor had brought Exeter City level with a neat finish. Unfortunately the second text reveals my wife needs a loaf of bread on the way home.

Then disaster. Whilst being told to speed up his goal-kicks by Mr Johnson, The Cat shouts "wanker" in his general direction. Despite the innocence of our Tourette-tormented goalkeeper, it's one "wanker" too much and the hard-nosed undertaker issues Danny with an automatic red card. To make matters worse, Kilbarry have only eleven players and Curly Power is forced to go between the sticks.

With eight minutes left the phone goes off. With just ten men on the field, I'm destined to spend the next few minutes wondering in agony at what drama has just unfolded at St James Park. Luckily, our hatchet man Nelchy O'Mara came to the rescue by driving Stradbally's sixteen year-old winger into the next field and adding ten minutes injury-time to the game in the process.

As the home side call an ambulance and send a search party to rescue their teenage winger from some bush, my joy cannot be tamed as I find out Steve Flack has scored on eighty-two minutes to give City a 2-1 lead.

With two minutes of injury time left, any medium of half-decent football has been squeezed from the life of this relegation battle and Stradbally versus Kilbarry has become a tennis match, with balls been served and returned into each other's half. By this stage I'm safe in the knowledge that Exeter have finally finished off Burton Albion, courtesy of Sean Devine and the Grecians can breathe easy.

There's one last moment of anxiety when a twenty-man goalmouth scramble in Kilbarry's penalty box results in at least half a dozen penalty appeals by the home side, but thankfully Mr Johnson waves five off them away (the sixth one was slightly dodgy as Stradbally's number ten had his leg severed off at the kneecap from a rogue Kilbarry leg). It ends seconds later amid bedlam and threats of retribution by shotgun.

AFC Stradbally 1-1 Kilbarry Rangers. Still second bottom. A job well done.

On the way home Davy Quilty loses the run of himself and treats the entire team to a nosh-up. Ten chips, three fish and a ribsteak are the spoils of war for his brave warriors, though this leaves Kilbarry's manager twenty-nine Euros out of pocket. It's a rush of blood that will cost Quilty again in the near future.

Exeter move up to ninth and crawl to within three points of the last play-off spot. That Saturday, Glen Cockerill's Woking come to town and use some awful spoiling tactics to frustrate the Grecians in a bad-tempered scoreless draw.

Despite this, Alex's men keep the revival going and string together two more useful results with a 2-2 draw at promotion chasing Morecambe and a somewhat laboured 2-1 victory against relegation-bound Farnborough.

April has always been the defining month in Conference football. With promotion and relegation matters still to be resolved throughout the country, the unofficial Division Four would draw to a close long before the triumphs and tears of a multitude of English league clubs.

A four-week run-in would see Exeter play seven games in twenty-one days. This punishing schedule would start away to Canvey Island and end with a daunting trip north to the borders of Scotland to play Carlisle. Barnet were already destined to life in League Two and the chasing pack included no less than ten teams after four play-off spots. City's challenge continued at Park Lane, the tiny home ground of Essex club Canvey Island.

The part-timers had caused an almighty shock early in the season by beating City at St James Park and the Gulls would give the Devon club another ninety minutes of torment at their ramshackle ground on the first Saturday in April. No sooner had I sat down with a hot cup of tea and vanilla slice, I was hurling my tasty treat at the nearest moving object (which happened to be Devil my cat), as the name Junior McDougal flashed on the Sky videprinter. A cross from ex-Ipswich player Neil Midgley landed at the Gulls striker, who beat Paul Jones and put Canvey ahead in the very first minute.

By the time Devil had strategically removed the remaining vanilla slice from his head and munched into my cake, the Grecians were still struggling. Flack and Devine had fallen out of favour and were-replaced by Jake Edwards and new signing Lee Phillips. The former Weymouth striker was strong, nimble and whole-heartedly committed to the cause, but neither striker was getting much change from the Gulls back-four.

A quick round-up of half-time scores made the day even more depressing. Sod's Law had intervened and dictated that every possible scoreline that could go against the Grecians - was.

Luckily enough I managed to pick up second-half commentary and share in the agony. If City were going to capitulate to a bunch of Essex part-timers again, at least now I'd be sharing in the blow-by-blow torment of it all.

With sixty-four minutes gone there was a better chance of Westlife writing original material than Exeter scoring that afternoon. Then City's young manager made an inspired substitution. Off came the ineffective Edwards to be replaced by the old reliable - Steve Flack. Sure there's times when the big man cant hit a barn door from five yards and have the turning capability of the QE2, but Flackie would soon be homing in on a hundred club goals for City and within sixty seconds of entering the fray, the Cambridge-born ex-boxer headed Exeter level, to cue a strange mix of relief and delirium among the Grecian faithful.

The expectant push finally arrived and City went for the jugular. Sheldon went close, a sea of Canvey legs blocked Sean Devine and Kwame Ampadu, having scored his first goal in 130 appearances for City, got a rush of blood to the head and attempted to notch again. When the breakthrough did come, it took a strapping young defender scoring his first senior goal for Exeter...Canvey Island's Dominic Sterling. The unfortunate own goal on eighty-one minutes by Canvey's number four, as a just - if slightly jammy - reward for City's persistence. Back home in the Kennedy household it's celebration time. The doughnuts are out; tea's on the boil and the cats a vanilla slice richer. Although there's still a few minutes left, I'm supremely confident that, having done the hard work, Exeter will close out the game and return home with the three points.

What's that they say about assumption being the mother of all fuck-ups?

With three minutes of injury-time played, Canvey win a corner and push everyone up. The ball is lofted into the crowded City goalmouth and pandemonium ensues. Unfortunately for the Grecians, Island's David McGhee displays a cool head and dramatically levels the game with virtually the last kick of the match.

There's just enough seconds for City to restart the game before the man in the middle calls a halt to proceedings.

Canvey Island 2-2 Exeter City. How much would that hurt come the end of the season? The travelling Grecians were in no doubt. This had been a damaging afternoon in Essex. Again City had lost ground on their rivals. Time and, more importantly, games were running out for Alex Inglethorpe's men. To be truthful, I should have seen the draw coming. Canvey had drawn ten of their eighteen home games and three of their last four games had finished level as well. Since falling into the Conference, every game had been a tiny stepping stone for Exeter back into the big-time, but being the proverbial big fish in a small pond; City found out all too quickly that teams wanted nothing better to put one over on the team that humbled Man United.

Three days later, Exeter's punishing schedule saw them line up at home to Halifax Town. The post-Man United crowds had disappeared and a more regular 3,500 adorned the stands and terraces of St James to see City dispose of the Shaymen on a brisk Tuesday night.

When betting on my beloveds, I always go for a lively outsider to notch the first goal. My stars had told me "luck would arrive in the form of a ginger stranger" - so I pumped twenty on Gareth Sheldon. No such luck - though I still felt a winner when the evergreen Paul Buckle steered home his second goal since rejoining the Grecians to give Exeter the lead. However, my money would have been safe on the next man to make the onion bag bulge. Lewis Killeen may not be a name for the purists, but the Halifax striker had constantly been a thorn in City's side ever since he scored the very first Conference goal against City on the opening day of the 2003/04 season. So at odds of 6/1, I'd let a tasty amount of mullah slip through my fingers when the beanpole hitman levelled just after the twenty-minute mark.

Given the circumstances of City's gruelling schedule, which had seen them play nearly once every four days, Inglethorpe's men could have been forgiven for feeling fatigued and lapsing in concentration, but the eleven weary troops picked themselves up, dusted themselves down and within fifteen minutes, Andy Taylor had slotted home what eventually turned out to be the winner.

Another tiring Tuesday. Another midweek match. Another back-breaking ninety minutes of football, but the reward of three priceless points for the mammoth Grecian endeavour. The games were coming thick and fast. No sooner had Halifax departed Devon, than City prepared for the visit of Northwich Victoria.

Sensing the perfect timing to get airborne and watch my beloveds take some part-time outfit apart, I decide its time to give my wife two days of solitary bliss and book a flight to Exeter. It's a special moment for my other half when I shift my posterior and vacate the Kennedy household for at least forty-eight hours. The wave goodbye - a mixture of sarcasm and excitement - starts a weekend of indulgence for my better half were she can kick back, down some plonk and control the remote without my fat ass around - whilst the milkman lurks menacingly in the background.

Before I can book a flight to the real St James Park (have some of that Newcastle), a meeting with my financial institution is on the cards. There's many a financial advisor who's contemplated suicide at the mere sight of yours truly in his office ushering those immortal words "re" and "mortgage".

Since my last re-mortgage (four on my last count - I think!), my bank manager had regained consciousness after a three-year coma and was back behind his desk. He's a loveable old codger and God knows I'd come close to putting him six feet under, but I needed to see Mr. Rodgers to keep me on the straight and narrow. Without someone cracking the proverbial whip on money matters, I could be just a credit card transaction away from sharing a cardboard box under the stars with my new friend Drunken Duncan the Alcoholic.

Thankfully our meeting doesn't result in a cardiac arrest for Mr. Rogers and his sound advice to cut up one of my remaining credit cards is reluctantly taken and my faithful old friend MasterCard bites the dust. In time-honoured fashion, my plastic pal is cremated and his ashes scattered over the Valley of Visa (my backyard).

Despite this, there's enough money in my daughter's piggy-bank (sorry, I meant my credit union account) to bale my sorry ass out and allow me one last trip to watch Exeter this season. There was always the distinct possibility of a play-off final to attend in a month's time, but I'd be saving the rent-boy idea for that.

Again I faced the Spanish inquisition about my ever-more-frequent trips abroad.

"How's the mistress?"

"Are the five kids all right?"

"Does your pimping operation extend to Tiverton?"

Now you can kind of see were they're coming from. It's not every man who'll spend twenty grand and re-mortgage a house three times for nothing more than eleven men playing non-league football in a different country. When you spend a solid seven hours travelling to watch a side that cannot attract Arthur Armchair and Barney Barstool from across the street, it does raise the odd eyebrow on the home front.

And although I'd love to boast about a female following or the odd psychotic stalker, I'm afraid my love interest in Exeter is confined to the playing field of St James Park and the utter devotion to the men in red and white.

96

Sad but true.

The Tuesday night three points from Halifax had pushed City to within two points of the play-offs and a win that Saturday at home to Northwich would actually push the Grecians back into the play-off zone. Exeter's recent revival had included four wins and three draws in a seven-game unbeaten run. The visit of a struggling Victoria side hovering just outside the relegation zone should have been the catalyst to launch City back into a prominent play-off position, one that the Grecians should hold onto under current form. Exeter had lost just four of their eighteen homes games to date, whilst Northwich had being defeated on ten different occasions away from the safety of their home turf. With over forty goals conceded on their travels (only two worse than the wonderfully inept Leigh RMI), Victoria should be ripe from a good old fashioned tonking, but the Vics lay in a false position.

Docked ten points for going into administration at the start of the season, manager Steve Burr had done an amazing job hauling the Cheshire club off the foot of the Conference table and, with a four-point cushion, another win would probably be enough to save a side that would be sitting comfortably in mid-table mediocrity had it not been for the pearls of administration - an increasingly more familiar penalty handed out to clubs in financial dire straits. For a change I touched down in Exeter on match-day instead of the night before. My reasons were threefold;

A - Arriving Friday coincides with a six-hour pub crawl that completely annihilates my unworthy carcass.

B - By the time I wake the next morning there's enough alcohol in my system to kill a herd of Buffalo.

C - In one night I've spent the entire financial budget of Microsoft.

So with this in mind, I make my way to Dublin airport and take the short forty-five minute flight to Exeter and avoid waking in a trashcan feeling like death warmed up and not out of pocket to the tune of Arsenal's annual transfer budget.

Hopes are high as I exchange chit-chat, read the programme and take my seat in the stand to watch the latest saga in City's season unfold.

And boy have I picked a humdinger.

The next ninety-three minutes encapsulate absolutely everything a lower league football fan can go through whilst standing on the terraces on a Saturday afternoon watching their pride and joy.

Five goals, sending offs, woeful defending, ten-man brawl, own goals and career threatening injuries. And Exeter City against Northwich Victoria had them all. City were one down before they could blink. Two behind by half-time. And down to ten men before they could mount a comeback. In between all this was a howler of an own goal and the final moments of Sean Devine's Exeter City career.

Typically it was classic City. A large expectant crowd had turned out only to see Exeter firmly aim the shotgun at their feet and take aim. Northwich (or "The Trickies" as they're aptly nick-named) took a shock lead on seven minutes when striker John Allan stunned the Grecian faithful by putting the visitors ahead. For six uncomfortable minutes we twitched nervously in our seats until Mr Devine resumed normal services by superbly heading City level.

Relief. The blip we expected has come and gone. Now we've equalised, this is where Exeter would push on, swamp the part-timers and deliver a predictable outcome.

Three minutes later Brayson scores for the visitors.

Exeter City 1-2 Northwich Victoria.

Gun cocked - aim at foot – fire!

Yet again City were determined to make even the most ordinary of opposition look like a team of eleven world-beaters. Victoria came forward again and Jones had to be alert to parry another Allan effort. Exeter were like deer in headlights. Just when you thought it couldn't get any worse Andy Taylor directed a harmless back-pass to Paul Jones who kicked nothing but fresh air and the ball travelled into the back of City's net to the horror of the keeper and the utter disbelief of 4,000 watching Grecians.

Sweet merciful Jesus. The scoreline stayed the same until half-time. Whilst sipping my half-time tea I reassure myself that however bad things look now, they'd surely be a dramatic upturn in fortunes in the second period - given the fact we all expected Inglethorpe to be roasting his men for the worst first half of football under his reign during the half-time break.

Then on fifty-five minutes the most crucial incident in the game and possibly the hardest moment of the season to take. It didn't involve a goal, nor a save, or even a sending off. In the fifty-fifth minute of Exeter's home game against Northwich Victoria, Sean Devine kicked his last ball for the club. The Irishman had gone down clutching his knee and never got back up. Although it looked bad at the time, little were we to know Exeter's record signing and top goalscorer for the past two seasons would never return to the St James Park turf again to kick a ball in anger. It was tough to swallow that the talismanic Devine, who'd hit forty-two goals in ninety-seven games, wouldn't play another second in City's already perilous play-off campaign and would ultimately leave the club at the end of the season.

For the last half-hour it was predictably one-way traffic. Exeter peppered the visitors' goal in a desperate attempt to get back into the game. Having conceded three woeful goals and lost their main marksman through injury, it was turning out to be a bleak afternoon for the Grecian faithful. Apparently not content with the level of depression in the stands, Jake Edwards decided to put the home fans on the verge of suicide by getting himself sent off within nine minutes of coming on. The substitute, in a moment of complete stupidity, lashed out at the Vic's left-back on seventy-eight minutes and got his marching orders.

Finally in injury time, Steve Flack got the goal City's second half work-rate deserved to belatedly give Exeter a few seconds of hope, but moments later the man in black brought an end to proceedings at the Park and a soul destroying defeat for the Grecians.

Three days later Exeter collapsed in an even more painful manner. This time Dagenham and Redbridge were the team to put another damaging nail into Exeter's coffin. Leading 1-0 courtesy of an Kwame Ampadu (yes - you heard right) goal on eleven minutes, City contrived to miss a hatful of second half chances, most notably Les Afful who managed to miss a one-on-one with the Daggers 'keeper Tony Roberts after having an entire half and at least ten seconds to decide where he was going to place the ball. Predictably in the last minute of injury-time, a dodgy free kick gave Dagenham a few seconds to launch a final attack. The ball was launched into the crowded Exeter area. Cleared back out. Hoofed back in and, well, do I really have to relive the agony?

Dagger's substitute Tony Boot beat Paul Jones with eleven seconds left to put 2700 fans on the verge of ending it all on the terraces of St James Park. A mass suicide by a legion of followers to rival any cult.

Waco in the West Country.

It was a sickening blow. You could just see the back page headline tomorrow; TONY PUTS THE BOOT IN.

As devastating a full force kick in the teeth that was. Inglethorpe managed to lift his players and four days later a Gareth Sheldon goal on the stroke of half time was enough for Exeter to nervously sneak past Crawley Town.

By the time of City's penultimate game of the season, the Grecians are still playing catch up, adrift of that all important last play-off place by just two points. The last home game of the season saw the Grecians comfortably take apart Gravesend and Northfleet with goals from Jeannin, Phillips and Flack in front of a crowd fifty-three shy of 4,000.

A successful end to the home campaign for Inglethorpe's troops. The players took their end of season lap of honour unaware that every possible result the same night had gone against them. Morecambe won comfortably at home to Forest Green whilst Stevenage had won away at Crawley. Even Aldershot, who'd been hanging onto that last golden play-off ticket for the last month, conceded three goals to Accrington, had a player sent off, but still somehow managed to grab a late draw at Stanley.

Fate conspired against City again.

The twenty-third day of April finally brought the curtain down on possibly the most important season in the history of Exeter City FC. A year that had begun with uncertainty of a future and tottering on the brink of a deep dark abyss was about to climax in yet another last day scenario for a club whose destiny had been decided by number sixty-four and two wonderful matches against the giants from Old Trafford.

The romantics among us insisted City would continue the Mills and Boon storyline by making the play-offs, beating all and sundry and complete the happy ending with a play-off final victory at Stoke's Britannia Stadium.

Alas, the Hollywood scriptwriters would be out of luck come five minutes to five on that cold afternoon in Cumbria. Exeter would impressively defeat Carlisle at Brunton Park with goals from Flack and Edwards, but all the possible permutations that would see Exeter grab the coveted fifth spot never materialized. Aldershot predictably beat struggling Scarborough, whilst Stevenage finally put the end to Leigh's season of slaughter with a routine 2-0 home win. Morecambe's failure to defeat Tamworth however, cost the Lancashire club and they slipped out of the top five at the very last hurdle.

And Exeter? Yep! For the THIRD season in a row ONE POINT had either caused a relegation or narrow miss from possible promotion. Even in a season of celebration, the heartache never seemed more than a kick of a football away.

The club had seen trials and tribulations and fought many battles in recent years, though when the dust settled that afternoon on the borders of bonny Scotland and the City faithful plodded home through cobblestone streets and hung their scarves and replica kit up for another season, many felt that the war had been won.

It may have meant another season outside the confines of League football, but it was, crucially, another season. And although we watched on as Carlisle secured their return to the league after one season in non-league, we could bask in the knowledge that there wouldn't be padlocks, decrepit turnstiles and uncut grass on Well Street after all - thanks to the support of the fans and the bravery of eleven men on the field of play.

The next day Kilbarry Rangers secured the coveted second bottom position in League Division Four of the Waterford Junior and District league thanks to an astonishing 3-1 away win against Tramore Athletic. One the way home manager Davy Quilty was forced again to shell out twenty-nine Euros for ten fish, three chips and a ribsteak for his victorious team. The three points had even put our side level on points with third last Saint Josephs. Only one small statistic separated us and Josephs - a goal difference of minus thirty-four.

Despite that technicality, Quilty was a happy man.

"Don't worry guys. It's all part of my five-year plan. By the end of the decade we'll be mid-table".

His blinding optimism was loveable.

Still, God loves a trier.

Chapter Ten

LIGHT 'EM UP...WE'RE GOING DOWN!

Anyone who tells you dropping a tin of dog food on you toes doesn't hurt is a blatant liar.

Sweet Jesus it hurts like hell.

The pain, similar to the experience of being kicked in the genitals, doesn't hit you for at least three seconds. In that time you've realised the object has struck the target and agonising pain is just a few short seconds away. The next few moments give the victim a chance to clench teeth and brace themselves for impending agony, which dually arrives like the stab of a thousand daggers. It will take a further five minutes of eye watering, nut-clenching discomfort before the sweet release of cold water and an ice pack finally kicks in.

My Friday morning hasn't started very brightly. However, the sun is shining, the birds are signing and the smell of fresh cut grass and a dozen barbeques is floating through the summer air.

Best of all I'm off to South-West England to continue a love affair. Since I last visited St James' Park, Exeter had brought down the curtain on their second season in the Conference, coming up short yet again by one point. They'd made the club solvent and in doing so secured their future. And for the second year in a row, they'd brought a country full of international stars to grace the lush green grass of St James Park - The Italian Masters.

Following on from the visit of the world cup winning Brazilian side of '94 the year before, Exeter treated their long-suffering fans to another international side when Italy's ageing veterans rolled into town. Again I travelled over and again I enjoyed. Sure it wasn't the star-studded Italian side we had been promised, the crowds didn't show and the game was forgettable (young Danny Seaborne's debut aside), but I got to meet an altogether different type of hero from that of the football variety with the first game that evening.

Before City took on Sergio Brighenti's Italian team, an Exeter side full of club legends like John Hore, Martyn Rogers, Jimmy Giles and Tony Kellow took on FDNY - the Fire Department of New York soccer team.

FDNY consisted of twenty-three men who played in the third division of the top league in New York state. Fire-fighters one and all. On the 9th of September 2001, the team beat a local rival 1-0 with a goal scored from Sergio Villanueva. Two days later all twenty-three were actively involved when American Airlines Flight Eleven out of Boston crashed into the north tower of the World Trade Centre. Forty-five minutes later when United Airlines flight 175 struck the south tower of the Trade Centre, Sergio Villanueva departed with Ladder 132 from Brooklyn. He never returned. The Argentinean-born former police officer was killed in the line of duty, sacrificing his life whilst trying to save his fellow New Yorkers. In honour of their departed friend - the team retired Sergio's number ten jersey.

At 6 pm that evening the FDNY took to the surface of St James Park, Exeter. They stood in unison to the strains of the American National Anthem. The sound of the Star Spangled Banner and the bravery of these humans sent hairs bristling on every fan's neck and reduced some to tears. At that precise moment you're nationality wasn't a deterrent. Everyone felt the pain, but immense pride of the men below us who selflessly risk their lives every day for the sake of the rest of the human race.

I didn't even remember the score. I just wanted to meet these men and offer a firm hand of friendship. Later that night I got my chance and struck up a conversation with Derek Harkin, a lieutenant in Engine 292 in Queens. His modesty after such obvious heroics was commendable.

"I'm not a hero. It's my job and I know what's expected of me."

The midfielder was an Irish-American and very proud of his Irish roots which stem from Offaly. We chatted for a while about Exeter, the States and our love of the Irish football team.

The main attraction was won 1-0 by Exeter, but it paled into significance with the pride, passion and raw emotion of the first game.

Now, less than eight weeks later, I was travelling back to Exeter to watch my very first pre-season game. Nottingham Forest were making the trip to rural England to lock horns with Devon's finest. The former European Cup winners had hit on hard times and for the first time in over fifty-four years were playing in the third level of English football. Former Norwich manager Gary Megson had come in January, but couldn't stop the City Ground outfit from being relegated from the Championship. Seven months on and Megson has brought a side brimming with new signings to St James Park. Gary Holt, Ian Breckin, Grant Holt and on-loan Nathan Tyson were brought into a Forest side already bristling with the experience of players like Gareth Taylor and David Johnson. Whilst the Grecians were basking in the glory of finally being on sound financial footing and trying out some trialists, Forest would have a huge weight of expectation around their necks which comes with the territory having won back-to-back European Cups less than three decades ago.

My route to Exeter - normally a not so healthy sixteen-hour round trip - is slightly different this time as I opt to fly from my home airport of Waterford and land in London, from where I'd take the three hour train journey from Paddington in a bid to cut time and give me a different change of scenery, even if it is green fields flying past my eyes at 120 mph.

This would be the first in a litany of disasters that would end two days later with a last will and testament at 20,000 feet over the Irish Sea.

On arriving in Luton and taking the short thirty-minute minute ride to Paddington, I find a certain train company wants to charge me £47 for a single to Exeter. That's SINGLE folks - one way - not return - SINGLE! If Dick Turpin had pulled up on Black Bess and robbed me at gunpoint - I'd have understood, but believe me highway robbery in the twenty-first century still exists, it's just changed from a horse and a pistol to a glass window and grumpy woman. Gone are the days of "stand and deliver" replaced with "shut up and pay".

Having been forced to fork out the single fare after several minutes of pleading, which gave way to several more minutes of condemning everything from British Rail to the monarchy over the price of a train ticket, I just about manage to board the 2.15 pm to Exeter St Davids. By now my blood pressure has been cranked up another notch on stepping on board and checking all thirteen carriages for a place to sit. Having spent almost forty-five minutes of the journey in vain hope of finding a place to rest my weary posterior, I make do with leaning against the counter of the buffet bar with two bags between my legs.

Oh and there's twenty-five of us here! The phrase sardines and can would aptly describe our predicament.

Predictably the remaining two hours and fifteen minutes travelling time felt roughly like five years of my life and I kissed terra firma at 5.12 pm when finally arriving in Exeter.

By the time City took to the field that night against Nottingham Forest however, I'd been desensitized with the help of my friend Jack Daniels. Gary Megson brought a strong squad with him and won the game 2-1 with goals from Holt and Gareth Taylor (who for some reason looked about nine feet tall on the pitch - five of which was pure hair). With many fans toasting themselves on the beaches of Spain or having the annual family barbeque at home for the relatives they won't see for another 365 days, the attendance that night at St James was just over 2,000. The balmy summers evening however, made it possibly the most pleasant experience I'd ever had at City.

No pressure, relaxed atmosphere and a game where the result was of no consequence. Such a refreshing change from pent-up frustration, eternal angst, the obligatory leap from your seat-eyeballs about to burst and a cardiac arrest just around the corner after watching City lose 1-0 to Gravesend and Northfleet.

The ninety minutes however, would prove to be the only peace I would experience that weekend.

On returning to Paddington two days later, the train was held up at a small town called Castle Cary for over an hour because of "falling debris on the rail-line that has disrupted services."

Briefly decoded; leaves on the track.

Leaves on the track... leaves on the fucking track! I'm going to miss a flight back to another country because of some deciduous trees that's foliage has somehow held up a juggernaut of transport that can reach speeds of 180 mph.

"What a complete and utter joke!" - growled the old man in carriage D.

"Count your blessings my friend." - I lamented.

"We're lucky they're from an oak tree. If they were spruce leaves we'd probably all be dead by now."

I didn't for a second give myself any lingering hopes of catching the flight and predictably arrived fifteen minutes after the gates had closed in Luton. Because of a few falling leaves I now had the privilege of forking out another 120 Euros to get the next flight to Waterford, which of course could only be the next day as I'd missed the only flight home.

I'd had enough of Luton airport by the time I boarded the 9.15 am to Waterford the next morning, but despite everything I'd endured over the past forty-eight hours the real drama started on the plane. This was when God, in his infinite wisdom, decided to attack my plane with twenty minutes of turbulence that drained seven pints of blood from my body.

At the halfway point of the flight, 20,000 feet over the Irish Sea, the Aer Arrann ATR 72 jolted erratically and - according to the gay flight attendant- "dropped a very unhealthy 2,000 feet in seven seconds". Imagine sitting in a seat and dropping a height four times the size of Blackpool Tower and you'll get an idea why I was picking my colon up off the floor after it jumped out of my body through sheer terror.

It didn't help proceedings that I was sitting next to the only person in the universe that picked today as his first day to fly and a set of flight attendants that smiled through the caked on make-up like it was just a slight puff of breeze. You got the feeling that even if we were plummeting to the ocean at the speed of sound, Terry, Joan and Aishling would still be grinning like

Cheshire cats and offering you the latest in duty free jewellery.

The crackling voice of our captain came over the intercom.

"Ladies and gentleman, we are just experiencing some mild turbulence and should be over it soon. Nothing to worry about - relax and enjoy the rest of the flight."

That's standard cabin crew talk for - "Light 'em up, we're going down".

The descent to Waterford airport is just as bad and by now even Terry the gay flight attendant has to reapply after the sweat had melted his foundation.

"Folks, this is your captain speaking. Might be a bit choppy coming into Waterford, but we'll have you on the ground in no time" (In 127 pieces and a ball of fire).

What Captain Connors really meant was "Smoke 'em if you got them folks, I've got five boxes of Silk Cut and a parachute - see you on the ground."

Thankfully moments later, flight E104 out of Luton and hurtling at 57,000 mph to the tarmac on Waterford airport's runway, landed with a thud and sixty-seven people could rejoice at not having plunged into the Irish Sea for a chat with Eric the Eel or Sammy the Basking Shark.

Summer saw the annual arrival and exodus of professional footballers the length and breadth of the country. Clubs from all over Britain were busy signing strikers, trying trialists and balancing the books. There was also a flurry of activity down in Devon.

With the departing Sean Devine heading to far away New Zealand, the gaping hole up front would have to be filled by the incoming Carlisle striker Craig Farrell. Marcus Martin would leave after his year long loan, but the arrival of Billy Jones (a man who single-handedly financed every trip I had to Exeter in 2007) in defence helped bulk-p the Grecian back-four. Former City favourite Chris Vinnicombe would arrive along with on-loan Tony Scully in October, but perhaps the biggest coup manager Alex Inglethorpe pulled off was the arrival of Aldershot's highly rated Jon Challinor.

Challinor had been a regular in Terry Brown's Aldershot side that had been unlucky to lose out to Carlisle in the play-offs the season just gone. The twenty-five year-old had struck the net fourteen times from midfield and would be a huge addition to a Grecian squad attempting to climb back into League football at the third attempt.

It all sounded promising.

By late September is would be astonishing.

For the first time since possibly their fourth division championship winning side of 1989/90 - Exeter looked genuine, bona-fide title challengers. City hit the ground running in spectacular fashion to stun even the most wide-eyed optimist of Exeter City fans. So much so, that by September fans where genuinely dreaming of a magnificent year which would surely be capped with a record points total, promotion and superlatives from fans and press alike for a runaway Exeter City title-winning side.

Little did any City fan think this when Exeter kicked off the 2005/06 campaign at a sun-laden Stonebridge Road, home of Gravesend and Northfleet on August thirteenth. The 'Fleet had been somewhat of a bogey side in City's short Conference life, however, two Lee Phillips goals either side of half-time clinically put an end to that hex.

Three days later, 4,000 fans watched a tight, tense game against freshly relegated Kidderminster Harriers, where new signing Craig Farrell scored to give the Grecians a narrow 1-0 win. The momentum kept going and two more wins, at home to Morecambe and away to Accrington Stanley - both 2-1, gave Exeter their best start in over eight years and made Alex Inglethorpe's men the early pace-setters. By the time Forest Green came to St James Park, the Grecian bandwagon was in full throttle and the minnows were expected to be little more than cannon fodder for City.

Ninety minutes later and 4,691 people filed out annoyed and frustrated from the home of the Conference leaders (I'm excluding the five happy-go-lucky Forest Green fans who danced their way through the entire game). The minnows from the tiny town of Nailsworth, who should have been lambs to the slaughter, had pissed all over the party at St James and became the first side not to concede against City that season.

The following Saturday, City looked to be slipping to their first defeat of the season against Dagenham and Redbridge. John Challinor had notched his first goal of the season for Exeter to level an early strike from Southam. A goal on the hour from Chris Moore seemed to have condemned Exeter to their first defeat of the new campaign. Then, in the last chance saloon, Chris Todd made a timely run into the Dagger's goalmouth and poked home an equaliser four minutes into injury-time.

At home the early kick-off had thrown me and BBC Ceefax was my only means of commutation. Just as I'd given up all hope of City rescuing anything from the capital, glorious Ceefax displayed the name Todd (94) for me just before I'd switched over to watch The Karate Kid for the 119th time.

Dagenham and Redbridge 2-2 Exeter City.

And that sweet, sweet, statistic - Todd (94)

Have some of that, Daggers!

High on the fumes of success emanating from the West Country's finest, I booked myself an outrageously expensive flight (with that "cut-price" airline again). I made my way across the Irish Sea, minus the mid-air mayhem this time and found myself back at the Mecca of my footballing fantasies - St James Park.

It was also a test of my worryingly more regular jinxing powers. To see how much of a crow I really was. Recently I'd bet on some of the surest things since blonde Essex girls in white stilettos only to find out it is possible for a supreme novice hurdler to break each of its four legs at the first fence in a horserace and a greyhound with a fifty-race unbeaten run to catch its paw in the trap and chew it off before the eyes of its suicidal trainer!

City had made their best start since the glorious Fourth Division title of 1989/90 and would make it five wins from seven if they could dispatch the visiting Cambridge United on tenth day of September.

I travelled that Friday with a pocket full of money and a new pair of jeans. I knew they were new jeans as I left the fifty-six Euros price tag from Topman on my arse from the moment I left my house to stepping foot in The Brook Green that evening. It was slightly disappointing to eventually find this out, as all afternoon I'd been convinced my arse had been the focus of attention to at least half a dozen women - and worryingly - a few middle-aged men.

A change of venue - and thankfully jeans - followed and my night was spent dividing time between a chicken satay and trying to recapture a youth, lost studying for meaningless tests, at the Arena nightclub.

By the time three o'clock rolled around the next day, I'd shaken off the effects of a chicken kebab and the awful, yet interesting, mix of rum and ginger ale and taken my place in the stand alongside my local cohorts.

The Grecians take to the field against a Cambridge United side spending their first season in non-league under the guidance of Rob Newman. The Us had made an average start to their first conference season, but arrived in Devon on the back of two straight defeats and one point from a possible nine. Nevertheless, United arrived with a merry little band of fans that positioned themselves behind the tiny open terrace facing Well Street and basked in the west country sunshine before their heroes donned their war paint and prepared for battle.

That battle lasted exactly four minutes and twenty-one seconds. On-loan Tony Scully drove his free-kick from outside the area - low and hard through a sea of legs that amazingly none connected with - which nestled nicely in the bottom right-hand corner of Darren Behcet's net. It was the Irishman's first goal since his loan move from Notts County and would spearhead a relentless Grecian assault that ripped the heart out of Newman's men (and his forty-five strong travelling Us army). - before fifteen minutes of the game had even elapsed. This would be due in no small part to Lee Phillips (or "super" Lee Phillips as he's slightly unoriginally known in these parts). On fourteen minutes Exeter's number nine latched onto a ball from Jon Challinor and drove his effort forcefully past the hapless Behcet and his ball-watching defence. It would take thirty-one more minutes before United would be saved from the onslaught by the sound of Mr. Malone's whistle to indicate the visitors had a respite of a mere fifteen minutes.

All things considered, I reckoned to possibly being the most contented human on the planet as I sat at half-time eating my Cornish pastie and gulping down my coke - bathed in the Devon sunshine. Now normally this is a moment that should be bottled and sold to every war-weary, relegation-haunted, survival-scraping fan that adorns the nailed-on wooden benches and waste-papered terraces of their chosen lower league team. Rare is the moment when after only half of a game is played that they can rest, relax and rejoice in the sheer unadulterated joy of their side's performance. All too few are the moments when the loyal fan of a lower league side can revel in the mercilessness of their side's performance - that you cannot wait in your chosen coliseum for the next instalment of a modern day massacre of the visiting Christians among the home side's lions.

Even with a two goal lead, Exeter never looked like letting Cambridge back into this match and midfield dynamo Paul Buckle effectively killed off the game with a bullet of a header on sixty-three minutes. The applause had hardly died down when Jon Challinor - fast becoming a cult hero with the Grecian faithful, not to mention a hit with the opposite sex - if the opinion of fifty-seven year-old Dorothy Butler in Row G Seat 7 is anything to go by - scores Exeter's fourth.

"Chall-la-la-la-la-la-la-nor!" sung the crowd to the tune of Tony Christie's "Is this the way to Amarillo?" A new hero had been born. A flurry of token substitutions followed and with it the closing of play at the St James Park love-in.

A four-goal humbling of recently deceased league opposition and another week as kings of the castle - or Conference as the case may be.

Seven days later and Exeter welcomed Conference newcomers Southport with a handshake, a smile and a three-goal beating, with new singing Farrell notching a brace just in case the Liverpudlians had any ideas above their station that afternoon at Haig Avenue. However, just three days later, Exeter would taste defeat for the first time at the hands of eternal enemies Stevenage and their seriously infuriating manager Graham Westley.

Recent rivalries had seen sending-offs, missiles and the obligatory twenty-two-man brawls and Tuesday night in late September proved to be just as miserable an experience for Alex Inglethorpe's men as once again Westley outfoxed the Grecians. Two goals in the closing twenty minutes gave the Londoners the three points. However begrudging the travelling City fans exiting Broadhall Way that night would be, it had to be said that Stevenage away was always going to be one of the toughest assignments in the non-league calendar for City.

This, of course, would be quickly remedied by the slaughter of Burton Albion at fortress St James a mere four days later. However, the expectant floodgates didn't seem to open that afternoon and with nine minutes left on the clock, all Exeter had to show for eighty minutes endeavour was a solitary Billy Jones goal and have a dozen guilt-edge chances (which is standard City procedure when playing struggling relegation sides that are fifty points off safety).

Burton were that archetypical side. Nine games into the season, one win, two scrapped draws and six defeats. Cannon Fodder.

Then, nine minutes from the finishing line, out comes the gun from its holster, the foot shows itself in all its glory and Exeter City take aim. Having had a nosebleed from travelling into City's area for three corners the entire game; Albion's Darren Stride beat Paul Jones to level the tie in front of a totally dumbstruck home support. Four minutes later, Exeter inexplicably let Jon Shaw steal in to astonishingly give Albion two goals in four minutes and the most unlikely three points Nigel Clough's side would earn all season long.

Having supported Exeter City for nearly two decades now, I'd like to have said I'd experienced all the absurd ways that my beloved club could turn victory into defeat. I'd want nothing more than to rely on an array of startling, yet depressing, statistics of last-minute capitulations at Leyton Orient on a Tuesday night to Saturday afternoons at Halifax turning two goal leads into 5-2 defeats, but at that present time, against such awful opposition in a game of total dominance, I simply couldn't think of a more woeful case of City shooting themselves in the foot.

All of a sudden doubts crept into Alex Inglethorpe's side. The midweek arrival of Woking at Exeter tested the Grecians' nerve even further and, although City took a 1-0 lead to the latter stages of the match courtesy of a goal from Tony Scully, Woking equalised from a controversial free kick which was dispatched by Murray and gave the visitors a share of the spoils.

Stuart had text me three minutes after the game had finished. I'd mistaken his lack of an update since the first goal as a sure sign the game had finished 1-0.

At 9.42 it came through. "Dodgy free-kick. Finished 1-1".

Cocknobs!

The sky-high confidence and feel-good factor that had engulfed a giddy Grecian support since mid-August had now given way to an altogether more familiar pessimism and a growing realism that Exeter City wouldn't just simply run away with the 2005/06 Nationwide Conference title.

Next stop...York City and the absurdly catchy Kit Kat Crescent. Many the pundit has used the home of the Minstermen in some God awful pun (I'm looking at you Jeff Sterling) to amuse the masses. So I'm not about to add to it by suggesting City were choc full of surprises etc, etc, in a game which saw the Grecians continue their recent poor run of form.

How is it things never seem as good as they are when you're winning, but always as bad as they are when you're losing? It's always fun when there's a winning streak put together, but it's never as dramatic and soul-destroying as a run of three straight defeats. That October afternoon in York proved another one of those soul- destroying days.

Though they tried valiantly, Exeter were second best to a York side that came out of the traps like greased lightning. The home side went ahead after Chris Todd had been penalised for a foul in the penalty area and York striker Andy Bishop struck away the resulting penalty. Despite this, Exeter where level within a mere 120 seconds through the evergreen Steve Flack. This was a brief respite for the ever-faithful City support who filled the away end terrace 300 deep to offer a rousing vocal support for their eleven men, but a goal by Stewart, seven minutes before half-time, gave the Minstermen (I do love these quirky historical nicknames) a 2-1 half-time lead.

The remaining forty-five minutes produced three goals, sadly two of those went to the home side, as Devon's finest ran out of steam and succumbed to our Northern hosts. On seventy minutes, the colourfully named Clayton Donaldson - a striker of dynamite potential - fired past Jones for 3-1, (not bad for a guy with a name like a character out of Dynasty), and although Billy Jones kept the visiting City fans on edge with a penalty four minutes later, Bishop netted his second of the game in injury-time to finally kill off a valiant, but ultimately morale-sapped Exeter City eleven. Heavy hearts and leaden feet shuffled from the Crescent that evening. Normally a trip to the Kit Kat would be a tough prospect and defeat wasn't exactly a surprise, but it felt like another unravelling of the early season rope of dreams that City had given their fans with their table topping conquests.

It was a flat week in work. All my exuberance and happy-go-lucky outlook had been replaced by a frown, mild narkyness and growing depression. City had gone from winning six of their first eight games to taking just one point from twelve, which included three damaging defeats to knock them off their perch at the top of the Conference table.

Suddenly the Grecians were beginning to resemble Kilbarry Rangers, except we weren't being paid good money each week to make a balls of things.

Halifax Town would prove to be the signpost back onto the road to recovery for Alex's men. An afternoon of high drama followed which included six goals, two great comebacks, a sending off and astonishingly, a Les Afful goal.

It was easy to be sceptical about the Grecians title credentials after such a recent woeful run and sixty-seven seconds after kick-off cautious optimism gave way to a depressingly familiar groaning from the terraces as Halifax took the lead when John Grant rifled home. However, Inglethorpe's men steadied themselves and got back in the game little more than seven minutes later when Jon Challinor was brought down in the area - allowing Billy Jones to make no mistake from the penalty spot.

I was acutely aware than in Lewis Killeen, Halifax had a player who just adored scoring against the Grecians. He'd been the first player to score against City in the Conference and had become the proverbial 'thorn in the side' ever since, so it didn't come as a surprise when the annoying sod drove home from twelve yards out shortly after to regain Town the lead.

The Shaymen's passing was slick and determined and City looked a distant second best. So what better way to put the kybosh on that than with sheer brute force and a sprinkle of controversy? And when you need a man mountain to shake things up, look no further than ex-boxer Steve Flack. With just seconds left in first half injury-time, Glenn Cronin's ball was launched in on Town's goalkeeper Ian Dunbavin. A suspiciously offside-looking Stephen Flack steamed in, saw his effort initially blocked, but then drove boot, ball and goalkeeper into the back of the net.

Mr Phillips pointed to the centre spot.

2-2! Cue pandemonium from Halifax. The protests were lead by Denny Ingram and Town's manager Chris Wilder who were incensed the linesman had not raised his flag and that Mr Philips had also allowed the goal to stand. Like a red rag to a bull, it was all a little bit too much for one Denevan Ingram and the Halifax defender was sent off for swearing profusely at the linesman.

Not content with this, Town manager Chris Wilder felt a longing to sit alongside his fearless, though slightly foul-mouthed defender, in the stands for the second half by continuing the abuse at both referee and linesman off the pitch and into the tunnel.

Result; Halifax lost a goal, whilst defender and manager was thrown in for good measure. What a cracking end to the half!

Forced to pile the pressure on, Exeter went for the jugular, though with a little less than twenty minutes left, it looked as even the advantage of an extra man (not to mention an extra manager) and a generous linesman to boot, City would still flounder. Cometh the hour-cometh the man...step forward Les Afful.

Les Afful?

That's right...Les Afful.

Yep little Les (I've found more ways to miss the target than Arsenal on a Saturday afternoon at the Emirates) Afful. The tiny Liverpudlian winger with a passion for almost scoring who had a single goal in nearly seventy-three games to his name, received a ball from Jon Challinor and drove home powerfully from the edge of the box to the sound of absolute ecstasy from Grecian players and fans alike.

The nippy little twenty-one year-old was mobbed by his team-mates (even goalkeeper Paul Jones raced the length of the field to hug him), as City had finally taken the lead in a game of never-ending drama.

Ninety seconds later the roof came off the Big Bank. A classic route-one goal (hoof from goalkeeper, one bounce, steaming striker finish) gave Exeter two goals in two minutes when Paul Jones mega-hoof was chased down and bravely headed in by Craig Farrell to give Exeter a fourth goal and compound the misery of our irate guests.

Exeter City 4-2 Halifax Town. At last, the sweet taste of victory had passed the way of the Grecians lips once again.

What is it they say about waiting for one bus and three come along? By the end of the month, Exeter had added nine more points to their impressive ten-win tally by winning away at Kidderminster 2-1 and comfortably disposing of Tamworth at home 3-0. The sweetest of the three victories however, would be Jon Challinor's two injury-time goals seconds from the end of normal time away at Crawley Town. Not that I had anything against the Sussex side, it's just sweeter than a sugar sandwich and sugar shake at Sugar Shack when your teams not played well, but still won a game away from home with two goals - seconds from full time.

Like my E104 flight from Luton, the mid-air turbulence, six decades of the rosary and pencilling out a last will and testament at 20,000 feet, City's short flight of fancy had seen them scale heights, dip under grey skies, yet return to auto-pilot and relative plane sailing.

A week later a 1-1 draw away at Altrincham returned Alex Inglethorpe's Exeter City to the top of table with thirty-four points from seventeen games of the 2005/06 Nationwide Conference.

Chapter Eleven

A CANVEY ISLAND CHRISTMAS.

DECEMBER 2nd 2005

There's not much to be said for cats is there? I mean they serve absolutely no use to mankind. Do they fetch, roll over, play dead or get your slippers after a hard day at the office? If the purpose of the feline community is to shed hair, bawl to get out at 4am, and urinate over every piece of fabric inside your four walls then generations of moggies have achieved their goal.

And yet we put up with it. As the saying goes - humans are hard to train, but they're the only slaves cats have.

Take this morning for instance. I've just opened the front door to find a mouse on the welcome mat. Now I use the word "mouse" in the loosest of terms. What's landed on my doorstep is the remaining carcass of a rodent that's been dragged through half a dozen fields and attacked by every cat on the block. Above the remains stands Devil - my pet pussy. Now I'm familiar with feline customs and recognize that a cat bringing home a dead mouse is supposed to be a way of appeasing their owners and proving they are great hunters, but I know Devil - and, put bluntly, he's full of shit.

The only predatory instincts my feline friend has shown was nicking the mouse from my neighbours cat across the road, putting it on my doorstep and grinning at me from ear to ear in a callous attempt to pass it off as he own. Whilst I'm begrudgingly giving him a rub and a half-hearted "well done," Tigger across the road is getting a kick in the arse and "piss off I've no food" from Mr Johnson in number 54.

I'd have had more respect for Devil had he came back with half an ear missing after a scrap with Jonesy - the trashcan rooting moggy from two doors down- with part of his leg in his mouth - (seriously that cat's got a bullet with his name written ALL over it the next time he fucks up my garbage). But for Devil to actually bring home a mouse would entail he had to hunt, and my cat's just too damn lazy. It's been a constant wonder to me that Devil even has the effort to open his eyes in the morning he's that lazy. His routine starts when he gets up at the crack of noon, bawls for three hours until he's managed to blag two tins of cat food and the remains of that afternoons dinner, before dragging his ass to the front porch were he watches the world go by for the remains of the day. As he stands above what's left of the dilapidated rodent, we exchange brief eye contact. In that split second we read each others minds.

"I know you didn't catch that mouse you lazy bastard".

"I know that, but where's the proof sucker - now give me the Whiskas you tramp".

Our brief chat comes on the morning of my trip to Exeter to watch my beloved Grecians take on Canvey Island. It's the beginning of the festive month and City are now third in the Conference table. It's a table Inglethorpe's men will be able to concentrate on after Exeter have been dumped out of the FA cup at the first attempt by arch-rivals Stevenage. The fourth qualifying round pitched Exeter against Graham Westley's Londoners at St James Park, however the magical mystery tour that was Exeter City's cup run of the year before, was killed off before it even begun with ex-Banstead Athletic (who-exactly!) defender Barry Laker's goal, to give Stevenage a first round tie with Kettering and leave manager Westley exiting the home of the Grecians with a smile that could been seen all the way back up the A30.

Bastard!

However that winter brought a lovely distraction, and a well earned ode to dedication, when Barry McConnell brought down Premiership Charlton Athletic for his testimonial.

A local boy all his life, Barry never wanted to play for anybody else but Exeter. In his time at the Park he'd played under 9 managers, tasted relegation and a string of unfortunate injuries, but if you wanted someone to score a penalty in English football you'd look no future than the Whimple Whippet (and I'm including you Matt Le Tisser). McConnell was a Grecian through and through, and though he was to move on at the season's end he still holds an affectionate place in every Exeter fans hearts.

In the league, City's top of the table clash against Gray's Athletic had drawn a crowd of 6,682 - our biggest Conference crowd to date. However despite Jon Challinor equalising and early goal by Athletic, some young pup by the name of Gary Hooper decided to ruin everything with a goal one minute into injury time to knock City off the top of the table , and replace them with his own side.

Exeter bounced back seven days later with an impressive 2-0 away win at Edgar Street against Hereford, but by now the infamous Accrington Stanley (no I'm not doing the milk advert) had muscled into second place as all top three sides shared a six point gap from the rest of the chasing pack.

Exeter's early season hot streak had kept Alex Inglethorpe's men in this lofty position despite some indifferent form in the past five weeks, however the pairing of City against struggling Canvey Island was, seemingly, perfectly timed. Jeff King's part-timer's were below mid-table, well off the pace and struggling financially with rumours abound that the club would be forced to withdraw from the Conference.

Manager and owner King had brought the club from the Essex Senior League in 1992 to the threshold of the Football League, but financially it had placed a burden on the big man - they would eventually resign from the Conference at the end of the season.

However until then they remained a Nationwide side, and with it a thorn in the Grecians side.

In their debut Conference season the seasider's had taken 4 points from Exeter - winning 1-0 at St James and scoring an injury-time equalizer at home in a 2-2 draw (incredibly Canvey would never lose to us in their tenure at this level). The draw at Island's ground hit hard as arguably it cost the Grecians a play-off place, so revenge would have been a priority for City this weekend.

After seeing City dismantle a hopeless Cambridge United on my last visit to the park, and given Exeter's lofty position, I was smugly dismissive of Canvey's chances of causing an upset at St James irrespective of the seemingly new hoodoo Jeff King's men had on the Grecians.

It rained that week. Cats and dogs. Rained so hard you couldn't see the road and inflatable dinghy's became the new must have fashion item. Poured so viciously that our River Suir burst its banks and we got flooded for three days straight. Even my frontyard was submerged.

I live on a hill. Go figure.

My time was divided between checking the Devon weather forecasts and swimming about the front garden searching in vain for Marmaduke-my pet rabbit. Frantic phone calls were made to Stuart, the club and the British

Metallurgical service to find out if Exeter would actually take the field this weekend against Canvey Island.

Even as I boarded my flight to Exeter that Friday morning it was really a toss of a coin whether City's brilliant ground staff could drain the excess water from the surface of St James Park to make sure the game went ahead.

This proved to be the wrong weekend to break in my new suede jacket. Not being a dedicated follower of fashion and not familiar with my fabrics, I was convinced that suede wasn't a fabric that stiffens up horribly when water is added, but rather some kind of super rain repellent that would ward off a monsoon and still retain its pristine condition. Of course I'm an idiot. Not that it had been the first time I would lose something suede to the weather. Ten years ago I decided I'd bring along suede boots whilst going on a boat trip. Innocent enough until you find out the boat trip was the Maid Of The Mist and the weather was Niagara Falls.

It was a miserable first Friday of December. Rain pelting down on the hundreds of moving umbrella's and scattering figures with weather-beaten coat's and men in suits, paper over head in a vain attempt to cover their pin-striped best from the elements.

Among these wet warriors I scurried, looking to do some half hearted shopping whilst ducking in and out of shops for shelter rather than checking out the retail hardware from Dixons to Debenhams. Every trip abroad would always be dominated with the purchase of the latest Barbie for one Leanne Lindsey Kennedy, the six year old loveable rogue and apple of her daddies eye. England to Italy, America to Accrington, no matter where I travel, the mental state of my daughter depends on her father returning with the latest Barbie doll or fashion accessory. It doesn't matter if the new Barbie to roll off the conveyer belt has the massive new feature of a pair of tiny plastic red heels and purple handbag, I'm still obligated to return home after being screwed for £25 by Mattel so my daughter can sleep under the stars with Percy the bear, a life size Pink Panther and 27 Barbie Dolls.

Shopping is brief. I cram in some CD's and a couple of movies - SNATCH for me and unfortunately THE MOMMY RETURNS for my wife. When I watch a film I like it to have the basic fundamental qualities required for a good night's viewing. A plot - fine acting, and some believable action. These are three things woefully missing in this picture. Everything is filmed against a blue screen, with cheesy one-liners and directed by a man who should have been put on the witness protection program for bringing out such a film.

Now this may seem a tad harsh on the sequel to THE MUMMY, but Cecile B. Demille had a cast of thousands and couldn't rely on some sweaty overweight mature student, boxed up in a studio creating millions of computerized screaming Egyptians for a quarter the price of paying a hoard of Hollywood extras.

Sod The Mummy - give me Moses. Good ol' Charlton Heston, now there's a man who could act, part the Red Sea, and fight for the right of gun-wielding Americans everywhere.

A hot shower, change of clothes and a tasty hot Italian (and a meal!) sorted out the rest of my Friday night and I retired to bed praying for St James to be bathed in sunshine on my awakening the next morning.

4.37am - God damn Pasta Carbonara. Better get the Bible, this could be a long stretch on the toilet bowl.

By the time daybreak enters my room I've finished Genesis and Revelations is just around the corner. My dodgy Italian has left me the worst for wear and weather conditions have worsened my mood. I didn't need the sound of dripping against corrugated iron and the rumbling of thunder in the distance to tell me that today would be a wee bit wet.

By midday weather had worsened and word had gone out of a pitch inspection at the Park. In all my visits to Exeter I'd been lucky not to be present when a postponement was announced, but on first sight of the mud-ridden, puddle laden St James' surface, it looked a forgone conclusion that I'd be heading back to the Emerald Isle with nothing more than some drink, banter with the locals and a Barbie doll.

By 2.15 the officials and both managers were out surveying the surface. The second pitch inspection was long and thoughtful but after much debate referee Mr. Malone decided the excellent morning's toiling of the dedicated, over-worked Exeter ground staff had paid dividends and the game against Canvey Island would actually go ahead.

Inwardly Alex Inglethorpe was worried. He made no secret of the fact he thought the game should have been cancelled, but now not only would the conditions be a leveller for a struggling Canvey Island, but the park's surface would be destroyed and might never return to it's pristine condition with a heavy fixture schedule and the incoming winter months of January and February still to come.

Despite the inclement (and that's putting it mildly) weather nearly three and a half thousand had made their way to the park and watched as Exeter make a purposeful start in simply awful conditions. With the ball either flying like a speeding bullet across the surface, or sticking like sludge in the mud, any type of passing continuity went out the window and route one became the formula of trying to unlock each defence.

The match, much like the conditions, degenerated by the minute. Exeter did force a handful of routine saves from Canvey's number 1, but the first half elapsed with the deadlock not been broken.

By this stage my match programme resembled a wet sponge. With the rain torrenting into the first ten rows of the main stand - yours truly being in row three, I made a vain attempt to keep my noggin dry and spent the entire first half hidden under a 64 page A5 size prize-winning programme and convinced myself it had the blanket effect of a golf umbrella.

Second half. Out came the teams. On came Steve Flack. On went the rain. Within minutes of the restart Craig Farrell failed to capitalize on a spilled ball by Canvey's goalkeeper and Challinor fired high wide and handsome. At 4.13pm we got 37 seconds of sunshine, before it disappeared behind a sea of black clouds and the heavens opened again. By now the game was a succession of misplaced passes, fresh air shots and some suicidal sliding tackles. Having endured almost an hour of this, people where committed to seeing the game out to it's pneumonia-inducing end. Then completely against the run of play Canvey took a shock lead. Winning their first corner of the game, a static City defence stood and watched as Island's Sedgemore nipped in to crash a rebound off of Paul Jones and into the back of the city net in full view of the horrified Cliff Bastin Stand.

"Call it off! Call it off!" - went the cry of more than 3,000 fans!!

All of a sudden a shock result was on the cards and with the prospect of

Exeter's title challenge being unexpectedly derailed, everyone pleaded with Mr. Barry Malone to sound his whistle, grab the ball and point to the dressing rooms. The delight in arriving at the park to find a football game would indeed take place, was now replaced with the horrific fact that little old Canvey Island were going to walk away with three points from St James' for the second year running.

At 4.37 I exploded.

Tired, cold, wet, frustrated , I snapped, got up , turned the air blue with a foul-mouthed tirade that required at least ten Hail Mary's and a visit to the confession box, and left my seat. In every fan's life there comes a pivotal moment where, just for a moment, they question their undying loyalty to their chosen team. A fleeting moment in time where you look to the heavens and wonder why, in the name of sweet divine Jesus, you actually lay your life down and open yourself to a lifetime of sorrow, pain & hardship for the sake of a football team.

And at 4.37pm on a miserable Saturday in December, among the huddled masses, drenched to the skin, and freezing to the bone, I had my moment of madness - stood up, cursed everything Grecian and headed for the toilets and the warmth of a hand dryer.

I hadn't reached the first steps when the ball hit the onion bag again. One time City player Kezie Ibe - it couldn't have been anyone else to complete this miserable day-picked up the ball outside the City area and strode on, beating two defenders, before cleverly producing a shimmy that left a bewildered Paul Jones on the seat of his pants and rolled the ball home for 2-0.

For all of Exeter's toiling up front and several half chances which fell to Flack, Moxey and the ever impressive Danny Woodwards - a recent signing and revelation at right back, City couldn't break down a stubborn Canvey defence who adopted that time-honoured Kilbarry Rangers motto "hoof first-ask question later".

It was the last straw. Hundreds poured out the gates and home to the safety of a warm fire and strong cup of tea. By this stage I was back in the sponsor's bar fuming. The soaking and subsequent week long flu I could take, but City's failure to kill off a struggling Canvey Island side, going into the crucial Christmas period, was maddening. Sure the conditions were more suitable to a mud-wrestling match but it's that old adage - two sides had to play on the pitch. The final whistle was greeted by a loud chorus of boo's. The City faithful had got used to seeing Exeter top the table and win a succession of games that season and 90 minutes of action against Canvey Island without a win, or even a goal, didn't fit into the C.V. of a would-be title winning side.

Hot whiskey's were lined up at the bar. One by one I warmed my throat, slurred my speech and tried my level best to erase the memory of what I'd just seen. Results did not go Exeter's way that day and Accrington Stanley moved ominously further away from the chasing pack. The rest of the evening was spent sampling the delights of Exeter's numerous nightclubs and attacking a KFC Zinger burger on the way home.

By the time of my flight home the next morning sanity had kicked in and the order of loved-up Grecian had been restored. Exeter were still third, injury-free, and fighting for the league status they'd relinquished three years back. Christmas was just around the corner. With no bonus at work - for the 97th year running - I knew Mr Visa & Mrs MasterCard were going to take a hammering over the festive period. With my daughter wanting the latest Barbie accessory and a new son of the way, the idea of fishnet tights, stiletto's and selling my body to a group of husky sailors down dockside was looking ever more appealing.

With children in the family, Christmas decorations now went up the first week in December. This of course meant a weekend of untangling fairy lights, checking spare bulbs and electrocuting myself in the name of our lord and the sanity of my daughter. Don't get me wrong I love the festive period, but I can do without hanging off a drainpipe 50 feet in the air with two tons worth of outdoor lights hanging from my teeth and nothing by a stone pavement to break my fall.

Luckily a week later City got back to winning ways. Scarborough were the victims who fell foul to a resurgent City and a Craig Farrell free kick gave the Grecians a narrow 1-0 win at the McCain Stadium.

League duties were pushed aside seven days later when Exeter entertained Conference South outfit Bishop Stortford in the third round of the FA Trophy. Unlike any other cup competition (except maybe the glorious Devon Bowl which City seem to win every year), Exeter would always be among the favourites for the non-league version of the FA Cup. Two seasons in the Conference had resulted in Exeter making the quarter-finals on both occasions so hopes would be high for another run.

Billy Jones set the City on the way in the fifth minute with a penalty after Lee Phillips had been pole-axed in the box by a Stortford defender. Five minutes before half-time Exeter debutant Anton Robinson side-stepped some challenges and side-footed a ball with pace and precision past the Stortford goalkeeper for a 2-0 lead. However to that point the visitors had looked meancing and just before the whistle could blow to sound the end of the first period a goalmouth scramble ensued in the City area and resulted in Roy (yes it's me - the Wycombe guy that scored in the FA cup, etc, etc) Essandoh cutting the arrears in half.

There was a festive feel to the match. Santa hat's were abound, free mince pies handed out at half-time and a spot of Carole signing broke out on this Sunday afternoon fixture , but Bishop's were calling the tune in the second half and in truth Exeter were very lucky to hold onto the lead and see out the game 2-1.

Christmas Eve was spent in front of the fireplace among a mass of wrapping paper and deciduous tinsel. Before going to bed Leanne had spent the most important 15 minutes of her year - presiding over the exact temperature of Santa and Rudolph's mince pies - before placing them along with the customary glass of milk on the fireplace for both of them to scoff on their rounds. My mind harked back to Christmas '74 when I'd done exactly the same, but Uncle Benji replaced the milk with a glass of brandy and convinced me Santa would rather some alcohol to keep him warm on his rounds despite my insistence Santa would never drink and drive. Of course Benji was an idiot and on a fast track to rehab and several thousand AA meetings.

It would be that same alcoholic Uncle first through my door on Christmas Day. He brought with him his wife Maxine, partner of 18 years and a woman with the longest running grudge in our family's history.

Despite marrying Benji in the late 80's and pledging a life of devotion to her husband, she never let him forget the brief twenty minute fling with a stripper called Carla on his stag night.

"Hello Uncle Benji. Hello Aunty Maxine. Come in, let me take your coat. Care for a drink ?"

"I'll have a sherry Brian. Benji would like his whore of a stripper but he'll make do with a Guinness".

Needless to say the afternoon was as quick as a tortoise marathon and as painful as a doze of haemorrhoids. Whilst myself and Sandra tried to lighten the mood with witty anecdotes and Nat King Cole tunes, our roaring relatives continued their tirade.

"I won't have to much turkey Brian. Maxine doesn't like my love handles- or as she likes to call them "I don't want to touch you anymore you fat bastard".

"Yes, my husband likes to watch his weight. He also likes to watch 19 year old trollops dance on poles ,take their clothes off for money, and screw them in the back of a Ford Capri."

St Stephen's Day arrived 24 hours later and with it probably the Grecians best performance of the season. Aldershot Town were the visitors to Devon and although the game was 15 minutes late in kicking-off due to an accident on the A303 it only delayed the inevitable, as the moment Paul Buckle and Billy Jones scored two goals in three first half minutes the result was never in doubt.

It would prove a personal triumph for City's dynamic midfielder Jon Challinor. The former Aldershot favourite, who'd surprisingly found himself surplus to requirements by manager Terry Brown, left to join a "bigger and better club" and rubbed further salt into his former managers gaping wound by launching an exocet past 'Shots 'keeper Nikki Bull just past the hour mark.

City were in full flow. Cronin back to his best alongside the tigerish Buckle. Chris Todd imperviously marshalling his defence, and Andy Taylor producing a man of the match winning performance. On-loan Gary Sawyer was still keeping Santos Gaia out of the side whilst Scott Hiley - our Ronaldo nutmeg maestro and all round Grecian legend, watched from the sideline with increasingly familiar regularity as the sublime young Danny Woodards kept his place. On 68 minutes Lee Phillips capped off a magnificent team display by seizing on a fabulous through ball from Taylor and firing past Bull to complete the rout 4-0.

By the time Phillips had turned to accept the adulation of the City faithful in the Bastin stand, the Aldershot fans has long given up any hope of even a consolation goal and started a conga-line lead by half a dozen Santa's and a bare-chested lunatic who'd whipped off his shirt in minus five degree weather and conga-ed their way around the away end.

A morale boosting win for the Grecians and just what they needed going into Friday's top of the table clash with Hereford United. This however created problems. Big television sized problems. It wasn't the fact that United were worthy adversaries and featured recently departed Grecian Alex Jeannin and the forever-agitating Graham Turner, but more to do with the goggle box that millions of us sit in front of every single night.

You see, although not a well known fact to everybody outside the football supporting city of Exeter, the Grecians have, since the invention of television over 50 years ago, consistently been truly awful when put on the big screen. The mere sight of a television camera or SKY pundit at St James Park is enough to put the fear of God into even the most optimistic of Grecian supporters. It didn't matter if SKY, BBC, or even Afghanistan TV had agreed to show Exeter

who could have been on a 55 game winning streak. The moment they'd made the decision to broadcast a game at St James it almost certainly coincided with a performance of truly cringe-worthy proportions.
Don't believe me? Here's a recent brief summary.

2001 FA Cup. Exeter City 0-0 Dagenham - When City were a league side. Graeme Tomlinson has the Grecians best chance after nine seconds. 89 minutes and 51 seconds of sheer misery followed. Sky showed a masochistic streak a mile long by actually televising the replay as well. Exeter were hammered 3-0.
2002 FA Cup. Exeter City 0-0 Forest Green - Played at The Lawn, and again featuring a City side still playing league football. BBC screen the game, Uri Geller hams it up and Glen Cronin captains City for the first time. The next 90 minutes had football fans nationwide reaching for the remote control for anything from Songs Of Praise to Murder She Wrote - and you know the footy is seriously bad if you're switching to watch an hour of Angela Lansbury on a Sunday afternoon.
2003 Conference tie. Exeter City 1-1 Dagenham - Again the Daggers feature. A sending off for the Londoners. A resulting Sean Devine penalty and 80 minutes against ten men is still not enough for the Grecians to win on television.
2003 Conference tie. Exeter City 1-1 Hereford. Battling performance away from home but the Exeter still can't find the winning habit on camera. Steve Flack scores and adds a contender for miss of the century when he hits the bar from two yards out.
2004 Conference tie. Exeter City 2-3 Chester City. A promotion battle at the Deva Stadium. Exeter arrive in bullish mood. Sean Devine gives City a shock lead. Everything's in place for our first televised win. Unfortunately Chester have other ideas and score three times in eight minutes. Sean Canham grabs a consolation.

So you could have forgiven the Grecian faithful for not jumping with joy when Sky announced plans to show Alex Inglethorpe's men to the entire nation. Although it was extremely useful for myself and fellow exiled City fans worldwide, I'd rather watch a painfully slow Ceefax screen post a 1-0 Exeter City win rather than sit through yet another ninety minutes of stage fright from the Devon's finest.
However that night I cracked open some beers, popped some popcorn and watched the drama unfold as a third placed Exeter City took on a Hereford United side five points adrift in seventh place.
Within five minutes Exeter had the lead. Lee Phillips tore down the right flank like a speeding bullet, outpaced a hesitant Hereford defender and fired low into the corner of the visitors net for the lead. Moments later a miscued Jeannin clearance ended with Glenn Cronin striking the visitors crossbar. Shortly after that Andy Taylor warmed the hands of the 'Bulls goalkeeper with a stinging free kick and Phillips again went close to extending the lead.
Hmmm - I wondered to myself. Could this finally be the end to this tragic curse of the camera at the ninth time of asking?
Nope.
From starting in a determined manner and dominating the opening exchanges, City amazingly found themselves 2-1 down at the break despite finishing the half against ten men.

On the half hour Guy Ipoua, despite being surrounded by at least four Grecian defenders, twisted right, left, and right again before firing from distance past the hesitant back four and Paul Jones for the equalizer. Shortly before the break Exeter gave away a free kick just on the edge of the area which ex-Grecian Alex Jeannin stood menacingly over.

I just walked out of the room. There was no need for me to watch the next five seconds to understand exactly what was about to happen. A bitter ex-player, released after not getting the contract he wanted, standing over a free kick on the edge of the Exeter area. Oh... and it's his birthday.

Sure enough the inevitable happens. The Frenchman curled a beautiful dead ball into the back of City's net to give Graham Turner's Hereford the lead. Moments later the visitors were reduced to ten men when goalscorer Ipoua was sent off rather harshly for supposedly inciting the crowd. This was followed by a rash of rather beefy challenges and the referee blowing up for half time (30 seconds early in my opinion - as the chances of a few snapped legs and a parade of ambulances to Well Street seemed extremely high at that moment).

With 45 minutes at home against ten men and a partisan crowd to roar you on I was still confident City would pin Turner's men into their own penalty area and eventually come away with the three points.

Of course I was an idiot.

Despite the extra man and a home support that would have gladly welcomed even a point at that stage, Exeter, despite vast periods of possession, never came close to breaching the visitors defence in a truly awful second half.

I'd like to say this was a total shock but I'd be a lying bastard. There seemed to be a pre-determined script written who's ending insisted on the Grecians coming out at the wrong end of a result.

I sat with a look of resignation on my face. It had been etched all over my mug from the moment Alex Jeannin had given Hereford the lead against his old club and although there had still been another 45 minutes of football to be played and a match to be won, inwardly I, the fans, and possibly some of the Exeter City staff knew whatever unfolded, the team were about to fall fowl of the dreaded curse of the camera for the ninth consecutive time.

Yet again I faced a barrage of criticism and questions from my friends.

"Are you off your tits?. Who's the bit on the side over there because you're sure as fuck not going for the football".

"Are the fans given a rope at the turnstiles to hang themselves from the rafters after a 5-0 defeat to a team likes Gravesend & Northfleet?"

"Do you get paid to sit in the ground?"

These are standard run of the mill questions. Normally they're extremely supportive but every morning after City have played on TV (and I used the word "played" extremely loosely) it's like the Spanish inquisition all over again.

New Year's was ushered in by the sound of sirens at no.29 where Mr. Murphy was amazingly arrested on suspicion of murdering his wife of 43 years. I suppose it's possible to do the gardening and let your pitchfork accidentally slip into your wife's back, it's just the 43 times this happened that the police were having a little trouble in believing. Can't say I blame the poor man. When you're married to a woman who's love of Tammy Wynette extended to her playing "Stand By You're Man" six hours straight every day for the last three decades you're bound to want a "D.I.V.O.R.C.E" at some point in your life. Pity Mr. Murphy didn't take the sane route of filing for separation inside of embedding a garden implement into his country & western loving spouse.

Exeter opened 2006 and finished off Christmas with a narrow 1-0 defeat away to Aldershot. City dominated early on, Challinor going close and Lee Phillips striking the bar, but Exeter looked shabby in defence thus a goal on 16 minutes coupled with a man of the match performance by 'Shots 'keeper Nikki Bull (he spells it like a girl) capped off a rather miserable end to a rather miserable Christmas. A period
that started with a defeat in atrocious conditions against Canvey and ended with Exeter five points off the top and further adrift of leaders Accrington Stanley.

The one bright spot had been the St Stephen's Day hammering of Aldershot which proved to be a false dawn as two successive defeats followed, with the 'Shots gaining revenge for that defeat less than a week later.

Online the City fans were starting the inquest. A post mortem was being carried out on EXEWEB - the biggest online forum for Grecian fans everywhere.

"We'll piss this away on this form. Sort it out Alex".

" I went to Aldershot and got a burger from a converted ambulance that doubles as the catering. Talk about stone age!".

"I hate Aldershot. 6 mile hike to the ground, death-trap cobblestones at turnstiles and floodlights that wouldn't light a hamsters bedroom."

Humorous to a fault, yet united in one common goal - supporting their team.

One fan seemed to capture the current mood.

" We've had an awful Christmas. We can't defend. I'm losing my sanity. It's enough to drive a man to drink."

I headed off to the pub in total agreement.

Chapter Twelve

THE STORY OF DJIMI TRAORE.

You've really got to wonder what kind of misogynistic bastard made the movie Watership Down? I mean here's a man who brought Richard Adams novel to the big screen and endured the wrath of parents worldwide whilst traumatising every dough-eyed toddler and pre-pubescent kid by presenting a film where there's an orgy of blood and violence with fluffy bunny rabbits being slaughtered at will.

I had the misfortune of being one of those wide-eyed innocent 9 year olds when I went along with my father to watch the movie in 1978. I was happy with a spot of male bonding with my dad and a story about a bunch of rabbits in a quite rural town in Berkshire. What followed scared the living shit out of me whilst breaking my little heart at the same time. I should have seen it coming the minute Fiver the psychic rabbit foresees an apocalyptic vision for the warren.

"The fields are covered in blood. BLOOD".

Now that had bad news written all over it.

At one point Blackavar - one of the leading rabbits - gets his ears ripped off for trying to leave the warren and is basically torn to shreds by the evil general Woundwort soon after. Through a flood of tears I watched as Hazel, Bigwig and Fiver battle it out for the right to stay alive and make a new life for themselves on Watership Down.

At the end of a bloodcurdling 90 minutes and Art Garfunkel reducing an entire cinema to tears with the beautifully haunting "Bright Eyes" , I left my seat a quivering wreck with just one thought on my mind….

What the fuck was my father thinking?

It's bad enough he introduced me to Bambi when I was 5 and gave me an entire month of sobbing after finding out Bambi's mother gets blown away - in the first 5 minutes, that he springs this upon me a month before my tenth birthday. What was supposed to be an idyllic afternoon with my father figure turned out to be a traumatic 90 minutes that still disturbs me almost 30 years later.

Just last year, whilst searching for some awful 80's slasher movies, my daughter picked up a copy of Watership Down and gave me the cunningly planned and expertly executed - dad will you please buy me this before I burst into tears - routine. As much as I wanted to appease my offspring, there was just no way I could even begin to tell her why she could never what this movie. I remedied the problem with the purchase of the SpongeBob SquarePants movie and resigned Watership Down to the bottom of the DVD pile, just in case some poor misfortunate child with the awful combination of innocence and curiosity about bunny rabbits happened to stumble across it.

I managed to forgive my father for his lousy choice (he could have brought me to see what he called "some ridiculous space movie" that same afternoon) but opted for the grim tale of rural rabbits tearing the shit out of each other in the English countryside.

By the way that "ridiculous space movie" that nobody wanted to see?

Star Wars.

We've never shared the same cinema since.

From that moment, any movie my father heaped critical praise on and suggested I should rush out and see has been taken with a severe pinch of salt. Only once after Watership Down did I ever get painfully hoaxed by my father again. Unfortunately it came less than two years after that, as at the tender age of 11 he let me say up late one night and watch - and I'll quote him word for word on this baby - " a harmless little film that's probably a bit spooky".

That film was Halloween.

I was eleven.

I didn't sleep for the next five years.

Around that time last year, when my daughter was giving me the Spanish inquisition on why a film about fluffy little bunny rabbits could induce a lifetime of trauma, all things Exeter was falling apart.

City entered 2006 in third position, well placed to strike should leaders Accrington and second placed Grays fold under questioning, but by March the Grecians had effectively killed off any hope of even a play-off place with a disastrous run which astonishingly produced six defeats in nine games and caused Alex Inglethorpe and his players to feel the wrath of a disgruntled City faithful.

Despite a patchy Christmas, Exeter had started the new year with a narrow defeat to Aldershot and a Lee Phillips goal nine minutes from time killed off visiting Gravesend a week later at St James Park. A last gasp Jon Challinor goal on the stroke of full-time away at Morecambe continued the mini-revival, before Exeter faced trail by TV (yet again) with a Monday night SKY SPORTS encounter against league leaders Accrington Stanley.

Having sat in my living room for years watching the Grecians snatch defeat from the jaws of victory and coma-inducing scoreless draws with Dagenham and Forest Green, I decided, although the game was being televised, I'd travel to Devon to watch the drama unfolding in person.

This naturally aroused even more suspicions among the conspiracy theorists in work. Why would a married man be travelling alone to watch a non league football team play on a frost-bitten winters night when he could sit in the comfort of his armchair and see them predictably lose in yet another televised terror.

"She must be some hot piece of ass to drag your carcass away from your living room sofa!".

Oh course they were idiots. My reasoning for travelling and yet again rocketing myself to the poorhouse was simple. By being at a televised league game I thought it might reverse the jinx and finally put an end to City's atrocious run of defeats and God awful draws. I'd sat like thousands of other Grecians, watching my side fall to pieces at the sight of a camera, so maybe, just maybe by actually being in the ground instead of at home with my head in my hands and looking between my fingers that Exeter might actually do the unthinkable and win a game.

The one thing my friends did get right was the weather. Siberia was a warmer place to be than St James Park on January 30 2006. It was one of those evenings were standing still for more than five minutes could turn your toes to icicles and only a pair of thermal underwear could stop a certain body part from shrivelling up even more than the unhealthy size it already was.

A win would bring City back to within five points of Stanley and re-ignite talk of a title that had disappeared with a poor run over Christmas. Sure Exeter were now second and it was a top-of-the-table clash, but realistically it represented City's last chance at reeling in an Accrington side swimming further down stream and disappearing out of sight from the chasing pack.

With temperatures struggling to stay on the plus side of freezing Exeter kicked off with an impressive 4,642 fans hoping to beat the would-be Champions elect and finally bury a ten year television ghost.

Predictably it was the visitors who struck first. A free kick on the edge of Exeter's area was wonderfully struck by Stanley's combative (that's a nice word for hatchet man) midfielder Gary Roberts into the back of Paul Jones net. 12 minutes in and the curse seemed as depressingly intact as ever. The Lancashire outfit had signalled their intentions after only six seconds when Matthew Gill was almost cut in half by a challenge that went unnoticed as the play was elsewhere and this theme continued when Chris Todd was caught by one of the most cynical tackles ever seen at this level (and boy that's a lot).

Put simply, the Exeter defender was lucky not to have his leg broken when Peter Cavanagh caught Todd thigh high with an act of sheer brutality. From the stand it looked truly sickening, but not as awful as Mr East's interpretation of the incident that warranted - for some insane reason - a yellow card. Todd received lengthy treatment - Cavanagh should have received a prison sentence. Things steadily got worse. Todd gave up the ghost five minutes later and City wasted several good openings to bring the game back level. Billy Jones warmed Elliot's hands with a wicked free kick, Jon Challinor drove narrowly wide and Jake Edwards drove straight at Elliot when well placed in the area.

With time almost up on an eventful first half a high ball was lofted into the Accrington penalty area. Up went an arm and a free-kick was awarded to the visitors. Harmless enough? Not really - when everyone inside the ground, watching at home, and even the Pope could see it was the Accrington defender who'd handled the ball.

To simplify - Exeter wore Red & White. Accrington wore blue.

There's not a colour clash there Mr East.

Astonishingly the man in the middle confounded the rules of football by giving a free out to the visitors. A stonewall penalty, missed by an idiot with a whistle from five feet and an even bigger fool with a flag ten yards away.

Half-time arrived and any sub zero pre-match temperatures were replaced by a white hot atmosphere and a home crowd seething for blood.

Naturally I got stuck in as well with a good humoured ditty as Mr East left the pitch.

Who's the bastard, who's the bastard….
Who's the bastard in the black….
Who's the bastard in the black?

By the time the officials returned to the fray the mood hadn't improved. Every time City had appeared on national television it had coincided with a disaster of Titanic proportions but this felt infinitely worse. A real sense of injustice not only about the scoreline but the disgraceful proceedings of the first 45 minutes. Roared on by the fiercely partisan crowd (and one psychotic Irishman with suicidal tendencies at this point), the Grecians set about righting a wrong. At this point Accrington showed exactly why they were league leaders. Hussling City all over the field and winning every 50-50 challenge, Stanley continued to take the game to their hosts and on 55 minutes Romuald Boco stabbed the visitors further ahead and put a two goal cushion between both sides.

2 became 3 ten minutes later when Roberts notched his second of the game after some under-11's Saturday morning defending by City's back four.

Exeter City 0-3 Accrington Stanley.

I searched for a litany of profound words and well worn hard luck sporting clichés to explain how I was feeling but one word summed it all up.

COCKNOBS.

A little light opened at the end of the tunnel when Jake Edwards pulled one back for the Grecians on 72 minutes but it proved to be a false dawn.

Whiskey was my alley for the rest of the night.

Good old fashioned, raw, burn a hole in my chest, knock me out for the night and repent at leisure Irish Whiskey.

The next six weeks saw Exeter completely fall apart.

Three demoralising defeats in a row followed. At Burton, City put in possibly their worse away performance under Alex Inglethorpe - going down 2-0 to Nigel Clough's men, whilst a week later they tamely surrendered to York City 3-1. The last defeat - the first time City had lost four straight league games - came three days later when Exeter headed east only to turn in a lifeless display in a one goal defeat to Woking.

There was total and utter disbelieve among the City faithful. How could a side who'd won six of their first eight games, led the league and consistently stayed in the top three placings of the division until early February, now be completely adrift of the play-offs ,six defeats in eight games and seemingly out of the running with eleven games still left to play.

Salvation came in the unlikely form of the FA Trophy. Having negotiated Bishop Stortford in round one before Christmas, City then accounted for an extremely competitive Histon side at the start of January (Challinor's goal 9 minutes from time securing a narrow 3-2 win against the Conference South outfit.)

Struggling Cambridge City then came to town and the Pope rescued Exeter - Neil Pope that is - as it was his own goal that secured a narrow one goal win and a place in the last eight for Inglethorpe's grateful men.

Having reached the quarter-finals for the previous two years Alex Inglethorpe knew this could be a season-saving trophy that would appease the ever more disgruntled Grecian faithful. Continuing the astonishing record of being drawn at home in practically every cup game they'd played since falling into the Conference, Exeter were given another St James' Park assignment and again drew lower league opposition.

Wiltshire based Salisbury City were riding high at top of the Southern League and arrived in Devon with just one defeat in 17 games and the scalp of Canvey Island (something we never managed) in the previous round. A big day out with nothing to lose, Salisbury were in a win-win situation.

Although the Grecians were overwhelming favourites nothing, and I mean nothing, could be taken for granted.

You see anything is possible in football folks. Exeter could win the Premiership, Ireland lift the World Cup and my very own Kilbarry Rangers take home the Champions League .

Why?

It's all down to just one man.

Mr Djimi Traore.

France has produced some of the finest exports seen in the English game. Pires, Desailly, Makelele and a certain Thierry Henry to name but a few. Managers latched onto the French revolution and an influx of everything within a mile of the Eiffel tower and the word "wee" in their vocabulary was hailed as the latest sensation from abroad.

However every so often there's a glitch and someone gets found out.

Stand up Djimi Traore.

Djimi started life at Metz- a solid French club with a proud history. To get to this point as a blossoming 16 year old Djimi must have been doing something right. I mean you can't buy your way onto a team and unless Djimi's dad had caught the Metz manager in lingerie, lipstick with a sheep called Suzy, you'd have to admit Djimi was there on merit.

From there Djimi moved to hometown club Laval where he made his first of five league appearances.

At the tender age of 17, with not even half a dozen games to his name, that master transfer market maestro - Mr Gerard Houllier - decided to spent half a million of Liverpool FC's pounds to bring the French-born Malian left back to the banks of the Mersey.

What followed was a living nightmare played out on the fields of the Premiership and in front of millions of viewers each Super Sunday. Poor Djimi was simply awful.

His mistakes opened him up to copious amounts of criticism. Memorably, his bizarre own goal against Burnley in the 2005 FA Cup were he somehow combined a Zidane style drag-back and Cruyff turn in his own six yard area to score a glorious own goal for the opposition.

But one thing Djimi had was heart. He had fuck all else going for him, but he never gave up. On the 25TH of May 2005, Traore lined up for Liverpool in the Champions League final. At half-time Benitez's men were 3-0 down and Djimi had been turned absolutely inside out by AC Milan.

But he never gave up.

The rest is history . Benitez's sacrificed seven dead chickens and made a pact with the Devil in the dressing room at half-time and Liverpool scored 3 goals in 5 minutes and eventually won the 2005 Champions League Final.

The world watched in amazement as the 25 year old French-born Malian kissed his winners medal, thus concluding the fairytale ending.

So when your team is facing an insurmountable object or you've got eleven men battling against seemingly impossible odds, never fear. Nothing is impossible my friends because if Djimi Traore can get a Champions League winners medal than absolutely anything is possible in this big wide world of football.

Salisbury needed a Traore-style inspiration that afternoon at St James but the Grecians killed that romantic idea stone dead with a thoroughly professional display on a gloriously sunny afternoon.

Lee Phillips opened the scoring on 15 minutes from the penalty spot after a clumsy challenge on Steve Flack which saw the Salisbury defender dismissed. By the half hour mark the big man had notched himself when Dean Moxey flicked on an Andy Taylor corner to the back post where Flacky made no mistake from a mere two yards.

City continued to hold all the cards after the break and despite Danny Woodards collecting two silly yellow cards and receive an early bath, Phillips wrapped up the win late on and despite a Salisbury consolation City marched into the semi-finals of the FA Trophy on the back of a 3-1 victory.

A week later an experience as rare as Haley's Comet and as spectacular as a solar eclipse was witnessed in Exeter .

A Steve Flack hat-trick.

Scratch that - a 15 minute Steve Flack hat-trick!

In the first 15 minutes!

I'd arrived home late Saturday afternoon (my diva of a daughter convincing me I needed to spent the morning shopping for new shoes for her precious feet) only to find there was a fault with my teletext.

You see, somehow the scoreline after 15 minutes in the Exeter's game against Southport read; Exeter City 3-0 Southport. But it was the neon statistic underneath that made my knees buckle and come over all faint.

Scorer; Flack 3, 5, 15.

I switch to Ceefax - same score. Gillette Soccer Saturday - same score. As a last resort I phone Stuart in his season ticket seat at St James Park.

"He hasn't has he?"

"He has you know!"

For the rest of the game I sat in awe listening to the radio as Jimmy Giles waxed lyrical on our giant strikers performance and his clinically taken hat-trick. City added two more goals from Phillips and Buckle to annihilate the hapless Southport 5-0 and complete our biggest win in our short Conference history.

Nevertheless the Grecians recent woeful run had seen them plummet from a title challenging second place to a pedestrian ninth. The hammering of bottom placed Southport proved to be a brief respite from recent results and Exeter got back into the losing habit away to Halifax a week later. This was followed by a ridiculous sixth defeat in seven games after Stevenage travelled to the West Country and left with a 2-0 win to leave Exeter with seven home defeats, a slip of seven places, and depressingly, seven points off the play-offs.

Thankfully St Patrick's Day rolled around and I had an excuse to drown my sorrow in several vats of whiskey and the Grecians could look forward to a date with Grays Athletic in the semi-finals of the FA Trophy.

There's an old Chinese saying that goes; before you start out on the road to revenge, dig two graves. This proverb would never be more apt then in Exeter's two-legged semi-final against Grays Athletic. The Londoners had handed out a painful footballing lesson among the low level stand and high rise buildings of Athletics' Recreation ground in last seasons tournament. The 4-1 mauling was still fresh in the memories of the Grecian faithful who travelled to the nations capital that afternoon to see City dismantled by the eventual winners. Revenge needed to be a dish served extremely cold as both sides met for the first leg at St James Park on March 18th 2006.

A crowd 51 over 3,000 watched Exeter display fighting qualities that were sadly lacking in City's recent league form as the Grecians came from behind to beat Athletic 2-1 and gain a narrow advantage over the Londoners. The visitors had taken a lead on 32 minutes from Jamie Slabber but a heroic second half display which included an insanely brave Chris Todd equaliser and a well worked Lee Phillips winner 14 minutes from time meant Exeter needed to just avoid defeat at the Recreation ground to contest their first ever major cup final.

Seven days later both sides met again. 11 V 11. Devon v Essex. The prize - a day out at Upton Park, home of Premiership giants West Ham United. It was so

126

close that the temptation to dream couldn't be avoided. One solid 90 minutes would see Exeter return to the capital, only this time to contest their first cup final in the clubs 102 year history.

In a rollercoaster ride season which continued to display City's bi-polar condition, Exeter saved the 25TH day of March to combine a cocktail of depression and bitter heartbreak to end their cup odyssey at the hands of Mark Stimson's Grays Athletic.

Exeter made an awful start. With their first noteworthy attack of the game the home side took full advantage of City's stuttering start and Glen Poole pounced to volley Grays one ahead. The next half hour saw City masquerading as a bunch of deer caught firmly in Athletics' headlights. Soon after the Essex club doubled their lead when the unstoppable Aaron Mclean swivelled in the area and placed his shot low and hard past the outstretched arms of Paul Jones. Exeter managed to survive until half-time and keep the game ticking over, just, as a contest.

The remaining 45 minutes were as tense and nail biting as anything Exeter experienced in THAT game at Old Trafford. Needing a goal to force the game into extra-time, Inglethorpe's men started to force the issue. The turning point came on 70 minutes. Challinor burst into the area and was promptly hauled down by Martin. The referee had no hesitation at pointing to the spot.
Penalty.

Lee Phillips placed the ball on the spot. Facing him ex-Exeter goalkeeper Ashley Bayes. 2693 people waited with baited breath for the outcome of this two man duel. Phillips strode up and stuck his spot-kick well but Bayes was equal to the task and pushed the ball out - and back to Phillips.

The less said about the rebound the better.

City had missed a guilt edged chance to bring the tie level and gain the momentum which would have surely swung in the direction of Inglethorpe's men. As I sat at home, nursing the worst post-St Patrick's Day hangover in my 36 years on this earth, my heart had sunk. Sunk to my feet, past it, through the floor and burrowed it's way to China.

Twenty three minutes of huff and puff followed and by 4.52 that afternoon the fist-pumping, back-slaps and celebratory high-fives belonged to Grays Athletic. The Grecians were devastated. From new signings Matthew Gill & Wayne Carlisle -at the club less than eight weeks - to the courageous Chris Todd and his crestfallen comrades.

Phillips was inconsolable. City's top goalscorer had ran himself to a standstill all season and his work-rate had been exemplarily, but his failure to beat Bayes from eight yards ended Exeter's chance of writing a glorious new chapter in the clubs career.

Trudging off the pitch, head bowed, tears running freely down his face.

He deserved better.

Exeter deserved better.

A month later we watched as Grays beat a pedestrian Woking side to lift the FA Trophy at Upton Park.

Both sides brought a combined crowd of 13,800.

City would have brought that alone.

Frustration really has no boundaries.

The rest of the season brought novel little landmarks. Exeter's quickest Conference goal - 49 seconds and scored by Jon Challinor against Tamworth. It

also proved to be our first game against nine men - and we still couldn't win!
Why? - because Mark Cooper scored Tamworth's goal.

Guess who Mark Cooper once played for?

Oh the irony of it all.

It never reigns but man does it fucking pour!

Thirty days into the month of March a stork arrived at the Kennedy household and dropped off a 7lb bundle of joy.

Callum Ryan Glen Exeter Kennedy completed the 2.4 household and added about 30 years to his dad's life in those first six months of constant nappy changes and 4am feeds. He very soon copper-fastened the nickname "Chompy" due to his infuriating habit of putting even the most inedible object into his mouth and chomping until it, or his three teeth, were in ribbons.

His name had been the source of many a heated argument among yours truly and my increasingly suicidal wife.

Not satisfied with filling my other half with murderous rage over everything from women drivers to the curves on my 18 year old next door neighbour, I decided to put her within a phone call of hiring a paid hit-man by contesting the name of our then unborn child.

Sandra had a shortlist of Ryan, Callum and Sean.

Mine was short and sweet.

The 1989/90 Exeter City Division Four Championship winning side.

She wasn't amused.

I tried a more suitable option.

The 2003/04 undefeated Arsenal Premiership winning team.

Finally we got it down to two. Callum and Dylan. I wanted the latter but my wife decided to give him the same name as the waste of a human life that is George Best's son.

The compromise would be I'd get the name of City skipper and good friend Glen Cronin and the title of Exeter on his birth certificate, thus avoiding the trouble of my wife paying several thousand pounds for a man in a balaclava to riddle my body with bullets.

Belatedly, after a decade of marriage, I finally realised there are several golden rules to obey in order to keep you're partner/spouse/mistress happy.

Never argue with women - it's a total waste of energy as they'll always maintain they're right - or batter you into submission with a curling thong.

When she says "does my bum look big in this?" - just say no even if it's the size of a small country.

On Saturday's never say "run along now and do the shopping, the footy's on" - unless you like the taste of hospital food.

Always leave the toilet seat down - unless you want your nuts permanently stapled to it.

Never, never get into an unmade bed. You may be on death's door with just minutes to live, but your other half will still roll you onto the ground to make sure every blanket is permanently wielded to the mattress.

Never belittle the programmes she watches. Just because she loves UK Drama on Sky (with films like the classic Not Without My Hairbrush - the story of one woman's struggle to be re-united with the only object that can keep her hair tidy), doesn't mean it's not entertaining to the female species. Further poking fun at said station could result in eyelids been super-glued to forehead, tied to a chair and forced to watch the next instalment of Murder She Wrote. Finally, the male species are always one word - WRONG.

Lucky enough my wife is an intelligent woman that never abides by the above rules (apart from the UK Drama bit), and has, for some unknown reason, decided to stand by her man for the last decade. A man that drives her insane and has been fundamental in four re-mortgages, but still not the worst in the world.

For the first time in three Conference seasons Exeter City's April was a month of sheer anti-climax. April Fools Day saw us make idiots of Altrincham (3-1) but a week later lose to a goal by a guy (Jamie Guy to be precise) in injury time against Cambridge at the dilapidated Abbey Stadium.

Not content with having heaped a lifetime of televised misery on our doorstep, SKY decided to screen the Grecian's away trip to Grays Athletic - a side becoming more infuriating by the day - on Monday Night Football.

City were lying in eighth spot but mathematically still had an outside chance of getting to the play-offs. The eight point gap could possibly be bridged should Exeter take at least 15 points from the last six games.

Lights. Camera. No Action.

Again Exeter failed in front of the cameras, though the final scoreline of 3-0 severely flattered the hosts. The Grecians fell behind to a Glenn Poole goal on 34 minutes and despite sustained pressure in the second half (were Lee Phillips missed a golden chance to equalize), City were caught twice on the break by Oli & Martin and fell to their fifteenth defeat of the season.

I sat perplexed at home watching our pre-destined fate.

Inevitable but awful. Even the cat wanted to cry.

The next morning, in-between sniggers and the Spanish Inquisition from my workmates, I decided to show another act of suicidal devotion and unswaying loyalty to my side.

In typical fashion ,when I should have been running a mile from everything Exeter, I decided to travel to England to watch the last game of the season - Scarborough at home.

The four week window would give me time to put together some money (with the help of the dreaded O word - overtime), and pay some money off the credit card so I could max it out again over in Devon.

Seeing the play-offs as a distant dream after the Grays defeat, Exeter put together a mini-revival which included draws against Forest Green and Canvey (we always score in injury time against Exeter) Island and some thumping home wins against Dagenham (3-1) and a penultimate day hammering of Crawley Town were Jamie Mackie, Danny Seabourne, Craig Farrell & Dean Moxey completed a rout that belatedly pushed the Grecians up to seventh place.

That Saturday I boarded a train, caught me a plane, and found myself back with the Grecians again. A weekend in sun-kissed Devon watching Exeter play out the remaining ninety minutes of their anti-climatic season.

I enjoyed the banter. Renewal of friendships. The taste of ice cold beer.

As for the match - City may have played at pedestrian pace but opponents Scarborough needed a stirring performance of pride and passion, not to mention three points, in order to avoid relegation from the Conference. Two seasons before 'Boro had been extremely unlucky to lose a fourth round FA Cup tie against Premiership Chelsea. Now the Seasider's stood on the precipice of the anonymity of Conference North football.

For the record, two goals in the final four minutes dictated the story of the game.

Unfortunately for Scarborough they only scored one of them. As the game wound down to a seemingly predictable scoreless draw, Jon Challinor latched onto a pass from Jamie Mackie and slotted the ball calmly past former Liverpool trainee Ian Dunbavin for the opening goal. Debutant Matt Bye then struck the Scarborough post and just as it looked like City had won, kept a clean sheet and delighted the crowd of 3,382, Tony Hackworth latched onto Neil (I've had more clubs than the entire European Ryder Cup team) Redfearn's cross and belatedly levelled the tie. A couple of frantic minutes later, as the visitors fought in vain for a winner, the whistle went and with it the curtain drew down on the 2005/06 league season for Exeter City.

Along with it went the familiar face of one Stephen Flack.

Tough-nut. Target-man. Trier.

Love him for his trademark powerhouse headers or loathe him for his limited ability with the leather object at his feet, Flacky was 100% City. A man who'd turned down the chance of league football in his final season with generous advances from Chester City and Grimsby Town in order to try spearhead Exeter's promotion challenge.

His astonishing 15 minute hat-trick against Southport had brought his goalscoring tally for Exeter to 98. Alas the big man never notched the remaining two goals needed to break a century though it certainly wasn't from the want of trying.

The Grecian faithful filed out of St James Park for the last time that season. Stuart headed for the bar. Bob cursed the six teams above us ("that sodding Morecambe are a bunch of seaside loving arse bandits"), and Kiss-the-seat-Pete reminisced with his plastic moulded friend about another season of highs, lows, and occasional soakings.

Rumours were abound of Alex Inglethorpe departing for higher echelons and the inevitable clear out of playing personal. Who'd stay, who would go? Matters to be resolved over the closed season and a month long World Cup.

What's another year? Well actually it's another eight months outside league football for the Grecians - our fourth season, and still not a play-off place to show for it.

Alex Inglethorpe's men had finished seventh. A drop of one place on previous seasons but a gap of 11 points separated City and Morecambe-in the last play-off place.

That May we watched on as Hereford won the Conference play-off final defeating Halifax in a five goal thriller to regain their league status for the ninth time of asking, Liverpool winning a classic FA Cup final, and Roman Abramovich PLC securing back to back Premiership titles.

However the real agony began in the last 15 minutes of the 2006 Champions League Final. My beloved Arsenal, having fought in the face of injuries and adversity to reach the Champions League final - creating a record for not conceding a single goal in eight European games along the way - were cruelly undone by Henrik Larsson in the final 15 minutes of Europe's showcase final.

Everything seemed to be going to script for the Gunners even though they'd had goalkeeper Jens Lehmann sent off after just 18 minutes and the reliable Thierry Henry had missed a glorious chance to put Arsenal ahead in the opening moments, when Sol Campbell headed ten man Arsenal ahead before the break.

Just when it looked as if Arsenal's fledging footballers were going to carry off mission impossible, Barcelona threw on Larsson.

The rest is painful history.

In hindsight I'd have much rather a comprehensive three goal win by the Catalan giants then two goals in the final 15 minutes against a wobbly Manuel Almunia and his jaded back four.

Hindsight is always better - depending on the hind you've sighted.

Summer brought the World Cup and four weeks of sheer bliss. Despite the fact Ireland hadn't made it to Germany, the nation picked out a fellow underdog to champion the cause. Trinidad & Tobago fitted the bill perfectly, especially as they would lock horns with the old enemy.

Yep - ENGLAND.

It's always been a source of astonishment to my friends across the water that when the Republic play, the whole of England support us, yet when three lions on a shirt appear on our television sets the entire collective weight of 4 million Irishmen & women from the Emerald Isle automatically side with whichever opponent is facing the Queen's eleven that afternoon.

The devil himself could have an XI that included Adolf Hitler at centre-half, Joseph Stalin on the wing and Jack The Ripper up front and we'd still cheer the murdering bastards on!.

To re-assure my Saxon buddies, this, contrary to popular opinion, has actually nothing to do with the England football team itself.

It's the English media and they're fascination with one particular year of the 2007 the world has evolved through since the birth of our lord Jesus Christ.

1966.

Alas for my friends across the water Sven's men suffered yet another penalty shoot-out heartbreak when a Liverpool duo and Frank Lampard (or KD Lang as my friend calls him - and trust me there's a striking resemblance) missed their spot kick's and England trudged off down the tunnel of the Veltins Arena in Gelsenkirchen to the strains of John Motson cursing English luck and Gareth Crooks insisting anyone of the '66 team would have finished off Portugal single-handedly in the first 15 minutes.

England were out .The combined Celtic nations of Ireland, Scotland and Wales rejoiced, whilst Alan Hansen smiled on smugly in the studio and Martin O' Neill tried to keep a straight face.

As for the Grecians? - they'd waved goodbye to league football (again), goodbye to Santos Gaia - who moved to Stevenage and most importantly, goodbye to manager Alex Inglethorpe who took up a prestigious coaching role at Tottenham Hotspur. I could forgive him defeat's to Burton, Woking and Canvey Island - but moving to Spurs!. A pox upon you Alex, a pox I say!

Inglethorpe had citied seven new arrivals for the coming season. Yet now our ambitious young manager had departed. With all too depressingly familiar regularity the Grecians informed the media they'd be looking for a new saviour. An influx of players hadn't arrived. Challenging times lay ahead, and yet again the club stared adversity in the face.

Still you know what they say about that.

He who smiles in the face of adversity, probably has a scapegoat in mind.

Chapter Thirteen
TISDALE - THE SUICIDAL HAMSTER.

The phone call came at 4 minutes past 5.
I'd just arrived home from the first fixture of Kilbarry Rangers new season - a pre-season friendly away to Carlow Town, which we'd actually won 1-0. I put this down to the fact not one single person could find the ball in the 22 man goalmouth scramble in the last minute. Not saying Carlow is behind the times but the lawnmower has yet to be invented in these parts. Having spent 89 minutes kicking lumps of grass in blind hope of moving the leather object buried beneath it, the game came down to that orgy of bodies in the Town goalmouth which resulted in new signing Pablo Gonzalez diving on the ground to punch the ball into the net. Given the fact the referee couldn't even see the ball, he assumed someone had made contact, put the ball in the back of the net and awarded the goal.
I picked up the phone, instantly recognising Stuart's voice on the other end.
"Check the Norwegian website....Big news".
Yes folks... Exeter City has a big Norwegian fan base... eat your heart out Ole Gunner Solskjaer and your teenage fan club of four 10 year olds!
The site had breaking news about the managerial vacancy at Exeter City FC. Over the month of July the club had advertised for a new man to lead the Grecians back into the promised land of league football. This, apparently, would be a "manager of league experience". Hopes were high and rumours abound of which tried and trusted old codger would be taking over at SJP. Danny Wilson ? Mark Wright? Some even predicted Ian Holloway would be on the road down to Devon. Two weeks later - three applicants arrived for a round of interviews - only one had previously managed in English league football.
Former Reading, Swindon and Shrewsbury boss Jimmy Quinn had taken the helm at league clubs, but more importantly had taken Shrewsbury out of the Conference at his first attempt in 2004. The other two applicants couldn't boast as strong a résumé. Shaun Taylor had made over 200 appearances for Exeter and was one of a handful of Grecian heroes' that had lead City to the historic 1989/90 Fourth Division title and Paul Tisdale was virtually unheard of as manager of Team Bath in the Southern league, though he had also played at City on a 3 month loan spell eight years ago.
Hardly an inspiring line-up, but the choice on the face of things seemed straight-forward. Given the club's statement of intent to find a manager of league experience and the lack of it from the other two candidates, Quinn seemed to be a shoe-in.
However on leaving down the phone and checking the Exeter Norwegian fans website I was left dumbfounded. Just 24 hours before the unveiling of the Grecians new manager, Quinn had phoned a Norwegian contact and announced he hadn't got the job.
In the words of my milkman Clumpy Brennan (when he walked into his bedroom to find Mrs Brennan with the 17 year old student next door);
"What in the name of Christ is going on here?"
In a three horse race, Quinn's pedigree should have seen him romping down the home straight whilst his competitor's where still clearing the first fence. With hours to go Shaun Taylor seemed destined to land the job at his former employers. The reliable centre-half in the most glorious season of Exeter's 102

year history had been head of Bristol City's youths and was assistant manager at Forest Green. He'd also narrowly lost out to Alex Inglethorpe for the hot seat last time around.

Monday morning opened in bright sunshine and an air of expectancy over St James Park. At 10am that morning Exeter City's eighth manager in the last ten years was finally unveiled.

Paul Tisdale was that man.

The seemingly complete outsider had impressed the selection committee enough to land the job as City's new manager.

To be truthful I didn't know what to think. Taylor would have been a safe choice for the fans, whilst Quinn seemed to have all the right credentials (though he showed a nasty patriotic streak in a certain world cup qualifier against the Republic in '93 which we don't forget - that goes for you too Mr. Dowie).

Whatever the feeling among the Grecian faithful about our new manager one thing was undeniable. Paul Tisdale was going to get all the support in the world possible. There may have been a feeling of letdown , in some parts disgust, at the boards failure to live up to their word and delivering a man of experience , but Tisdale couldn't be made the scapegoat.

A competent pre-season followed , along with the arrival of some fresh faces. Adam Stansfield from Hereford, Bertie Cozic from Team Bath, and the welcome return of an old favourite in defender Jon Richardson, who spent six years of the 90's at St James. However Tisdale pulled off a pre-season pickle with the signing of Rob Edwards from Blackpool. The former Preston defender had made over 400 league appearances and been capped 6 times for Wales. An impressive coo by the astute young Grecian manager. With every piece in place, Exeter opened up their fourth season in the Conference with a tricky away tie at York City.

It was a typical opening day encounter - tight, tense , no quarter given. There are easier places to start a Conference campaign then the Kit Kat Crescent, but City's new line up were chockfull of surprises (sorry couldn't resist) and could count themselves unlucky not to take all three points. Both Stansfield and the energetic young Jamie Mackie forced point blank saves from Evans in the home sides goal, but York's goalkeeper was then astoundingly just yellow-carded for handling outside his area - a decision that earned derision from the travelling City faithful.

Scoreless but satisfied, City built on the opening day draw with 2 home wins against Forest Green and Altrincham. The Grecians new striker Stansfield opened his account with the sole goal against our neighbours Forest Green whilst a late Jon Challinor goal was enough for the points against Altrincham in a game I'd been lucky enough to see.

I had made an early pilgrimage to Devon that afternoon to see how City's early season form was shaping up. I'd incurred the wrath of my wife by forgetting to book online tickets for a forthcoming Bon Jovi concert, and losing my mum in law's 100 Greatest Country Hits CD. The concert I could live with (paying 75 Euro to see a man in a perm sing as if his testicles have been clamped with a pair of pliers is simply criminal), but the lost of a compact disc which included the suicide-inducing Crystal Chandeliers by Charlie Pride could have serious repercussions on my health should my mom-in-law have found out. After four hours of searching online and a further three rummaging through the bargain bins of every record shop in town, I finally found the album - on QVC - the shopping network.

Success? - not really. Whilst I could replace the CD that I'd inadvertently used as a weapon to sever the head of my cat for attempting to eat my steak dinner, it would mean a wait of 28 days before my wife's mom could listen to Charlie warbling on and Dolly Parton telling Jolene not to take her man.

Naturally Maggie was not a happy woman. By the time Glen Campbell got to Phoenix I'd still be waiting for the sodding CD to come in the mail.

Escaping the self-inflicted turmoil, I arrived in Bristol and took a quick 55 minute train journey to Exeter. I've always varied the many ways I travel to Devon. The natural explorer in me will seek out an overnight stay in Barnstaple and Bridgwater before paying over the odds fares from so-called "low cost" airlines. Today a short trip over the Svern and a scenic journey through the South West proves the perfect antidote to the musical mess I'd left behind me in the emerald isle.

Saturday afternoon rolled around and with it a Canvey Island-like downpour of biblical proportions before the game. I'd already enjoyed pneumonia from that fixture and with the seemingly incessant rain teeming down I didn't fancy a week long stay on a hospital bed as comfortable as a bed of nails anytime soon. Lucky enough that loveable duo - Mr sun & blue sky appeared over the horizon just in time to brighten up proceedings at the park.

Unfortunately my overactive bladder cost me a view of the first goal. With the mere sight of a running tap enough to have me dashing to a urinal for at least 3 hours, I'd missed the first attack and subsequently the first goal of the game. It didn't fall to the home side.

Barely 2 minutes had elapsed when Martin Rice was forced to produce a superb save from a stinging Altrincham effort. However his parry landed at the feet of an incoming Robbie Lawton who gleefully accepted the rebound to put the visitors ahead.

Exeter couldn't get out of first gear. With almost 20 minutes on the clock the home side still hadn't produced a shot in anger. Finally Adam Stansfield aroused a muted home support by tumbling in the area after a mysterious leg sent the Exeter man onto the surface, but referee Linington was having none of it.

Thinking we weren't having a miserable enough time, the Lord decided to hit Exeter with another deluge. By this stage I was pretty convinced it was just a matter of moments before Noah arrived up Well Street in the ark looking for a missing pair of penguins. The restless natives were briefly stirred again by the sight of Chris Todd's header being cleared from under the visiting side's crossbar and a sweet Matthew Gill volley which flew past the post.

With the watch showing 41 minutes parity was finally restored courtesy of another effort from Todd. This one however was a laser guided missile from a Billy Jones cross. City's captain arrived late into the area to deliver a bullet header and bring the game back level.

Half-time arrived and with it a welcome cup of hot coffee to roast my lungs.

Thankfully Exeter came out of the blocks quicker at the start of the second half despite a rash of substitutions which briefly fragmented the Grecians. A point would have been considered a setback against our northern counterparts, so with that in mind Jon Challinor proved to be the deciding factor in the resting place of three points that afternoon.

With just 4 minutes left on the clock the Grecian midfielder collected a superb pass from Andy Taylor and drove an unstoppable effort into the roof of the visitors goal to effectively wrap up the points and send 3,345 fans home happy. That night being slightly adventurous I attempted a chicken vindaloo - the mainstay of Saturday night English pallet's and apparently the most popular dish in Britain. This decision would cost me a night's sleep and a five hour appointment with a toilet bowl. To put things in context, I break out in a sweat just looking at a chilli. I perspire dramatically at the touch of a spice.

However, determined to taste a cornerstone of British culture I walked into the nearest Indian, ordered myself a vindaloo, and worked my way through the dish with the aid of two jugs of water and a coke.

What in the name of Lord Jesus Christ was I thinking? Had I gone through my usual routine of chomping down my nosh under the safety of my bed sheet blanket I could have left this time bomb on the bedside locker and slept it off, but when you're smack bang in the middle of a restaurant full of hungry punters scoffing down their meals and an extremely friendly Indian host asking me why I'm picking at the meal his chef has lovingly slaved over, you really don't want to disappoint anyone.

Of course I disappointed my bowels, the toilet bowl, and the subsequent hotel cleaner the next morning by surging on in the face of such fiery opposition but at least it taught me a lesson. When you're scared of spices and pissed on a Saturday night, never go within 50 feet of you're nearest Indian or curry house.

The win had pushed Exeter up to fourth in the table and I'd returned home confident that weekend that City would add another three points with their upcoming away trip to lowly Tamworth FC.

On my return home I found a new member had been added to the Kennedy household. On a trip to the local pet shop to stock up on fish food, my daughter Leanne took a liking to a hamster. Being a persuasive little minx she conned her mum into bringing home the furry little friend and spending about 100 Euro on cage, toys and general hamster friendly gadgets.

The novelty wore off after about 25 minutes and yours truly became the guardian of our new housemate.

I'd never had a hamster before. We already had two dogs, two cats, rabbit, a fish and a large filthy rodent living in our attic that tries to attack me once a month when I feed him his favourite meal of rat poison though he's not really a pet.

Seeing as we'd had him a few days and he'd still not been given an official name, I took it upon myself to christen our new housemate. This was never going to be straight forward. Given the fact I used to own a dog called Asshole (my Uncle named him that after he ate his false teeth) a fish called Bergkamp , and presently had a fridge-raiding cat named Devil in my house, I would be taking my time naming another member of the weird and wonderful animal kingdom in the Kennedy household.

Another Saturday afternoon. Another away day, and with it yet another long journey for the dedicated Grecian army.

Staffordshire in the West Midlands would mean a solid three hours drive. From there the negotiation of roads and roundabouts would lead the travelling Devonians to The Lamb - home of perennial strugglers Tamworth FC.

With no mobile updates or radio coverage I sat pensively at home. Just me, a cup of coffee, and the hamster with no name.

135

Unfortunately for Exeter, the home side had Dick Turpin among the starting line up. That was the only way to explain the smash & grab scenario that followed over the next 90 minutes.

City dominated but failed to score. Controlled the game but couldn't net. A frustrating afternoon was compounded by a goal ten minutes from time from Tamworth's Adie Smith completely against the run of play to delight the tiny home crowd and send Exeter to their first defeat on the 2006/07 season.

A funny thing happened that afternoon.

I found a name for my furry friend.

At the exact moment- Tamworth 1-0 Exeter (Smith 80 mins) flashed on my screen, the hamster with no name got out of his miniature house, climbed to the top of his cage, clawed his way to the middle of it, hung there for a moment , then threw himself to the bottom of the cage taking out a carrot out the way down before landing in a heap of lettuce.

Ten minutes later, and the confirmation of Exeter's defeat, brought a repeat of this psychotic act.

Had my new housemate some kind of death wish?

Was he depressed with a life of caged captivity?

Did he yearn to run amok among the roaming plans and riverbanks?

Or was it the fact that Exeter City made him want to take his own life?

Convinced that it was the latter, I named my new four-legged friend after Exeter City's new manager.

From 4.55 on that August afternoon he became Tisdale - the suicidal hamster. To this day he still throws himself off the roof of his cage with wild abandon anytime the footy's on. Good thing he wasn't around in our relegation season - that would've been to much for the crazy little rodent to bear.

Despite the defeat Exeter remained in the play-off places despite another slip-up at home to visiting Crawley Town that bank holiday Monday. That game saw the return of Scott Hiley to St James Park. Having fallen out of favour under Alex Inglethorpe, the patron saint of nutmegs found a new home at the West Sussex outfit and lined out that evening against the club he'd made over 300 appearances for.

Exeter were made to work for their point- coming from behind with a Dean Moxey goal on the hour giving the Grecians a share of the spoils despite constant pressure in the last quarter of the game.

Even at this early stage two clubs were setting the pace. Freshly relegated Oxford were looking to bounce back at the first attempt whilst Dagenham had turned themselves from last season also-rans into a competent squash-buckling side under the guidance of seasoned campaigner John Still.

Having not qualified for the play-offs in our first 3 seasons at Conference level, this would be a hugely significant season.

A fourth consecutive year outside the top five would be beyond comprehension, whilst City's new manager was only on a 1 year rolling contract. With fans getting anxious at Dagenham's progress, not to mention the title winning Accrington side of the year before (who also finished nowhere before taking the league by storm), the collective weight of 5,000 City fans rested firmly on the shoulders of Mr Tisdale and his playing staff.

Luckily for our fledging manager and the suicidal hamster of the same name, Exeter took four points from their next two games to steady the ship (my furry friend focused on Arsenal for the next few weeks - the Gunners were currently giving him plenty of scope for a rodent with suicidal tendencies).

A Friday night trip to the Abbey Stadium saw Exeter fall behind to Rob Newman's Cambridge United before producing a barnstorming second half display to see off the struggling U's.

A disputed free-kick on 20 minutes ended with a hesitant City defence falling asleep for the exact amount of time it needed for Mark Peters to nip in and slot the ball into the Grecians net.

That was as good as it got for the hosts. Exeter cut Cambridge open seemingly at will soon after and it was no surprise when Lee Phillips equalized 5 minutes before half time after some terrific work on the wing from Jamie Mackie.

Exeter wrapped the game and three points up midway into the second period. This time Phillips turned provider and after a lovely run at the United defence he set up Challinor to drive past the despairing grasp of Crichton in the home side's goal. Although Cambridge did strike a post against the run of play, City gave themselves a two goal cushion from the resulting rebound and attack when Phillips' drive was put into the back of his own net by goalkeeper Crichton.

It was the final straw for a seething home crowd who turned their anger on manager Rob Newman in a verbal onslaught that lasted long after Hanlon had been sent off for United and the ensuing final whistle.

The mob had spoken.

Newman was sacked immediately after the game.

I felt sad for him. The game had changed so much. So far beyond all recognition in fact that a man can get sacked on the back of four defeats and be out of his livelihood just six games into a season. This wasn't a man who could agree a wealthy severance fee, move to another Premiership club and write his memoirs about former employers in a wealthy book deal. This was a man humiliated just moment's after a game of football and out of a job.

Rob Newman was only going one place - the job centre.

The cynics will say it's a result-driven culture but stability and sensibility seem out-dated words, almost frowned upon by millionaire chairman in a game of soulless outsiders in a world were sponsorship rules and television rights are paramount.

Tradition has become an ugly word. Everything counts to these corporate clones except what really should - the man through the turnstile.

A week later the Grecians played out a tight scoreless draw with Aldershot. The game was memorable only for the fact it was City's biggest attendance of the season so far - six short of 4,000 - and John Challinor had a late chance to put one over on his former employers.

However the result maintained an unbeaten home record and kept Exeter in the hunt.

The next seven days saw City explore a whole range of emotions and experience three different results in three different games.

First up, a trip back to the capital and a visit to the Kassam Stadium to play league leaders Oxford United. Jim Smith's side were looking to bounce back to league football at the first attempt and made a perfect start when Steve Basham put the home side ahead. Martin Rice was called upon to save a penalty soon after but the rest of the game was all about the Grecians. Tisdale's side notched up close to 19 different efforts at the Oxford goal but couldn't find a breakthrough. A frustrating evening for Exeter and one the home side can count their blessings for all three points.

Devon's finest vented their anger on an unsuspecting Gravesend side just four days later but still found themselves out of luck. Within the first 50 seconds Matthew Gill served notice by narrowly firing wide before Jamie Mackie warmed the hands of the 'Fleets goalkeeper Cronin. Finally on 19 minutes Exeter did take the lead. Billy Jones corner was floated into the home sides box and Rob Edwards was there to score his maiden goal for the club and put City ahead. Shortly before half-time Exeter doubled the lead when Andy Taylor's deep ,hanging cross was expertly met by James Smith to hammer into the net.

Unfortunately for James, he plays for Gravesend.

15 minutes and a tongue lashing later from temper-tantrum ,cup-throwing, vain bursting coach Liam Daish, the home side started back on the road to recovery. Winning a free kick on the edge of City area, Hawkins floated in a cross which was neatly glanced on by Sodje and past Martin Rice in the Grecians goal for 1-2 with 60 minutes gone.

The mood suddenly changed as Paul Tisdale's men spent the last quarter of the game on the back foot. Again City conceded. And again from a set-piece. Keeling's corner was again glanced in by a head. This one belonged to Ross Graham-Smith to set up an extremely tense last ten minutes. What was supposed to be a routine City away win at half-time, to set up a happy evening in the Kennedy household, now had that gut-wrenching feeling of a second half collapse and a night of kicking the cat off the four walls in my place of residence.

In the last minute Stansfield was bundled over in the area but no spot kick resulted. What did result was an instant break by the home side, a panic-stricken defence and a magnificent point blank save from Martin Rice to deny Gravesend a last gasp victory.

Listening in on the radio, I'd clinically died for 2.7 seconds at that point.

The dog revived me an hour later by licking my face with his ice-cream laden tongue. Nice of my four legged friend to perform this service but the bastard was cute enough to eat my dessert first before he attempted to revive me.

Man's best friend my arse.

The last of Exeter's trilogy took place a mere 72 hours later but this time at home.

Having been unlucky not to take maximum points against fellow title challenger's in Oxford and Gravesend, the Grecians hosted Conference newcomers St Albans at St James Park.

Although the pride of Devon had only played a mere nine games of the new season this was already being described as a must win game for Paul Tisdale's men. Having just set up an online account with a betting shop I decided this would be a good match to have a punt on. Exeter were clear favourites at 4/7 but the odds for the first goalscorer of the match were extremely generous. Either BET365 were feeling strangely charitable or they hadn't a clue about Exeter City.

I decided to lay my main bet on Jon Challinor. For a midfielder with a fantastic strike rate he was an astonishing 16/1.

Criminal.

There's people behind bars for carrying out less crimes.

This betting shop just HAD to be made an example of.

I rounded off my flutter with five Euro on Chris Todd (at a tasty 40/1 it could be a very handy 200 notes) and another three on Exeter to win 4-1.

The city slickers of St Albans came to stifle. For part-time folly trying to just avoid relegation and eventually establish themselves in the Conference this would be a tactic employed at many an away ground by the minnows.

Tonight was no different. The emphasis was on containment from the start. The Grecians started like a virgin in a brothel and the nerves were clear for all 2,494 to see. It took 15 minutes before a shot was registered, half an hour before a save and with a minute to half time the teams seemed destined to walk back to the dressing room scoreless.

Then a move of World Cup pedigree (I kid you not!) which involved Edwards to Gill - Woodards to Cozic, Phillips to Taylor, a ball back to Cozic and the sublime finish by French Bertie (as he's known) puts the Grecians 1-0 up with just seconds to spare.

A glorious let off that should have been the catalyst for City to drive on and secure three points.

Of course this is Exeter so in keeping with our club motto "Do things the hard way, it keeps the fans on their toes", the Grecians let the lead slip and on 55 minutes the visitors drew level with a goal from Dwayne Jackman.

Queue a seizure of epileptic proportions by yours truly.

"Fucking imbeciles! - They'd fuck up a cup of coffee!"

I think Matty Gill heard me. Seeing an injustice at St James, and a potential homicide in the south east of Ireland, Gill drove a 20 yard daisy cutter into the visitors net on 65 minutes to regain City the lead and restore some sanity in the Kennedy household.

After Phillips notched for 3-1 I'd put the wrist-slashing idea to one side and by the time Billy Jones scored I'd completely given up the idea of throwing the television out the front window.

4-1. Challs may not have bashed the bookies with his pre-match price but I was still looking at a tasty ton with my 3 Euro bet on Exeter to win 4-1 at odds of 33/1.

With 15 seconds left Lee Clarke scored for St Albans.

Que sera sera.

May you die roaring Clarke.

Exeter entered October desperately clinging onto the top half of the table. A scrambled Billy Jones equalizer 2 minutes from time kept the home record intact against Stevenage whilst a Paul Buckle winner on the hour away at Southport continued a revival of one defeat in six games.

Bogeymen Grays Athletic proved a nightmare for the umpteenth time a week later, coming from behind to take a 2-1 lead into the final moments of Exeter's league encounter. Then , our first bit of luck EVER against the bank-rolled boys of suburbanite London. With just seconds remaining Exeter won a corner which resulted in a goal-mouth melee and a ball breaking on the edge of the area to Billy Jones, who shaped, studied, and hammered the ball back with interest into Athletics' net.

The draw rejuvenated Paul Tisdale's side. October would see victories over Halifax and the triumph over adversity that is AFC Wimbledon in the FA Cup. A Lee Phillips goal insured no capitulation to lowly Northwich at St James', whilst City continued their hoodoo over Morecambe (7 games and counting) with a pulsating 2-2 draw away at Christie Park.

Although not setting the league alight, unlike 12 months previous under Inglethorpe's table-topping Grecians, City had managed to move unnoticed into fifth place and with it a slender hold on that oh so important last play-off place.

Even by late November it seemed as if one club would be wrapping up league title proceedings and breaking open the bubbly several months early. Although Dagenham were hanging on desperately to second place, Oxford looked a class above the chasing pack.

Before the arrival of Jim Smith's squad, Exeter could rightly claim to be the best attended, best supported club in the Conference. However the arrival of United, their millionaire chairman, and swelling hoards at the Kassam Stadium, frequently hitting double figures, meant City had to play second fiddle to the recently relegated Londoners.

Having got themselves into the play-offs Exeter looked to push on and ruffle the feathers of those above by putting another three points on the board against Stafford Rangers.

I felt uncharacteristically confident.

Maybe it was the sweltering sun, protruding through the clouds, unaware it was winter. Maybe it was the sexy smile of the outrageously flirtatious Mrs Allen at number 9 (still a classy act at 54). Or maybe it was the fact Tisdale-the suicidal hamster didn't feel the need to climb his cage and hurl himself off from a frightening height thus insuring an x-ray at the vets and a monstrous bill for his agitated owner.

Football logic suggested that if a team is promoted they will almost certainly have beaten sides the ilk of Stafford Rangers along their travels. And although Exeter had made a mockery of that statistic by falling apart at the likes of Burton, Woking and, more recently a God awful collapse to Tamworth, today would be a day that suggested logic would once again take over.

90 minutes later I was forced to rethink things. You see logic - much like whiskey- loses it's beneficial effect when taken in too large quantities. And boy did I want to sink my head in a vat full of Jameson after this game. City would not only confounded the theorists by snatching defeat from the jaws of victory, but in doing so had tossed in that time honoured adage - you're only as old as you feel - by letting a 67 year old striker score twice in the closing minutes and give the rather illogical Stafford Rangers a shock win at St James Park.

Alright so Neil Grayson was slightly younger than a man collecting his pension(23 years younger to be precise),but the fact City had succumbed after Adam Stansfield's opener on 55 minutes to a side just promoted and happy to be locking horns with a former league club, flew in the face of any logic that suggested City should win.

As defeat goes it was quite truly awful.

The Staffordshire side outclassed Exeter all over the park. Overrun in midfield, wasteful in attack, woeful in defence. Despite the injury-time winner from the mature marksman, City were forever second best.

Yet again, yet fucking again, in front of our biggest crowd of the season.

I slumped back in my chair, opened some whiskey and drank away the memory of the last ninety minutes.

In the corner a creature stirred.

Tisdale was out of his hut and making his way to the top of the cage.

God love him the poor thing.

God love him.

Chapter Fourteen

IT NEVER RAINS, BUT IT POURS..(AND POURS)
The great St Albans soaking.

How lovely it is to live life in your own little world. How splendid things are that, when the daily grind and struggle against the tide of life gets to much for us, we can shut ourselves out into our own little make-believe world and act out our secret fantasies and guilty pleasures without fear of reprisal from the outside world.

I'm of course talking of Trekkies.

Yep - the phenomenon that are thousands, nay millions of dedicated Star Trek fans that travel the world over, convention after convention, in support of their unswerving dedication to the television series that spawned an iconic following.

Having a day off work, and hailstones hammering against my window pane outside, I'm stuck to my sofa, boiling hot cup of tea in one hand, remote in the other.

In front of me - the God of my household.

Television.

Teacher. Mother. Secret lover.

It's here the world of the Trekkie has unfolded before my very eyes.

Middle-aged men dressed as Klingon warlords speaking insane dialect. Women sporting beehive hairdo's and proclaiming themselves to be Shahna - alien mistress of Captain James Tiberius Kirk.

Every now and then someone takes it too far, like the Idaho factory worker who turned up for jury duty in her best first officer uniform, complete with phaser and demanding to be addressed as "commander".

Or the Wyoming antique store owner who invented a complete Klingon language and dictionary for his fellow alien allies to engage in everyday topical debates on everything from Spock's logic to the price of spuds down the local market.

"Jay-kuck Gardack Can-dag" (that means I'd kill for a Chinese take-away apparently).

There are certain rules however to be obeyed when keeping fact and fiction separated. By all means dress up as Spock, style yourself on Scotty or become Kirk for a weekend at a Las Vegas convention, but popping down the local offy in full Klingon costume looking for a six-pack of Budweiser is probably best avoided. You may be able to tell your USS Enterprise buddies to go "Kag-dak" themselves, but dressing as a television character at an off-licence will get your ass kicked faster than you can point out you've tried to kill James T. Kirk on at least 17 occasions.

Don't get me wrong, I'm a big fan of Gene Roddenberry's creation and always found it superior to Star Wars, but when you're a 45 year old Alaskan male being interviewed on TV dressed in wig and full make-up to honour a female astronaut killed in an episode of Generations, it's probably time to seek serious medical help (especially when you've wrote a song in her honour called - Free now my love).

I sit in wonder as Jay Rogers from Bakersfield, California became the first man to write and produce Hamlet - entirely in Klingon.

I kid you not.

You have to wonder exactly what William Shakespeare would have made of it

all. Do you think the Bard would have been impressed , repulsed or seriously bewildered to here a group of middle-aged American suburbanites take to the boards and replace "to be or not to be" with "jum-bok ack-tack hackanack!".
You got to love them really!

Star Trek may have spawned a legion of fans somewhere between slightly strange to boarding on daily medication and a psychiatric evaluation, but they follow a phenomenon that's enthralled the world for over 40 years now.

Sappy it may have been in it's heyday of cardboard scenery and planets full of aliens that happen to have the same fashion sense as their earthly counterparts, but at least it escaped the "all's well that ends well" endings of the Star Wars saga.

George Lucas - "Hey Steve, this Darth Vader bit isn't working out. I mean he's the epitome of evil but people just don't like the idea of a guy in a black suit and Oakland Raiders helmet going round slaughtering people."

 Spielberg - "Make him Luke's dad."

 Lucas - "Works for me!"

I sometimes too live in my own imaginary world. A world were Exeter seduce the football-loving public with silky skills and a never say die attitude that wins the Grecians worldwide acclaim.

From Tiverton to Toronto. Bridgewater to Barcelona, they'd come in their droves to watch and worship at the alter of Exeter. We'd rise from the confines of the Conference to the pinnacle of the Premiership, winning a new army of fans and causing the pundits to praise us with a multitude of superlatives every time we'd take the field of play.

Unfortunately this is the real world.

And the real world meant Crawley not Chelsea.

Burton not Barcelona. Morecambe not Madrid.

Exeter continued November with two more games of equal frustration.

Our FA Cup saga started and ended at the hands of League 2 outfit Stockport County.

Despite the potential for a cup shock and a step closer to round three, City looked strangely out of sorts. Although Tesfaye Bramble- cousin of Titus, but not half as calumitous, put County ahead early on, Exeter drew level in first half injury time through "Super" Lee Phillips.

However with 8 minutes left and a welcome reply beckoning, former Wolves striker Adam Proudlock notched to send Jim Gannon's men into the next round in front of a healthy 4,500 at the park.

Next up Kidderminster and a 1-1 draw which helped neither side. Harriers took the lead after only 90 seconds when Russell Penn (you know Sean Penn? - well he's nothing to him!) slotted home, but Billy Jones continued his impressive goals tally from the penalty spot by drawing the Grecians level on 28 minutes. It was as good as it got. Despite Harriers having a man sent off with 25 minutes left Exeter couldn't capitalize on the extra man and the game filtered out to a predictable draw.

Perhaps City were distracted by the announcement that SKY had planned to screen Exeter's upcoming away trip to Burton Albion.

Having a game on television was as helpful to City's cause as a ticket on the Titanic and with Paul Tisdale's men struggling to keep afloat in the Conference tide we needed the game on television like a hole in the head.

I tried to play down the TV link by suggesting because it was game number 13 on the big screen that we'd finally break our jinx - ironically on the unluckiest number available. Fate has a funny way of throwing up oddities like that.

Fate however didn't give a toss at the Pirelli Stadium on the night of November 27 when City turned in another predictable stage-fright performance in front of Sky, the nation and several thousand mortified Exeter fans by going down to a single Andy Corbett goal on 28 minutes.

City had their chances- most notably Lee Phillips spurning a great opportunity just after the hour mark, but in truth the game suggested nothing more than the fact Exeter City would be playing Nationwide Conference football in 2008. Before you could say "Jesus where's the year gone?", the festive season reared it's commercialized cranium again, sending millions of housewives to the shops, and several million more men taking out a second mortgage to last the holidays whilst looking worryingly over their shoulder at their bank manager lurking in the distance.

Exeter City seemed to be at a crossroads. Languishing in eighth, five points off the play-offs and facing a Christmas period that would probably shape their own, and Paul Tisdale's fate over the coming month, the Grecians came to the crossroads unsure of what direction to take.

One route suggested sticking with their controversial choice of manager and fund his requests to bulk his frail side up. The other implied should the Grecians drop further out of the play-off chase tough decisions would have to be addressed. A dwindling support, an unhappy campaign after the table topping high of 2006, and a Grecian jury still out on their final verdict on a manager completely unheard of before he'd taken the City hot seat.

What made matters worse was the fact both runaway leaders Oxford United and Dagenham were due at St James in the next two home games. Throw in a tricky derby with high-flying Weymouth and an accident waiting to happen away to St. Albans City it was safe to say Christmas would rekindle or kill off City's season.

It was around this time I'd toyed with the idea of throwing in an away day trip to see the Grecians at pastures new. Although I'd been to see Devon's finest in the humble surrounds of Accrington's Frazer Eagle Stadium to the grandiose settings of Old Trafford, I thought a trip to the tiny Clarence Park, home of St Albans, might be a romantic reminder of what non-league footy is all about (not to mention a stark reminder of the teams we're still playing against in this God-forsaken league).

Unfortunately I'd completely forgotten the small matter of my best mate's wedding the same day. Charlie Cummins may be slightly dim, wore a wig and was marrying a re-incarnation of the devil himself in Laura Long, but I couldn't let him down on the afternoon of the biggest mistake of his life.

Especially since I was the best man.

I couldn't attempt an excuse. Even if I faked my own death, absconded to Bolivia and married a horse name Sonita - Charlie would hunt me down and kill me like the unfaithful dog I was.

What made matters infinitely worse was the fact I couldn't see a TV, listen to a radio, or receive a text from anyone that afternoon as I'd be handing a ring to the most gullible man on the face of the earth and toasting his union to the money-grabbing, multiple-personality wife who had the bare faced cheek of claiming she was saving herself for her wedding night.

Not saying Laura's been around but there's bikes in China haven't been rode as much as Ms. Long.

We all have skeletons in our closet.

Laura's got a graveyard in hers.

Before all this matrimony took place there was the small matter of Exeter trying to get back their league status. The first of City's tough December assignments started at home to high-flying Dagenham & Redbridge.

John Still's men were locked in a table-topping battle with Jim Smith's Oxford and came to St James on the back of one defeat in nine games.

The first goal came as early as the fourth minute.

Predictably it went to the visitors.

Paul Benson, a little known forward who'd been plucked from total obscurity whilst playing at Essex Olympian League side White Ensign, put the Daggers ahead with goal no.14 in 19 league games when he latched onto a delightful back-heel to smash past a bewildered Paul Jones and give the visitors the lead. Even with a mere four minutes gone it was no more that Dagenham deserved. City had got off to a sluggish start and were made pay early on.

It did nothing to warm the Grecian faithful on a bitterly cold December evening in Devon. Jamie Mackie tried to raise spirits on ten minutes by testing Roberts in the Daggers goal and Paul Buckle threw in some trademark crunching tackles to shake up the visitors midfield. Shortly after Tim Cole returned the compliment-and then some- by attempting to separate the lower half of Jon Challinor's leg with a tackle worthy of a drunken Sunday league centre-half and incurred the wrath of the home crowd.

Then as it looked as if Tisdale would have to launch into a rousing half-time team talk, City's eleven gave themselves, their manager and the paltry 2,900 crowd a morale boosting shot in the arm when Adam Stansfield collected a Billy Jones pass, twisted and turned before rifling home via his trusty right peg and level the scores up at 1-1.

It got better on the hour. Despite having to replace the squash-buckling Danny Woodards with Lisburn-born Wayne Carlisle and dropping Andy Taylor into an unfamiliar right back role, the Grecians surged forward and on 60 minutes Jamie Mackie put City ahead for the first time. A sweet, dipping cross by Carlisle into the Dagenham box saw an incoming Mackie rise majestically and force a magnificent point blank save from Tony Roberts. Unfortunately for fat Tony the rebound landed back at Mackie's feet and the 21 year old Scottish midfielder hammered the ball back into the onion bag to the delight of the home crowd.

I'd barely been able to revel in the score-line and switch on the kettle when the Daggers equalised almost immediately.

Forcing City on the back foot, Dagenham won a corner. The resulting kick was delivered straight onto the head of Dave Rainford who rose completely unchallenged to bulge the back of the Grecian's net for the second time. Cocknobs!

Despite a 2-2 draw being an acceptable result against our high-flying visitors, City knew a win was needed if they were to get back among the business end of the league. Exeter took the game to Dagenham but it was end to end stuff. Stansfield dragged a shot across goal, Dagenham replied with a smart turn and shot from Craig Mackail-Smith. City countered again through Challinor's long range drive whilst Jones was again called into action to keep out the pesky Benson.

But there was still time for one last twist in the tale. Deep, deep into injury time, a Jones cross was cleared as far as Matthew Gill. Standing on the 18 yard box he drilled the ball back into the visitors far post were a combination of a bulldozing Challinor, a marauding Stansfield, and crucially the outstretched right leg of Dagger's defender Shane Blackett, resulted in the unfortunate (though clinical finish) of the defender's shot past a helpless Tony Roberts.

Seconds later Mr Sainsbury blew his whistle (and headed back to his supermarket.)

Exeter City 3-2 Dagenham & Redbridge.

Have some of that you southern softies!

It was a big win. A hugely significant three points for Tisdale's men. A long road lay ahead and it was still baby steps at St James but at very least City had proven they had what it takes to upset the applecart and inflict defeat on the big boys.

There was a break from league proceedings to dispose of Isthmian Premier League outfit Heybridge Swifts in the FA Trophy. The trophy had been a tournament Exeter had featured heavily in the latter stages since their drop into the Conference, and given the lower league opposition and the astonishing fact Exeter never seemed to get drawn away from home, it wasn't unreasonable to expect another interesting campaign from the Grecians in 2007.

Christmas arrived with much excitement in the Kennedy household. This was due to the fact Santa had been accidentally seen wrapping presents and swigging brandy late on Christmas Eve night. Leanne Lindsey Kennedy had awoken at midnight in a cold sweat having inadvertently forgetting to leave out some mince pies and milk for Rudolph and the rest of the reindeers.

Fortunately Santa was in full attire complete with flowing beard and was gladly able to cater for little Leanne's request for a kiss, cuddle and a premature present before she went back on a one way ticket to the land of nod leaving this daddy truly delighted he'd hired the suit and not scarred his daughter for all eternity. To this day I still blame my wife - I'm convinced she just wanted it to play out some sexual fantasy involving Santa.

Santa may have a big sack but he only comes once a year!

The following morning (6am!) 365 days of waiting paid off big-time for my daughter in the guise of a new bike, helmet and 16 different pieces of padding should daddy's little girl break her leg before she's even pedalled down the road.

It was all knew to Callum. The tree, the tinsel, the warbling of Nat King Cole and his awfully sarcastic - The Little Boy That Santa Claus Forgot. When you're nine months old you don't know about Santa, life, or the fact you've got the word EXETER in your name.

I was beginning to feel my age. When you're 17 you want to discover booze, girls and a permanent solution to acne.

When it's 27 you're at a crossroads wondering whether to plunge into the world of marriage, mortgage and 2.4 children or travel the world and conquer as many of the female species as humanly possible whilst avoiding a dose of the clap.

However when you're 37 you just want two things.

Peace and quiet.

The roads are a death trap, you're thinning on top and the latest music drives you insane. You hark back to yesteryear and the anthemic tunes of Queen, Kershaw and Spandau Ballet.

Christ even Shakin Stevens rocked me the odd Saturday night in '84.

After the endless unwrapping, the stuffed turkey and undying love over the phone from Auntie Ellie, you collapse on the sofa and relapse into the same coma you had exactly 365 days ago.

St Stephens Day meant one thing. Football. Exeter were making their first trip to the Wessex Stadium, home of Conference newcomers Weymouth FC. The Dorset based club, owned by millionaire hotelier chairman Martyn Harrison, had been promoted from the Conference South, thus giving Exeter their first bona fide derby match since we'd left Torquay United in League 2.

Despite being the newcomers to this, their highest level of football ever, the Terras had made an astonishing start to the league campaign and occupied the lofty position of third, five points off automatic promotion, but crucially almost a full eight points clear of the Grecians.

The novelty of a West Country derby brought the fans out to the Wessex Stadium. City could always be assured of a solid following but with Weymouth a mere 50 miles away the Grecians numbers swelled to over 1,000 before kick-off.

The Terras set a good tempo and the unpronounceable Chukkie Eribenne tested the nervy City defence more than once in the early exchanges. However it was to be a future Grecian connection that opened the scoring to the delight of the home support.

Richard Logan - fresh from a transfer from Peterborough United - sent a fine downward header past Paul Jones after a superb cross from Lee Elam. As I cursed the duo to high heaven from the obscurity of my house in Waterford, little was I or the assembled City faithful to know both players would be on the road down to St James Park within a mere three weeks.

Exeter responded well and within 2 minutes should have silenced the home crowd. Paul Buckle, City's tigerish midfielder, latched onto an Andy Taylor knock-down but his eight yard effort was superbly blocked by ex-Grecian Jason Matthews. Exeter continued to do an "Arsenal" (plenty of precision passing, flicks of flair and attempting to walk the ball into the net), but it took 7 minutes into the second half before the Grecians levelled.

It came from a dead ball scenario and once again the trusty left foot of Billy Jones delivered when it mattered most. His in-swinging free kick eluded everyone and nestled in the back of the Weymouth goal to send the sizeable away crowd into raptures.

Five minutes later the Grecian defender so nearly repeated the trick, though this time his free-kick smacked off the home sides far post. It was a full-blooded frenetic local derby played in front of almost 5,000 enthralled fans. City piled forward in search of three points but all they found was a strong stubborn home defence.

With time running out, City seemed to surrender territorial advantage to the home side. Challinor was replaced by a more defence-minded midfielder in Bertie Cozic as City looked to catch their hosts on the counter.

Alas there was one twist left in the tale of this West Country derby and it didn't favour the men in red & white.

With just 8 minutes left, a high swirling ball into the Exeter defence resulted in a frantic goal-mouth scramble in which Weymouth midfielder Ben Smith managed to poke home the ball from no more than 3 yards out and regain the lead for Weymouth.

Tisdale countered by replacing Patrick Ada and shoving on Danny Woodards in a makeshift forward role. There was still time for Adam Stansfield to have his shot well saved by Matthews and a Jamie Mackie effort which cleared the home sides crossbar. Conformation it wasn't to be City's day came in the last ten seconds when former Exeter 'keeper Matthews produced a fabulous triple save to deny Gill, Mackie and Stansfield.

If ever that old chestnut about ex- players coming back to haunt their former employers could be applied, then this St Stephens Day encounter would top the list. Even former Weymouth man Lee Phillips was injured, thus cancelling any chance he had of putting one over on his last employers.

The Grecians trudged off the field dejected and inconsolable. An eleven point gap now separated themselves and third-placed Weymouth. Exeter dropped back a place and even at the half-way point of this season play-off hopes were rapidly deteriorating. The last thing Exeter City needed now was a banana-skin away day at St Albans City.

The last thing I needed was a wedding.

Having agreed to turn up as Charlie's best man during a drunken work night barbeque which involved the consumption of 15 rum & black's, I was now seriously repenting at leisure, especially since it had cost me a non-refundable plane ticket to Luton Airport and a ten minute train journey to watch Exeter play at the homely confines of Clarence Park - home on the struggling Hertfordshire side.

The morning of December 30 opened with foreboding dark clouds and a howling wind over the South East of Ireland. It was the same in Exeter as the Grecian army made their way east up the motorway for Exeter's crunch away game at St Albans. Having lost their first real derby in four seasons to Weymouth (Forest Green was close but hardly a bona fide West Country derby), City just simply couldn't afford to return from the capital without three points.

By midday the heavens had opened on St Senans Cathedral - official church of the Cummins/Long wedding. By the time City were kicking off at Clarence Park poor Charlie would have his new wife's claws firmly embedded in his substantial wallet.

As I stood in the Lords house , ring in hand, painted smile of face, I wished for a Mrs Robinson moment to end this unholy union. For some last-gasp deluded sap to declare his undying love from the balcony before whisking away Charlie's would-be bride into the back of a bus to the strains of Simon & Garfunkel.

Unfortunately the VD clinic would have been the first port of call the morning after a night with Laura, thus making the chances of a last-minute declaration of undying love by any man in front of a packed church highly unlikely.

The irony of it all was that Laura was marrying the one man in town she'd actually not slept with yet. Six months of celibacy and a ten grand reception would finally end in a wedding night Charlie was unlikely to forget.

By the time we were cutting the cake and bedding in for a night of alcoholic bedlam, an injury-ravaged Exeter were kicking off in monstrous conditions over at St. Albans.

There's an unwritten rule for away day supporters that dictates- the more open the terrace, the worse the weather.

St Albans had 800 seats, a wooden stand , and a shit-load of terracing.

Queue the rain.

With the option of relative warmth and safety in the 84 year old West stand (quaint, loveable but a Bradford - Valley Parade in waiting) dashed by the fact of a terrible view of match proceedings, options were limited. The only other option lay in the east side Coca-Cola stand (25 years ago Coke put up two tiny advertising hoardings and the name stuck - talk about maximum advertisement for £50!), but with few remaining seats - not to mention being heckled for leaving the Grecian faithful to take refuge with your opponents - the merry man of Tisdale's army were left open to the elements in the tiny seven step Hatfield Road end.

The game kicked off in a monsoon and somehow progressively got worse. Rain not seen since Noah launched his ark poured down incessantly on little Clarence Park. Proceedings on the pitch did little to lighten the mood. Exeter were missing key players and the home side caused one or two palpitations among the City defence in the opening 45 minutes.

Back home, I'd managed to grab an eyeful of Soccer Saturday. Enough of an eyeful to tell me City were drawing at half-time and scoreless against the struggling part timers.

Just up the road Watford's game at Vicarage Road had been called off just before half-time. I knew the Premiership strugglers were not to far from St Albans and with several games in the capital already postponed down the leagues, I wondered was exactly were the playing conditions at Clarence Park? "Fuckin' unplayable!" - roared the fat man with the duffel coat by the toilets. Since the restart the surface water had almost doubled making tackling treacherous and playing conditions near impossible. Unbeknown to all and sundry Stephen Eames - St. Alban's kit-man, secretary and main groundsman (brilliant!-just what the love of football is all about) had asked the referee exactly what the situation was.

"I'll give it two minutes"- replied Mr McCann.

That was seconds after half-time. 15 minutes later both teams were still playing. And Exeter had broken the deadlock.

Jamie Mackie sludged his way into the home side's half but was tore down on the edge of the box. Wayne Carlisle spotted a gap in the wall vacated by a home side defender and ruthlessly exploited that fact by hammering home to give Exeter the lead.

Finally something for the pneumonia-bound Grecian army to cheer about. A crucial lead at a crucial time in a crucial game.

The sun came out for 37 seconds shortly after, but as if being punished for almost a full minute of sunshine, the heavens opened even harder within seconds and there was serious concern that the players, pitch and entire stadium could just sink into the Hertfordshire ground, disappearing from sight, taking 1300 souls with it.

The lead didn't last long. Shortly after the hour mark a completely unmarked Matt Hand was able to fire home unchallenged past a stranded Paul Jones to level the scores up.

Again everyone looked at the man in the middle. Again Stephen Eames -St Albans overworked, underpaid, jack of all trades asked is the match being abandoned.

"I'll give it two minutes." - came the reply.

The match had degenerated to farcical proportions. Players couldn't see a ball, let alone kick it, and several hundred travelling Devonians were standing, soaked, tired and extremely pissed off in the uncovered away end.

Credit to Mr McCann for wanting to give everyone their £12.50's worth but I don't think there'd have been a rush to the ticket offices and turnstiles to claim a refund had the man in the middle called a halt to proceedings that second.

Cut to wedding and the news St Albans had equalized went down like a lead balloon. A day of complete frustration was close to boiling over - the Best Man's speech was immanent, and I'd have to stand in front of 250 people and lie through my teeth about my dim-witted friend and his home-wrecking harlot of a wife.

Back to the monsoon, and desperate to capture all 3 points, Tisdale was forced into a last-gasp gamble. Challinor had been replaced by Dean Moxey and City's stalwart defender Jon Richardson had come on as an emergency striker for Bertrand "French Bertie" Cozic.

By 4.45, having played almost 88 minutes in truly, truly horrendous conditions, the chances of D.J. McCann signalling to his linesmen, grabbing the ball and abandoning the game at this stage looked highly unlikely and the depressing fact that Paul Tisdale's men had thrown away another two points was beginning to sink in. Maybe it should have been called off. Maybe it was unfair on a plucky home side who'd played their part. Maybe we just weren't damn good enough.

Maybe Dean Moxey had other ideas.

With the game entering injury-time (ironically everyone did escape without several broken limbs), a cross from the right was headed on by Jon Richardson. The danger looked over but somehow Moxey managed to turn the ball in from an impossible angle past a bemused Paul Bostock in the home sides goal and start an explosion of utter delight on the seven step Hatfield Road away terrace.

A lucky break. A last minute goal, with more than a hint of offside about it- but crucially three points. Exeter defended the remaining moments like their life depended on it whilst the home support renewed the call for an abandonment! The call's fell on deaf ears.

Back home I rejoiced in the name of Dean Moxey and the scoreline that flashed in front of my eyes.

St Albans City 1-2 Exeter City.

Annoyed that I'd missed the game, but thankful of having avoided pneumonia, I returned to the wedding party and prayed for alcohol to get me through the night.

Wet, weary and almost washed away, the Exeter City army retreated to the safety of their cars and the warmth of a heaven sent heater.

As the home side's faithful trudged away from Clarence Park bemoaning their luck and the lack of a competent referee, Stephen Eames looked forlornly at the remains of his pitch.

"It'll take me three weeks just to find the grass on it!".

The road back to Devon was full of many a story. Fans who rung their clothes out whilst strapping themselves to the nearest radiator, and stopping at every service station for the warmth of a toilet blow-drier.

None however came even remotely close to Mr Y.

Mr Y - as he shall forever be known - walked back to his car with two friends, decided not to sit on a dry seat in wet clothing, stripped completely naked in the car park, and drove three hours down the A30 bollock-naked with his two bemused friends in the back seat.

To be honest it made perfect sense. Why, after ninety minutes of the soaking of a lifetime, would you spend a further three hours in the same clothing only to find your hospitalized with a severe case of double pneumonia.

The journey back to Devon must have been a novelty for Mr Y. Praying to avoid a five mile tailback, crouching at every red light whilst the heater done a bang-up job warming his testicles. The mind boggles as to what would have happened if he'd got a puncture, crashed the car or run out of petrol.

Me thinks pulling into the nearest service station, asking them to fill it up on pump number two, and driving off in the nip might get you the attention of the poor 16 year old attendant asking you do you want leaded or unleaded.

However the trickiest part of the journey had yet to be negotiated. With his house in a well light suburban area and the police station a mere 400 yards away, Mr Y had to time his entry into his street to absolute perfection. Planning ahead, he phoned his wife to tell her his predicament and asked her to keep watch until every one of their neighbours were indoors and no police cars were in the immediate vicinity.

Can u imagine the phone call.

"Hi honey. Listen I've drove back completely naked with two men in my car for the last couple of hours, do me a favour, let me know when Mrs Smith at number 42 has gone indoors and the kids are off the street. Also keep an eye out for the cops and be a love and put the kettle on, my testicles are beginning to prune."

After an hour of driving around Exeter city centre and waiting for a phone-call from an extremely curious wife, Mr Y managed to pull up in his driveway, run out naked into the cold night air and retreat to the safety of his household with his two friends doubled-up with laughter and expecting the Spanish Inquisition from his other half.

The next day the fans could reflect on a long away day, a well earned three points and being to laugh about the 90 minute soaking they'd received in Hertfordshire. Exeter followed up those three points against relegation haunted St Albans with a magnificent win against high flying Oxford United in front of their biggest crowd of the season.

Having got past league-leaders Dagenham with a last minute own goal, the double was completed over the top two with the Grecians best performance of the season to date. Paul Tisdale's side were still missing key personal - Jamie Mackie was forced into a makeshift lone role striker in a 4-5-1 formation - but Jim Smith's men were also short a few bodies.

It was a rip-roaring performance by City. Oxford were smothered all over the park, particularly in midfield were Buckle and Cozic owned the middle for almost the entire game, snapping tenaciously at every ball and working themselves to a standstill. United applied very little pressure and it was no surprise when the opening goal came after just 14 minutes.

Some smart interchanges by Jones and Moxey resulted in the latter delivering a superb low cross across the face of the Oxford goal. It fell to Carlisle who side-stepped a challenge and drove the ball off the incoming Rufus Brevett and into the back of the visitors net.

A fantastic start by the Grecians in front of over 4,700 screaming fans.

Amazingly Oxford seem to have no immediate reply. The rest of the half was played out by an Exeter side hell bent on completely finishing off Jim Smith's men before they even got to the refuge of the away team dressing room for

15 minutes respite.

The onslaught continued after the break.

Oxford, despite being just one goal down, had the look of a side who'd won just once in seven games. Smith's men, who'd looked absolute certainties to bounce back to league football at the first attempt since the very first game, were now struggling to keep up with Dagenham and a gap was beginning to appear.

City, despite being wasteful and flagging in the last quarter, looked to have killed off the game 13 minutes from time.

Paul Jones launched a kick Johnny Wilkinson would have been proud off deep into the opponents half. With Oxford defenders dallying or falling over themselves in an attempt to clear, Jamie Mackie remained focused, trapped the ball, and slid his effort under the body of Billy Turley from no more than ten yards out to instantly double the home sides lead.

Then, finally at 2-0 down and 75 minutes played, Oxford remembered the rules of football implied you need to score to beat your opponent.

Exeter were predictably forced to weather a storm in the remaining quarter. On 89 minutes Andy Burgess gave Smith's men a glimmer of hope from the penalty spot after Challinor was adjudged to have handled, and an astonishing SEVEN MINUTES injury-time was then added. Somehow, despite the pressure, City never looked like conceding an equalizer. Had there been an equalizer after 7 minutes of injury time I think the chances of Cambridgeshire official Mr Lewis making it back to his dressing room in one piece were slim and none.

A cracking way to open the New Year.

The first day of 2007 had seen the two biggest sides in the Conference lock horns and City rightfully prevail.

Maybe it was a sign of things to come?

Maybe Exeter were just about to hit form and go on a ten match winning streak?

Maybe I was a bit high from the smell of two gallons of paint I'd been using to tart up the garden shed?

On thing was certain. The crucial Christmas period had produced 9 points from a possible 12, and included crucial victories against the top two.

Tisdale's men had a break a week later - our FA cup conquerors Stockport would travel to Walsall and get absolutely hammered - but returned to cup action with an FA Trophy home tie (what else!) against Kidderminster Harriers.

Despite a solid trophy record and being installed as third favourites when the competition began, Exeter couldn't break down the visiting Harriers in blustery conditions at St James. The writing seemed to be on the wall when Billy Jones missed from the penalty spot when normally so clinical.

Unless it's against the Harriers.

I'm convinced you could bring Billy on in the last minute of a World Cup Final for England to take a penalty in front of 100,000 fans and 2 billion armchair critics, and he'd bury the spot kick with devastating precision past Italy's Gianluigi Buffon.

But put him opposite his old club Kidderminster and a penalty against Scott Bevan, and the last thing Jonesy will hit is the back of the net.

Brazil, France and Germany no problem - Jones wins the World Cup.

A Conference club from the Wyre Forest region - forget about it. City go out!

Still, 2,000 souls went home without any lingering thoughts of suicide. A cup competition it may have been, but everybody knew where the bread and butter football would lie.

So the festive season didn't prove to be as disastrous for the Grecians as it may have looked back in late November.

Than again if you call getting double pneumonia at a small club in Hertfordshire a disaster then you've achieved your goal.

"CITY TILL WE'RE DRY"- they sang at the tiny terraced ground.

To all those road weary warrior's who travelled that day to St Albans I salute you.

But none more than Mr Y.

You my friend are truly insane.

Chapter Fifteen

CHOCOLATE SALTY BALLS and THE FIGHT FOR FIFTH

January became one of the mildest winter months in recent Irish history. The mere fact we hadn't 16 days of constant hail, sleet and snow and 25 minutes of sunshine was normally enough for an Irish weatherman to declare 'We're having a scorcher folks!' However, there was a suspicious lack of clouds in the sky and an alarming amount of sunshine in the air.

Many will put this down to the ozone layer.

I put it down to Uncle Terry (aka - Mr Ozone).

Terry's never been one for the preservation of Mother Nature and the world at large.

Aerosol cans, industrial waste, nitrous oxide.

You name it- he's burnt it.

With every known chemical being toasted in his weekly backyard bonfire, Terry is quite possibly single-handedly responsible for global warming, greenhouse gas and the hole in the earth's ozone layer.

He's avoided the clutches of environmentalists for over a decade and is on the Green Party's ten most wanted list.

The toxic gases wafting into the air from Uncle Terry's weekly bonfires, might damage the ozone layer beyond repair, but when the locals are popping along to the beach and sunbathing 19 days in January, you won't have too many people wanting to grass out Terry to the local fuzz and Green Party activists anytime soon.

Despite basking in a mini heat wave, I flew my way out of Costa Del Waterford and over the Irish sea to watch Devon's finest continue their battle to claim a play-off place and return to league football, fours years after they'd last left it.

Exeter welcomed Gravesend and Northfleet to the hallowed St James turf. Though the festive period had been kind to Paul Tisdale's men, City were still outside the play-offs and today entertaining the form team of the past month. Liam Daish's outfit came to the South West on the back of 5 straight wins and had pushed themselves one place ahead of City in the race for one of the four remaining play-off places. Dagenham & Redbridge had pulled away for Oxford so it now looked as if eight clubs would have to battle it out and take their chances for promotion in the lottery of the Nationwide Conference play-offs. The Grecians new signing, Lee Elam warmed the bench for the first time.

Elam had been a pivotal architect in the Weymouth side that defeated Exeter on Boxing Day, but thanks to the Terras chairman putting the entire squad up for sale that month in order to guarantee the long-term financial future of the club, Elam was poached by the Grecians and issued the number 22 jersey at St. James.

It was a bright and breezy January afternoon at the park (all they needed was a few weeks of Uncle Terry's toxic bonfire's, and we'd have been in our underwear splashing on sun cream in the stands), and hopes were high after recent form.

However, if one thing had plagued Exeter over the season, it had been the lack of a natural goal scorer.

Not since the departure of Sean Devine to New Zealand had City been able to produce a striker who could guarantee twenty goals in a season. Adam

Stansfield may have had a healthy strike rate at both Yeovil and Heresford, but the squad rotation up front, and Adam's tendency to miss a multitude of 1-on-1 efforts, meant the Tiverton-born striker hadn't reached double figures since his summer transfer to Devon's finest.

That was a problem Gravesend hadn't got. And boy, did they show it that afternoon.

25 year-old Londoner Charlie MacDonald had been a revelation since joining the Kent side, and it was the Gravesend striker who broke the deadlock after only 17 minutes. Martin Rice took a touch too much with a routine clearance and was closed down by Luke Moore. The rebound fell kindly for MacDonald and the 'Fleets danger man put the visitors ahead.

It was the start of a truly awful afternoon for City's man between the posts.

No more than ten minutes later, Ricey was picking the ball out of his net for the second time that afternoon after Moore chested down a cross and lashed a devastating volley past the hapless City goalkeeper for 2-0.

The natives were restless.

With the Grecians all out of sync, and Charlie MacDonald about as easy to control as an outback forest fire, Tisdale would have to drastically tune up the misfiring City engine before the chance of even grasping a draw went out of reach.

He never got the chance.

One moment of madness four minutes before half time saw to that.

An innocent Chris Todd back-pass ended up in Martin Rice taking his eye off the ball and completely miss-kicking, leaving MacDonald to win a race with Rob Edwards and gratefully slot home number three.

If ever the phrase 'beam me up Scotty!' could be attached to a single moment in the young shot-stoppers mothballing life, then this would be it.

But there was no heavenly beam of light. No engineer with a dodgy Scottish accent. No Starship Enterprise.

45 minutes had elapsed.

Exeter City 0-3 Gravesend and Northfleet.

There really wasn't much you could say.

Bury your head in the programme.

Clutch that half-time draw ticket in vain.

Munch a pasty and drink your Bovril.

The second half was a non-entity until six minutes from time when Jon Challinor latched onto a Lee Phillips ball to drive a daisy cutting 25-yarder past Cronin in the visitors goal to give instil brief home.

The handbags came out two minutes later when a scuffle broke out after Phillips was dragged back just outside the area, and this was followed by six uneventful minutes of injury-time, before the final whistle was blown to bring a sorry end to a sorry days proceedings.

I was beginning to attract several anxious glances from my Devon comrades. Another visit, another defeat. My proud record of attending City games with favourable results had quickly diminished with the turn of the millennium, and gone rapidly downhill since our relegation.

I'm a superstitious heterosexual and take these oddities extremely serious. Sure, at the end of the day, it's about eleven men in red & white, but if there's a 5' 10" lanky Irish Jonah in the vicinity of St James', it probably doesn't help proceedings.

I wasn't just a monkey on their back.

I was beginning to become Planet Of The Apes.

Thankfully I got the hell out of Dodge 24 hours later, as the Grecians renewed local bragging rights against visiting Weymouth FC.

With the monkey safely tucked away in the Emerald Isle, City set about repairing the damage Gravesend inflicted less than 72 hours earlier.

The charge of the Grecian brigade was made, by their newest recruit.

Playing against his former teammates, less than three weeks after helping them beat City; Lee Elam had an astonishing Exeter debut.

A 30-minute hat trick in his first outing for Devon's finest coupled with a late Challinor goal saw the Grecians romp to an impressive 4-0 tonking of Weymouth.

Despite the score line, the opening goal didn't arrive until first half injury time. Challinor, where the Bradford-born blonde stole in unnoticed to put City ahead at just the right moment, headed Wayne Carlisle's corner back across goal. 15 minutes after the restart he repeated the trick. Again Jon Challinor was providing the ammunition with a defence-splitting pass, which allowed Elam - with greyhound like speed - to run on and chip former City 'keeper Jason Matthews to double the lead.

The record-breaking hat trick arrived on 75 minutes. A training ground corner resulted in a goalmouth scramble where City's newest recruit came up trumps and so became the first player in Exeter's history to hit a hat trick on his full league debut.

Five minutes later, Lee Elam left the field to a standing ovation from his new club's fans. Proud of his effort. Delighted with his display. Warmed by his hat trick on a bitterly cold night.

A half-hour instant hero. Not bad Mr Elam. Not bad at all.

With nine minutes left, Challinor got the goal his work-rate richly deserved after Carlisle dodged some lumbering tackles to leave City's number 9 with a simple finish for 4-0.

Great team effort. Fantastic acoustics from the City faithful, and even the prawn sandwich brigade rounded off the night by actually nominating a player worthy of the 'Man Of The Match' award.

Yes, it was Lee Elam; though I was astonished 'French Bertie' didn't nick it for the ten minutes he was on the field. Trust me folks these guys could fuck up a cup of coffee!

I sat at home, drink in hand, delighted but completely paranoid.

Less than three days after turning in their worst home performance of the season with yours truly in attendance, City do a complete 180 and destroy their nearest rivals with the biggest win of the season.

Bastards!

Delighted, enraptured, overjoyed, but Bastards!

City under Tisdale was still an enigma. Hard to beat, yet not capable of stringing together a decent run.

Uncompromising yet underachieving.

Was this to be our fourth consecutive year in the Nationwide Conference without even tasting the play-offs?

Exeter were still lying eighth, six points off the play-offs and looking anything other than a team capable of stringing together some much-needed victories.

Probably the wrong time to be playing Dagenham and Redbridge 4 days later.

You can take that to the bank and mail it.

Our London counterparts - a massive 33/1 to lift the Conference title back in August-were now 7 points clear of chasing Oxford, and a full 16 points ahead of City as the Grecians travelled East to test the Daggers on their home turf - Victoria Ground.

The first half seemed promising. Plenty of endeavour from the visitors, the odd crunching tackle, and the usual abuse for the rotund figure of Tony Roberts. The Daggers goalkeeper has endured his fair share of, shall we say, 'good humoured banter' over the years from opposing fans, but beneath it all there was a grudging respect for the former Millwall and QPR shot-stopper.

Mr. Roberts would have the last laugh this afternoon. Having more then held their own in an evenly matched first half, Exeter fell behind within 50 seconds of the restart, courtesy of Dagenham's goal machine Paul Benson.

A long throw into the City 18 yard area, saw the Dagger's striker react quicker than Chris Todd and fired home the opening goal of his salvo past the outstretched arms of Martin Rice. Ten minutes later Mackail-Smith knocked an inviting ball into the lurking Benson and the young Englishman drove past Rice to double the lead.

Despite this, Exeter continued to battle bravely and take the game to the home side in front of a crowd of 1800 (makes you wonder what they'd have to do to get a cool 3,000 into the ground - win the Champions League maybe).

Wayne Carlisle made things interesting on the hour mark by halving the deficit with a neat finish after a strong confident run from Lee Phillips.

It proved a temporary respite.

Dagenham restored the 2 goal lead through Mackail-Smith and finished off a torturous afternoon in the capital when Benson completed his hat trick and rounded off the score at 4-1.

Excruciating but expected. Despite the margin of the defeat, City had simply come up against a Conference juggernaut that showed no signs of abating until it took it's rightful place in League 2 football.

With 18 games still left to play, and some extremely indifferent form under their belt, nobody was quaking in their boots at the prospect of locking horns with an out of sorts Exeter City.

Back home, Sandra broke her ankle, Leanne got the mumps, and Callum found a new use for the lawnmower - riding it!

Should have known my offspring would have some weird trait. Most kids can't wait for their first toy truck or digger to sit in.

My child wants to climb aboard a Flymo and ride around while I cut the front lawn.

Handy when it comes to Christmas however. I'll ask my wife for a present of a brand new lawnmower and keep the child happy as well.

February had to be fantastic if City were to entertain any thoughts of playing league football again in the new season. A month of magic was required by Tisdale's troops if the Grecian faithful were to get excited about anything other than summer brochures and the annual family barbeque.

City took themselves and their travelling entourage of diehard fans to Marston Road next - dilapidated home of Stafford Rangers.

Called 'The Marsh' - mainly because it's falling down into one, the ground has been home to Rangers for over 110 years. Despite a half-decent main stand and 500 gallons of paint through the years, Marston Road still looked and reeked classic non-league ground.

The crowd matched that. 970 times the turnstiles turned on a bright, crisp, sunny day over Staffordshire.

It was this sun that blinded almost every travelling City fan's view of the one and only goal of the game. Having dominated the opening exchanges, Exeter took the lead when Lee Phillips fired home, having initially driven his first effort accidentally off both Carlisle and Challinor.

Having beaten Exeter at St. James Park, Stafford didn't take things lying down - instead they got Jon Challinor to do it for them. Within a minute of taking the lead, the home sides hatchet man Lovett scythed down the Grecian midfielder, leaving him rolling around in agony and in need of attention (and possibly a new ankle).

Note to Mr Lovett; magicians saw people in half - not footballers.

A rousing away support carried Tisdale's men over the finish line and out of the ancient ruins of the Marston ground with three valuable points.

The Grecians registered another single goal win in their very next fixture. Woking came to town, but left empty-handed thanks to Jon Challinor. It was the dark-haired destroyer's goal on 53 minutes from all of 25 yards that clinched a nervy victory and launched renewed vigour into City's campaign.

If the two previous victories didn't exactly cause a play-off race earthquake, then the Grecians next victory would make its mark on the Richter scale.

Kidderminster Harriers with seven straight wins were, without doubt, the form side of the 24 teams in the Nationwide Conference.

'Hmmm', I thought, 'Seven straight wins. 20 goals scored. Just 4 conceded'.

'Think I'll take a dull, boring 0-0 draw,' thought thousands of likeminded City fans.

'Balls to that,' thought Chris Todd, as the Welshman led his team of Grecian Gladiators into the Coliseum of Kidderminster.

Ninety minutes later they returned home having slain the home side lions and three points to boot.

Exeter controlled most of the game, and home goalkeeper Scott Bevan was by far the busiest man on the field, early on denying Matt Gill and the recently re-signed Steve Tully. The Paignton born defender had returned to Exeter after two seasons as part of the Weymouth trio (Elam and Richard Logan) who City scooped in January.

The deadlock was broken just before the hour when Paul Buckle, making a rare start, set up Challinor to fire home and delight the travelling support.

Exeter made sure of the points with two minutes remaining via Lee Elam who steered home a Jamie Mackie cross to notch his 4th goal in his first five games for the Grecians.

An inspired performance by City, with two quality second half goals and even a Rocky Balboa style fisticuffs between Harriers manager Mark Yates, Lee Elam and several players on both sides, capped off a barnstorming day-out in Worcestershire.

Feeling tired after another evening of praying in front of the television set, I retired to bed early that night, foregoing the chance to party with some scantily clad beauties at my next-door neighbour's house-warming party.

With Sandra away on a family wedding weekend and the kids staying at my mothers, it seemed the ideal opportunity to strut my stuff with some nubile young females, but being a man in a monogamous relationship I shunned this opportunity for an evening in the sack.

Real translation; I was tired, broke, and not appealing to women half my age.

Sure, I could get drunk and ponce about, but when you still listen to vinyl and count 'Saturday Night Fever' among your favourite albums, there's a distinct chance I'd be as out of place at my neighbour's party as a black man at a Klux Klux Clan A.G.M.

Not that I got a good nights sleep.

At 4.23am I was awoken by the sound of Isaac Hayes. The dulcet tones of the Motown singer were instantly recognisable, but the song certainly wasn't.

Though groggy and half asleep I could clearly make out the words of the song pulsating from another yet unconfirmed room.

'Suck on my chocolate salty balls,'

Put 'em in your mouth and suck 'em.'

What the fuck?

Raising my head from the pillow and vigorously shaking myself, I squint my eyes, tune my ears, and listen to the lunatic lyrics of this noise, which I've now recognised as coming from beneath me.

'Say, everybody have you seen my balls

They're big and salty and brown

If you ever need a quick pick-me-up

Just stick my balls in your mouth.'

The penny dropped.

The combination of Leanne's 'South Park' album, the stereo timer and Callum's meddling fingers, turning the volume button to window-shattering full pelt, resulted in Isaac Hayes waking the entire neighbourhood up at 4 in the morning.

Before I'd had a chance to get dressed and start a libel claim against Sony Hi-Fi, Isaac Hayes and the entire Motown record label, a knock comes rapping on the door.

Yes, it's my friendly neighbourhood policeman, armed with a baton, frown and Mr Alder, the 78 year old war criminal from No.18 that everybody's afraid to shop.

We exchange pleasantries.

They agree not to charge me with noise pollution, waking up half the street, and subjecting them to novelty songs from Isaac Hayes in the middle of the night. In return I plead my innocence, ask them to arrest my 13 month old son, and tell them Mr Alder is actually Gustav Von Frick - propaganda minister for the Nazi party from 1942-45.

The next morning I replaced my 18-year-old stereo and retired my turntable for good. It marked the end of an era in the Kennedy household. I thought vinyl would always be here to stay. I'd fought compact discs invention with all my might in the 80's and was mortified when Mp3 players and computer downloads made vinyl ever more obsolete. But unfortunately, I was forced to drag myself into the 21st century.

Nothing stays the same does it?

Nowadays people's eardrums are permanently clogged with hi-tech headphones and you don't even have to go to the trusty record shop to pick up the latest album from Fleetwood Mac.

Now its plug in, download, and spend 23 hours of the day walking around in a zombie-like trance with the latest 'Chemical Brothers' CD on your I-pod. Who knew the art of conversation would become obsolete in the 21st century?

Exeter returned to St James, back to the die-hard faithful and back to an old foe.

Graham Westley - former Stevenage manager and self-styled scourge of the Grecians, returned to Devon in charge of his new club – Rushden and Diamonds. Graham was always an outspoken chap, which didn't win him many friends among managers and chairmen alike and seemed as popular in Devon as a Big Mac at a supermodels party.

Always good for a sound-bite, Westley announced he had a delightful hoodoo over City and was more than willing to prove it again in his latest trip to St. James Park. As per usual, he proved true to his word.

Despite having won his first five games in charge of the club, Westley's spoiling tactics were plain to see right from the first whistle. On a pudding of a pitch, Rushden delayed, dallied, and broke up any rhythm of play the home side struggled to put together, to effectively strangle the life out of the game. For their part, City weren't really much better. Reduced to knocking long balls and praying a set piece might come off, Exeter did manage a last minute goal, which was somewhat harshly ruled out on Richard Logan.

At the final whistle, a frustrated City following filed out of the park, momentarily distracted by a gleaming beam of light that was Graham Westley's smile as they trudged out the gate and home to a warm fire.

God was a Grecian that night however, as results (for the fourth week running) had gone Exeter's way. From looking down and out a month ago, Paul Tisdale's men were now in fifth place and hanging on, by goal difference, to that last play-off space ahead of Sammy McElroy's, Morecambe FC.

By now the games, much like the snow at home, were coming thick and fast.

Although it was almost March in the Emerald Isle, we had been giving an unexpected 4 days of sunshine in mid-February, so therefore had to pay for being dry for a couple of hours by spending the next ten days snowed into our houses.

Whilst Uncle Terry's single-handed destruction of the ozone layer, meant 40 degree heat in Bognor Regis, the length and breadth of Ireland was under a blanket of thick white snow.

Not that it meant anything to yours truly, only hassle. Fine if you're a 6-year-old child with an allergic reaction to a classroom, but when you're 37 years old the chances of the boss calling you and saying, 'stay at home buddy, and toast your nuts,' are about one zillion to one.

Not that it didn't deter me from ringing work, announcing I'd done my back in carrying out the trash on ice, and thawing my testicles for the next few days. Let's get things in perspective folks, you only have to do one thing in this life, and that's die. Work is an evil mistress you're hopelessly drawn to, whilst bills and taxes are ultimately cancelled out by good old life insurance the minute you're six feet under. Spend what you like - re-mortgage - repent when dead!

That's my theory. Not very scientific and likely to give your wife and bank manager a mild stroke, but if I should unexpectedly get run over by a combine harvester whilst out picking blackberries, I'll be able to say 'I've had a fun time on this planet.'

A bad day finishing still beats a good days work. SOMETHING PROFOUND WORK.

Exeter finished off a very productive February with an impressive 3-0 victory over fellow promotion chasers Burton Albion. The result was still in the balance until the last twenty minutes, but a Billy Jones penalty, a second by Richard Logan and an insurance goal by Adam Stansfield, made sure Nigel Clough's men returned home north with nothing but 150 miles of lament.

Finally, City were in a battle royal for a play-off place. At the very least Exeter would have something to play for, going into the last few weeks of the 2006/07 season. It may have been a nondescript first few months under Paul Tisdale's reign but the Grecian faithful seemed content with it compared to last season's topsy-turvy eight months under Alex Inglethorpe. Exeter may not have topped the table under Tisdale, but this time last season, City's title ambitions were disintegrating with a record amount of straight defeats in this division, under a manager who would soon leave Devon for the bright lights of London.

February should have brought the manager of the month award for Paul Tisdale, however it went instead to City's arch nemesis Graham Westley, who'd taken a relegation threatened Rushden side, to mid-table safety with an impressive five wins in an eight game unbeaten run.

Graham posed for the cameras, collected his award and was promptly given the sack!

Delighted with his sides progress, but unhappy with the style of play imposed by it's manager, Diamonds chairman, Keith Cousins announced a parting of the ways with Westley. At Christmas, his side was slipping to further non-league anonymity, now Rushden would at least compete in the conference for another season thanks to Westley. His reward, - a shrug of the shoulders, pat on the back and his P45.

Former Dagenham and Weymouth boss Garry Hill, whose first game in charge would be hosting Devon's finest in the first week of March, next grasped the thorn of nettles at Nene Park.

Now the unwritten law of football dictates that whenever a new manager takes over the helm at any given club, there will inevitably be a brief upturn of fortunes. City took to the field that afternoon needing to nip Rushden's flower firmly in the bud before it was allowed to bloom.

Exeter, in a word, was steamrolled.

Two goals in the first twenty minutes and one more just after the break to shatter any deluded thoughts of an unlikely comeback told the story of a miserable ninety minutes for the Grecians. No disgrace, just beaten by a resurgent Rushden side whose change in manager didn't mean a change in form.

Greys Athletic popped along to St James' the following Tuesday, frustrated the living shit out of the home side, and looked to have got away with an unlikely point until one of sports most glorious pleasures popped up - the injury time goal.

With four minutes of added time almost up, and the visitors stifling wave after wave of Exeter attacks, City's swash-buckling (not to mention top goal scoring) left-back Billy Jones, latched onto a botched clearance and drove home an unstoppable thunderbolt past ex-City stopper Ashley Bayes, to burn a hole in the visitors net and send 2,894 fans into a state of euphoria with virtually the last kick of the game. No sooner had the visitors taken despairing hands off heads and hips to restart the game, the referee blew for full-time.

Christ, life can be sweet sometimes.

And boy, did we owe Greys that misfortune. For the away day mauling in the Trophy. For the embarrassing surrender in front of television cameras a season later. For the semi-final heartache and the missed penalty that stopped us reaching the final of the FA Trophy for the first time in our short non-league history.

From last minute levellers to former players hindering our heroism.

On behalf of every City fan, and the left foot of Mr. Billy Jones, take that, you London scoundrels!

There was a spring in my step and a smile on my face as I arrived that Saturday for Kilbarry Rangers away tie against Blue Star Buccaneers in the first leg of the highly prestigious Howley's Homemakers League Cup. My beloved Junior League Club had forced its way into the quarterfinals of the cup by virtue of a 1-0 penalty shoot-out win over St. Josephs. Both legs had finished scoreless, and even a further 30 minutes couldn't separate the sides (the stats told the story of the tie - 240 minutes of football - 3 shots on target, and two of them came from the ref messing about with the ball during half-time). This was followed by ten penalties, six of which were sent into orbit, two which hit the bar, and one which completely took out Mincy Roberts, who'd been standing behind the goal whilst his dog, Skip, went for a piddle.

Fortunately Curly Power did manage to close his eyes, and toe-drive us into the next round where we'd meet the Buccaneers - a full two divisions higher than us.

Nobody was interested in Exeter's last gasp winner against Grey's. Not one person gave a toss that the Grecians were currently fourth and staring at a play-off scenario that could result in a final at Wembley.

Everything was Premiership, FA Cup and the impending Champions League Quarter-Finals.

Boring prattle really.

Kilbarry were inspired that evening, and for the first time in the club's 37-year history managed to score four goals. Unfortunately Blue Star scored six (completely against the run of play! - with a ref that was paid off with 50 Euro and the promise of a blow from Susie Suck before the game.)

Ironically, Kilbarry still won through to the semi-finals when Blue Star failed to show up for the return leg after turning up at the wrong ground. This clever ploy was down to the clubs secretary, Josie Malone, who'd given directions to our fierce rivals and local enemies Kilbarry Wanderers ground. By the time Blue Star realised they'd been duped and finally arrived at our pitch an hour later, the referee had awarded a walkover to Rangers.

A walkover in Waterford Junior League Handbook is always deemed as 3-0.

Final Score (over one leg and a no-show from our opponents)

Kilbarry Rangers 7-6 Blue Star Buccaneers. Sweet revenge.

It may have been downright dirty of our club secretary, but at least we hadn't conned an official with some cash bribe and the promise of a wank at the back of the bookies by the town tramp.

By the time Rangers lost their resulting semi-final 14-1 (ironically to our local enemies Kilbarry Wanderers), Exeter had gone through a topsy-turvy March which saw the club rise and fall out of the precious play-off places and give their stressed-out soldiering army several more grey hairs.

Defeat to Halifax was followed by a nerve-wrecking 1-0 win at home to Morecambe, courtesy of a stunning Richard Logan goal 15 minutes from time. However 90 minutes of solid endeavour against McElroy's men was completely wasted with a thoroughly awful display away to lowly Northwick Victoria.

Despite the Grecians continually chasing honours at the right end of the table each Conference year, there's one thing in a City season that seems as inevitable as Jade Goody's mug on a glossy rag, and that's a thoroughly awful ninety minutes against a soon-to-be-relegated Conference side.

Step forward Northwick Victoria.

A cold night in Cheshire. Dodgy pitch. Paltry crowd.

Among them, a trusty band of travelling supporters, brim full of hope. Optimistic to the end.

On their first visit to Northwicks new Victoria Ground, City turned in a nervy lack lustre performance. Both sides cancelled each other out in a tedious first half. A crowd of 754, 150 of which belonged to the Grecians, bedded in for what seemed destined to be a scoreless draw before a harsh handball decision against Chris Todd gave the home side a fortuitous penalty. Paul Jones guessed the right way but Carr's shot was paced just out of reach of the 'keepers reach. Exeter rallied late on through Stansfield and Gill, yet six minutes of injury time and a point-blank header missed by Logan, couldn't even rescue City a point.

There was an air of depressing inevitability about it all. I wanted to get annoyed, kick the cat and curse the day I'd set foot in Hulls Boothferry Park and laid eyes on a woeful side from Devon getting slowly executed 6-1 by the home side, but I couldn't move my fat arse to register a protest that involved standing up and shaking my fist like a deranged lunatic at the moon.

Not that I should be complaining. As I argued with the wall, and downed some whiskey to calm my nerves, a small band of war-weary supporters were driving their convoy out of Burton-On-Trent, destined for Devon in the wee small hours. By the time I'd accepted defeat and was tucked up in bed, 150 members of Paul Tisdale's Grecian army would still be stuck in the middle of nowhere-miles from home.

Passionate or plain psychotic, it didn't matter. Without these supporters, football clubs would not exist. From being caged like animals behind barbed wire in the pre-Taylor report 1980's, to ten hour round-trip coach drives to Carlisle in the 21st century. Supporters like this should be given a permanent directors box at their club. Football is about fans, not the prawn-sandwich eating, two-matches-a-year, corporate clients with as much passion as a stone, and whose interest in the box and buffet outweighs anything on the field of play.

City's rollercoaster ride continued with three more games of varying results. York City proved a tough nut to crack when the Munster men visited Devon. Despite playing most of the game with ten men and going behind to a Billy Jones penalty, the visitors grabbed a share of the spoils when ex-Grecian, Craig Farrell fired home from a second-half free kick. Another evening of missed chances. Another evening of frustration.

Things got worse before they got better. Facing the first of three consecutive away games, 600 fans travelled to Forest Green in an effort to cajole Exeter into three much needed points. However ten minutes into the game and one goal behind the mood changed among the normally supportive City faithful.

Every missed chance, every misplaced pass, was met with howls of derision as City struggled to get to grips with their hosts playing in their new home ground. Just on the stroke of half-time Lee Elam, calmed the crowd by scoring and the stage was set for a barnstorming second half.

However, City's finishing was akin to a regular Kilbarry Rangers afternoon - beyond comprehension - and a series of chances went a begging. Matthew Gill,

Lee Elam and Patrick Ada all missed decent chances; whilst Adam Stansfield was incredibly denied a magnificent double save from Green goalkeeper Robinson.

A night of high drama in the Stroud Valley concluded with a sucker-punch winner from the hosts. With injury time beckoning, Forest Green won a corner. The ball was swung in. Queue and almighty goalmouth scramble, in which Paul Jones made two excellent point blank saves, but John Hardiker managed to agonisingly squeeze home the winner and break the hearts of hundreds of travelling Grecians.

Four hopeful minutes followed, but alas, no equaliser.

The result hurt Paul Tisdale and for the first time, Exeter's manager was publicly critical of his players.

Speaking to the press, Paul gave a professional interview with hidden meaning.

'We cannot defend like that from set pieces. It's simply not good enough.'

Translation: Get the fucking ball cleared or you'll be playing for Margate reserves in a week's time.

'We're playing catch up and need to stand up and be counted away at Altrincham.'

Translation; Don't even think of pulling the same shit at Alty, or you bastards will be out of here like spit through a trumpet.

'Whatever happens, we will keep fighting right to the end of the season.'

Translation; Remember, half of you are out of a contract, so if you don't want to go back plumbing or climbing a ladder, I suggest you get the fucking lead out.

Mr Tisdale's polite interview had the desired effect.

Four days later, Exeter claimed only their second away win of 2007 when coming from 1-0 down to beat in-form Altrincham. Despite an early setback after falling behind to yet another set piece after only 18 minutes, City showed tremendous tenacity to produce a second half fight back with goals from Richard Logan and a crucial late Billy Jones penalty to secure a crucial 2-1 win.

Afterwards Paul Tisdale was full of praise for his team.

'We had to dig deep, but the boys showed some great character.'

We all knew what he meant.

'About fucking time!'

Chapter Sixteen

WEM-BER-LEE!, WEM-BER-LEE!

April brought angst. A month of birthdays, bereavements and temporary unemployment. 30 days, which would see me forget my mum's birthday, spend two days on a toilet, and indulge in twelve straight hours of mind-numbing slasher flicks.

Of course April would also be the four weeks, which would determine the fate of Exeter City's season.

Week one didn't start too well. Rumours were abounding in work that a strike may be imminent because of the company's failure to announce a bonus - for the 19th year running! It's not that we're a money hungry workforce, but when your last bonus is paid out the same year Wimbledon win the cup, a pint is £2 and the mullet is king, you tend to get slightly annoyed.

Life had passed us by in work. The last time a hefty bonus had been doled out to the work force of Porters Plastics, money was actually worth something. Wow -the things you could do with £300 in 1988.

Buy a microwave. Get the latest top loading video recorder. Nip down to the clothes shop and buy that snazzy lemon pin-striped suit, complete with six-inch shoulder pads.

Two hours in the hairdressers getting a mullet & ponytail combo and a can of hairspray that would hold the Great Wall of China together, and you were ready to wow the women. Throw in a pair of black slip-ons and a leather tie and the opposite sex would practically be throwing themselves at you.

You thought you were Don Johnson at the disco that night. Bopping away to Duran Duran and Curiosity Killed The Cat without a care in the world.

Who needed Miami Vice? We had the Horse & Tavern Saturday night over-18's disco. Eat your heart out Crocket and Tubbs.

Whilst we stood on the abyss of unemployment, Exeter where on the edge of the play-offs, in grave danger of ending their season on yet another bum note. Despite a crucial win away to Altrincham and a timely return to form, City was beaten in a five-goal thriller away at Aldershot in that first week of April.

The trip north to the recreation ground had started brightly with a Lee Elam goal after just 8 minutes, but the game turned, on the sending off of goalkeeper Paul Jones soon after. A slip by Rob Edwards allowed Aldershot in, Jones came rushing out of his area but was beaten to the ball before the Shot's striker who then skewed his shot wide.

Queue classic conference refereeing. Mr Lewis, having spotted an infringement, blew for a free kick, waltzed up to Jones and astounded every one of the 2250 people in the ground by pulling out a red card for apparent dangerous play.

City never recovered. Despite having been excellent to that point and appearing to have exorcised their away day demons of late, Exeter surrendered the lead soon after and by the hour mark were 3-1 behind with the Shot's striker Dixon being chief tormentor. Danny Seaborne made a rare Exeter appearance and it was the 19 year old defender who brought City back into the game soon after, and so set up a nail-biting finale which included some great saves, missed chances and the quickest sending off in football history.

With 12 minutes left, Ryan Scott entered the fray for the home side. And about eight seconds later he decided he'd had enough. As City won the ball,

Scott launched himself into Jon Challinors midriff with a horrendous studs-up challenge.

Red card. Early bath. Not even a mud-stained shirt. Quite possibly the quickest (not to mention dirtiest) sending off in the history of football.

For all effort, for all the stretching of every sinew of muscle, Exeter came out on the wrong end of a 3-2 score line. However, results (yet again) went our way. If God wasn't a Grecian he had a funny way of showing it!

With the threat of closure hanging over our factory, and my latest credit card bill through the letterbox making a giant crater on my porch floor, there seemed only one obvious solution.

Go on holiday to Exeter.

With just five games left and the stakes enormous for the Grecians, I felt the need to visit St James Park for possibly the last time this season.

I'd grown tired of sitting at home, waiting on a screen to change or a phone call from the park, unaware of events unfolding in front of my eyes. The timing could be better and the cost would see me rocketing to the poorhouse (yet again) but the tension was killing me. If City was going to make a balls of things, then I'd rather see it with my very own eyes. Despite the employment enigma, things were great at home. Sandra had booked a holiday, Leanne had got over her short attention span problem (wonder where she got that from), and we got a new lawnmower, which cheered Callum up no end.

The old Flymo had been a wedding present and ten years of chomping through the forest that is our backyard had taken its toll.

Besides, Callum wasn't happy with the seating arrangements on the Flymo for weeks now and needed a new lawnmower to ride around the block on.

We duly obliged with a Lawn-Boy Platinum 500, which our deranged lawnmower-loving son loves to death. He spends more time on it than with us.

The second Saturday in April I flew into Exeter for the Grecians crunch home game against Tamworth. It was a crucial bank holiday weekend for City, as less than 48 hours after playing relegation strugglers Tamworth, Exeter would travel east to greater London and take on Crawley Town. With the Grecians 1 point outside the play-offs, 6 points would do very nicely thank you.

I was fully aware that my recent record of watching Devon's finest wasn't exactly awe-inspiring, but if the Grecians were to make it out of this God-forsaken league, they'd have to win against teams like Tamworth.

Friday night was dinner, movie and the obligatory visit to Mega Kebab - my favourite late night Exeter eatery. Despite having wolfed down a beef satay only three hours earlier, I purchased a chicken kebab and proceeded to orally rape it in the privacy of my hotel bedroom.

Per usual the next morning my bed looked like a crime scene. To the untrained eye the tons of taco sauce and ketchup could easily fool the average person. Christ, if you were a crime scene investigator with a hangover you could easily mistake my kebab-chomping exploits for the work of a serial killer who just murdered someone in room 57 of the Three Trees Hotel.

By the time I'd exchanged pleasantries with my friends and taken my seat in the stand, a nervous apprehension had engulfed me.

The Grecians made a habit of struggling against such teams as Tamworth and with the added pressure of yours truly in the crowd, this could be an uncomfortable, edgy ninety minutes.

By half-time, nothing had changed.

You could feel the tension among the 3,500 all around St James Park. Moans from the big bank. The noise of a thousand nails being chewed from the Doble. Over in the old Grandstand, they fidgeted uncomfortably.

Was Exeter going to disappoint yet again against lesser opposition?

The answer came in the 75th minute. And I scored it!

Okay, well Wayne Carlisle was actually the man who put the ball in the net, but the man above and myself know I could claim an assist.

You see, there's a simple fundamental way to break the deadlock in a scoreless draw; go to the toilet. And if there was a world championship for watching 90 minutes of football, yet somehow missing the six goals in the game, I, my friends, would be champion of the world, 27 years in a row.

It started when I was ten. Whilst watching the 1979 FA Cup Final. I'd seen Arsenal race into a two goal lead against Manchester United. With five minutes to go I decided to dispense some urine before getting ready to celebrate a comprehensive victory for the Gunners. Before I even had time to get to the top of the stairs, the Red Devils had pulled a goal back.

Not particularly worried about Gordon McQueen's goal, I carried on regardless and took my time in the toilet. By the time I'd reached the bottom of the stairs, Sammy McElroy had made it 2-2.

Cocknobs!

Insane with fury, and overcome with a need to swim the Irish sea, run to Wembley and crack an iron bar over McElroy's head, I ran out the back, sulking that what looked a catwalk five minutes ago was now a game that would give me nightmares for the rest of my adolescent life.

Thank God for Alan Sunderland.

No sooner had I ran out into the garden, cursing United, and swearing a lifetime of vengeance against the Lord Almighty, the man with the world's biggest afro had stole in at the back post and drove home past Gary Bailey to give Arsenal an amazing 3-2 win in possibly the best five minutes of a Wembley Cup Final.

So it came as no surprise to myself and the man above, that the very moment I was standing over a urinal in the Doble Stand, Wayne Carlisle was bundling Exeter City into the lead.

A sigh of relief was breathed in unison around St James's Park.

Despite a nervy last 15 minutes, City hung on to their slender lead. Tamworth had the look of a team already condemned to life in a lower league. It finished 1-0.

We stood, applauded and retired to the bar to start the post mortem on the ninety minutes we'd just seen and where City's season was going from here.

Back into the play-offs for one. The three points coupled with Burton Albion's defeat at home to York City meant Exeter were back in the coveted fifth spot. That night we eat, drank and were generally very merry as we celebrated long into the night. Unfortunately this meant a trip to The Timepiece nightclub, and a walk straight into a rave.

Now there are plenty of fun ways of spending a Saturday night. Dinner. Movie. Night with your lingerie clad mistress when the wife's away (so I'm told!), but standing in the middle of over 2,000 students whilst MC Trance & DJ Wank, blast out 5000 watts of noise and distort my hearing for the next ten years is not one of them.

Worse still my so-called friends did a Linford Christie and made it out the door

166

faster than Ben Johnson on steroids.

Before I had time to say, 'get away from me you bunch of tax-dodging parasites,' Stuart, Bob, Ian, 'Kiss-the seat Pete' and his sultry wife Sandy Ample Charms - called that for two obvious reasons - were on the way home with a chicken kebab and the promise of a warm bed. Even Crazy Greg, the last bastion of southern comfort induced fun, the person who lived to party - who was down in Devon for the night -announced he was turning in to study for a test he had on Monday.

Determined not to give up the ghost I was forced to befriend Dave the Rave - a pill popping walking homage to techno music who spent the entire night enlightening me on virtues of Pete Tong whilst proceeding to lose 4 stone on the dance floor.

Don't get me wrong, I didn't want to spend my Saturday night listening to guest artists called DJ Uzi and Chuka Spanner, but it happened to be the only club in town open, and a bar that didn't close until 2am.

The next morning I phoned every one of my English mates at the crack of dawn then headed home; safe in the knowledge I'd actually seen the Grecians win for a change.

48 hours later, and an inspired Exeter City won again! Despite what should have amounted to a dodgy day at Crawley, the Grecians blew away the Red Devils on their own patch, with possibly their finest away display of the season to date.

What should have been a nerve-jangling ninety minutes, turned out to be a stroll in the West Sussex sunshine as goals from Lee Elam (3), and two from an on fire Wayne Carlisle, gave Exeter a comfortable 3-0 win against Scott Hiley and his new Crawley team-mates.

All of a sudden, Exeter were the team with momentum. That bank holiday Monday win, was followed by another inspiring performance against Cambridge United were Logan & Stansfield had the points wrapped up before the hour. Ironically, the opposing manager that day was one Jimmy Quinn - the odds-on favourite for the City job last summer. Whilst all and sundry were ready to embrace the former Reading manager as the club's new saviour, Paul Tisdale nipped in to take the hot seat at St James whilst Quinn sat around until Cambridge came calling.

What had seemed a strange managerial choice was now turning out to be an inspired appointment. Despite Quinn's experience as player and manager, it was well know he wasn't the most loved of people at the clubs he had frequented.

We went up in spite of him, not because of him - one Shrewsbury fan once told me on the Shrews return to league football.

Tisdale was now proving an astute hand at management.

Calm yet confident, whilst not afraid to make changes with any personnel at any time in a game in order to get a result.

His personnel were needed to produce a big ninety minutes in their next game - away to Stevenage in the penultimate game of the season.

With the mathematicians calculating every scenario possible for City over the next two games, the Grecian faithful could easily have taken, and passed, a university degree in maths. However one equation kept things simple.

Exeter needed 4 points from their final two games to be sure of a play-off place.

A win and draw would see City contest their first ever play-offs in any sphere of English football since the club was founded in 1904.

The general consensus was, that with a final day home encounter against almost relegated Southport, and Exeter would need a point at Stevenage before confirming their play-off place with three points against the struggling Merseysiders.

That week I got so stressed and nervous I got something I'd never experienced in my 37 years.

Hemorrhoids!.

Well singular actually.

Having a pile is a thoroughly uncomfortable experience. Especially when you find out what treatment is needed for it. Call me naive but I thought a dab of cream and a comfy pillow would do the trick, it was only then I really found out what the word suppository means.

The pretty blonde at the chemist explained it in thoroughly embarrassing detail.

I was less courteous.

'You mean I stick it up my ass?'

Saturday rolled around and with it, Exeter's penultimate game of the season - the crunch away tie at Stevenage.

This would make for an uncomfortable afternoon for several reasons.

1 - City were up against a side that could still make the play-offs.

2 - Exeter had never won away at Stevenage.

3 - The dog had eaten my suppositories.

With all the pressure on the Grecians, history standing against us, not to mention the partisan atmosphere of the Broad hall Stadium, it would be a testing afternoon for Exeter, their fans, oh, and my arse.

Radio was my friend for the next ninety minutes, though this only cruelly heightened my sense of imagination. When there are not 22 men and a round leather object to follow around the pitch in front of your eyes, you mind works overtime trying to piece together the action on the other side of the water.

Despite the bias commentary and the home sides heckling whenever City attacked, the score line stayed 0-0 at half time.

15 minutes relaxation before the battle recommenced.

Shortly after, Exeter got the chance to give both myself, and their long suffering fans some breathing space when Matt Gill hit an absolute thunderbolt towards the home sides goal from a rebounded corner. From the edge of the area, the Grecian midfielders cracker was acrobatically tipped onto the underside of the bar by Stevenage keeper Julian, who threw himself full length to keep the shot out. The ball flew down and dramatically hit the inside of the post as well before flying back across the six yard box and amazingly, rolling to safety.

Buoyed by that effort Exeter stepped up a gear. Moments later Mackie crossed and found Gill again, but Fuller managed to controversially clear the ball with a part of the body you use to wave 'hello' to your mum.

Outstanding clearance by Barry Fuller there - using his chest to full effect.

Lying bastard. Clear handball.

In the last quarter both sides went hell for leather to win the game. Cole and Dobson went close for the home side, and Patrick Ada had to make a fantastic last-ditch challenge to keep the lethal Steve Morrison from going clear.

With three minutes of injury time played, Stevenage won a free kick deep in City territory. It was at this point our mouthy co-commentators decided to

stop describing the action and let my imagination go hurtling into overdrive.
'Now, lets see what happens from this,' crowed the commentator.
And that's just what the bastard did!
Watched what happened!
For some unknown reason they forgot there was a listening audience in England and a hemorrhoid-hurting Irishman across the sea who needed them to describe in crystal clear detail the dying seconds of this hugely important game.
I listened to the cries among the 3,000 strong crowd, as the ball was whisked into Exeter's area.
Get in!
Get out!
It must be a goal.
'Hoof the fucking thing away.'
The sound of a whistle echoed seconds later.
It hadn't gone in.
It had been cleared.
It remained 0-0.
The wave of relief was awesome.
EVERY fan knows that feeling.
Like a last minute reprieve from a firing squad.
The discovery of that lost winning lotto ticket.
Finding late night porn on the TV.
Exeter had done what they'd set out to do. The scoreless draw at Stevenage let City's fate, for the very first time since their arrival in the Conference, firmly in their own hands. A win at home to Southport would give the Grecian army their first taste of the play-off pie.
The following Tuesday, Exeter's job was made somewhat easier by the fact Southport was officially relegated as results that night conspired against them. The Merseysider's had been on a hot streak which had staved off impending relegation for a few weeks, but with fellow strugglers Greys and Halifax winning their respectful games, it meant a return to Conference North for the part-timers.
That following Saturday over 6,600 people piled into St. James's Park for the final game of the league season. I was back on familiar ground. Home commentary, text updates from my friends, and a hemorrhoid free ass, thanks to a new box of suppositories and two full days on the toilet.
I've no idea if dogs get piles but if they do, my one is extremely well prepared having chewed its way through a full pack of them.
Paul Tisdale's men were ninety minutes away from a play-off birth, but not one person crammed into St James's Park was taking three points for granted.
Me, I sat at home, hoping, praying for a simple text message saying we'd taken an early lead and sewn the game up by half-time.
On 39 minutes I got a text all right.
It contained profanity - never a good sign.
'Fucking ballsed up again. 1-0 down.' Muppets.
On a rare foray into Exeter's half, Southport had taken a shock lead through Tate's deflected shot. It was the first goal Martin Rice had conceded in almost 400 minutes of play.
More grey hairs accumulated during the break. Another 20 years had been

added to my life. If I'd counted the amount of years that had been added to my life through worry, I'd be approximately 357 years old.

With Burton Albion drawing at half time, and Exeter needing to match their result, the equation was simple. City had to hit the back of the net.

This would be Paul Tisdale's most important team talk since he'd taken charge of the helm at Exeter.

Someone needed to shake City. Someone needed to grab the game by the scruff of the neck and drag Exeter past the finishing post and into the promised land of the play-offs. Having gone nine months and played 45 games to get to this point, it would be a devastating blow for City. Tiring trips to Stafford and Altrincham, winning by a single goal. Away days at York and Gravesend grinding out gritty draws. Keeping St James an impregnable fortress - breached only twice all season.

The walloping of Weymouth, the soaking at St. Albans, and that last gasp winner whilst pneumonia set in. All this would be irrelevant if Exeter couldn't turn the last 45 minutes of their season around against relegated Southport.

With just 25 minutes left, Tisdale made three dramatic substitutions. A decision that required balls of steel to change the outcome of the tie. On 66 minutes, having swapped Phillips for Logan, City's boss shocked everyone by taking off captain, Chris Todd, throwing on Jon Challinor, and going 3-4-3. It was a massive, massive gamble.

Within 5 minutes it paid off BIG TIME!!!

Just 127 seconds after Challinor came on, going into attack, and completely changing the formation, Adam Stansfield finally found his range and drove home from inside the area to level the scores.

Three minutes later the roof came off St James's Park. With Southport in disarray and Exeter sensing blood, Stansfield doubled his tally and won the freedom of the City by firing home from a tight angle to completely turn the game on its head.

The relief was overwhelming. With a 2-1 lead, and news of Burton now losing to Rushden and Diamonds, the Grecians were in the driving seat.

Again Tisdale made an inspired substitution. Almost immediately after Stansfield had fired Exeter ahead, the manager threw on defender Jon Richardson for winger Lee Elam, reverting back to a flat back four and changing back to 4-4-2.

With the fight taken out of the visitors, Exeter comfortably closed out the game and sent six and a half thousand fans into pure ecstasy.

Players hugged. Fans cried. Management embraced.

'Glory, glory, Hallelujah - Exeter City made the play-offs,' - roared the radio.

Paul Buckle clenched his fists.

Mr. Tisdale chatted to the press.

And Steve Tully summed it all up with two well-chosen words- live on air;

'Fucking brilliant!'

Ironically, in the end it didn't matter. Burtons loss to Rusden meant Exeter could have been steamrollered 17-0 and the Grecians would still have made the top five.

Thoughts now turned to one destination.

Wembley.

The grand old stadium had gone through a six-year re-vamp at a cost of some £757 million and was to host its first FA Cup final since 2000. However, the fact some Premiership giants would slog it out for bragging rights on May 19 meant nothing to Exeter City fans. It was the day after that the Grecian army had their sights set on.

On May 20th, one day after the first FA cup final at the re-vamped stadium, Wembley would play host, for the very first time, to the Nationwide Conference Play-Off Final.

What a colossal incentive for Exeter City. A chance of a lifetime for eleven men in red & white to walk out on the hallowed turf in the world's most famous football arena.

Of course there was the small matter of three other Conference sides all chomping at the bit, not only to ply their trade at Wembley, but to enter the promised land of league football.

The semi-final line up was simple. Morecambe would play York, whilst City would meet pre-season title favourites Oxford United.

On paper Exeter seemed to have drawn the shortest straw but having nipped into the play-offs on the back of four wins and a draw, City were the form team of the four.

With the prospect of a Wembley appearance a mere 180 minutes away, I simply had to sample the live atmosphere of Exeter's first leg against Oxford - at home in a rafter-rousing St. James Park. Sure, it would cost me yet more money. Sure, it would critically damage my credit card, and yes, divorce proceedings were now just a solicitors phone call away, but I just had to be in a corner of England that is forever Exeter that coming Friday. In explaining this to my long-suffering wife I tried to explain my logic simply.

'A- honey, Exeter won't beat Oxford United. I'm only going over to sample the atmosphere before Jim Smiths men walk all over us.'

B - honey, if we do make Wembley you can file for divorce, take the dog, cat and burn my entire record collection - even that ultra rare copy of Jimmy Hendrix's 'Voodoo Chile', and my entire Gilbert O Sullivan back catalogue. Even the 7inch vinyl of 'Ohh Wakka Do Wakka Day.'

Seemed a fair trade for Sandra.

If we lost she'd have her hubby back in double quick time. If we won she could burn every Gilbert O Sullivan record I'd drove her insane with and start a new life with Troy Benedict - the hunky new American milkman on our street.

The things I do for the love of one woman ..and the worship of eleven men.

The following week I worked the dreaded eight letter word - overtime - in order to have a couple of days off to enjoy my trip to Devon to watch the Grecians do battle with Jim Smiths Londoners.

That Thursday, having worked in two days and time on my hands, I paid a visit to my friend Video-Nasty Norm who was having his legendary annual 'Horror-thon', A 12-hour slasher flick-fest with some of the crudest horror movies ever to make it onto film. However, not just anyone could pop along to Norms house and watch a day of debauchery and sinister violence. No, it took a special kind of weirdo to gain entrance to 57 Hazelbrook House.

In order to be accepted you needed to bring a movie that was officially banned by the British Censorship Board. I brought a double bill.

'Microwave Massacre' and 'Evil Dead'.

Tame by these days standards but still on the hallowed list. It's guys like Pentagram Pete and his cousin Henry 'the-choke' Cleary that really had issues. With Pete owning films like 'Mutilation At the Monastery' and the 'Devil Takes

A Whore', you know these guys are playing for keeps. Anyone who asked their girlfriend to have sex in a pentagram is not to be trusted.

Cousin Henry got his charming nickname by insisting on choking his girlfriends during the act of making love. This apparently heightens the sense of sexual pleasure. Fair enough. But strangling a female whilst you're watching 'I Spit On Your Grave' is not exactly standard dating practice.

I sat through the first three films - 'Slumber Party Massacre', 'Slutbag Slaughter' and 'Maniac' before falling asleep. I woke several hours later, had another beer and took in 'Sorority Serial Killer 3', before calling it a night.

Despite the hoards of weirdo's and even weirder movies, it was a fun way to pass a day, even if my company preferred snuff to soccer.

The following evening I was among 8,659 football fans all united in one goal - to see their team stride out 16 days later at Wembley.

The travelling Oxford contingent had arrived en mass, and filled out the Well Street away end terrace.

A crescendo of red and black balloons greeted both sides as they entered the arena. This was what it was all about. Standing on a terrace, sitting on a seat, cheering you're side on - whilst the world watches on.

Yep - that's right. Sky was televising the game.

Fucking Brilliant. The goggle-box, a jinx responsible for bringing out the absolute worst in Exeter City Football Club, was back at the park.

14 games and counting. 14 games since City was first televised. 14 suicide-inducing performances that no City fan wanted to recall or relive. If this amazingly awful jinx was to be laid to rest, surely tonight had to be the night. Lights. Camera. Action.

Unfortunately as the author of this book, I'm obliged to write about the following 90 minutes. Let me just go on the record and say I'd rather face a full frontal lobotomy before I'd comment on this game again. I would use my nuts as a break on a rusty blade or sleep with my psychotic ex-girlfriend before I'd write another word in print of Exeter's first leg play-off against Oxford United.

The first half was simply awful. The second marginally better. For a game of such magnitude, Exeter produced one of their stalest performances of the season.

Maybe it was nerves. Maybe it was the attendance. Maybe it was yet again the sight of a television camera within a mile of Well Street. Whatever the reason, City weren't at the races. Sticking Richard Logan up front and bombing the ball into the air at any given opportunity just played into the visitors' hands.

The warning signs arrived early.

With just five minutes gone, Rice was required to make a smart save by his right hand post from a header. 15 minutes had gone and a Zebroski effort had the City keeper scrambling across his goal as the ball just cleared the Grecian's crossbar.

Exeter created very little. The one chance ground out fell to Stansfield who should have done better from a header no more than six yards from goal.

United forced seven first half corners in 30 minutes - all to no avail.

Then on 40 minutes, the eighth, and final one of the half.

A corner was driven into the Exeter area where Hargreaves headed powerfully against the bar. The ball rebounded into play where Jones cleared it with a header. Rose then drove the ball back off Todd, only to see it then strike Andy

Taylor on the chest and loop into the top corner.

Poxed is the correct term, ladies and gentlemen.

Two minutes later Oxford should have sown the tie up. A long ball over the top saw United's Odubade outpace the home defence and with only Rice to beat and the goal gaping, the Oxford striker fluffed his lines and drove wide of the near post.

A collective sigh of relief exhaled around the park.

Moments later the half-time whistle sounded with City looking as far off Wembley as AFC Wimbledon from the Champions League.

Again the manager tried some bold substitutions. Challinor replaced Carlisle, and the injured Edwards made way for Richardson. The formation went into more attacking, and City finally managed to create some chances. Stansfield was denied twice by Turley and Billy Jones hit a 30-yard thunderbolt on the volley that, had it hit the net, would have blown the roof off not only St James Park, but every house within ten miles of the ground.

But by far the best chance fell to Richard Logan. With City on top early in the second half, Adam Stansfield collected a short pass and fired in a fantastic ball onto the head of the Exeter target-man. With a free header from just six yards out, Logan planted his effort the wrong side of the near post to bring 8,000 Grecian fans collectively to their knees.

It would be the closest City came. But not the most important miss of the evening.

That my friends, belonged to one Chris Zebroski. With a minute of normal time left, the on-loan Plymouth striker arrived into the City box and latched onto a quickly taken free kick from the edge of Exeter's area. As the ball arrived to the lanky hit man, the travelling Oxford fans were already celebrating. Then, in a scene that will make any compilation of the worst misses of all-time, Zebroksi somehow managed to screw his effort wide from no more than four yards out.

It was a shocking effort. Somewhere you just knew Ronny Rosenthal was smiling to himself. Not since the Liverpool's strikers howler at Aston Villa had anyone witnessed such an awful clanger.

Zebroksi held his head in his hands.

So did 1200 travelling Londoners.

Ditto Jim Smith.

It was hard to describe the feeling as the full time whistle sounded. There was obvious disappointment at the defeat, but it was coupled with an overwhelming relief that the Grecians were still in the tie.

Truth be known, Exeter should have been dead and buried. Some banter with the travelling Oxford fans confirmed that. Despite the Londoners obvious joy, there was concern that they couldn't return home and book their seats at Wembley just yet.

City should have scored one.

United should have scored four.

Disappointed but not downhearted, we returned to the bar, started the post mortem and used alcohol to erase the memory of the 90 minutes just witnessed.

Later that night we sweated the night away at a local nightclub and got some much needed rations at a local burger van.

It was here that the fun started. With everyone of the party hungry enough to eat a horse, there was a vast array of food on option. Chinese to the left. Indian to the right. Kebab shop straight ahead.

However, we managed to stumble across the only burger van in the western world with no food and met the Joseph Stalin of Exeter's burger franchise.

Looking at this man the wrong way could result in him visiting you in the early hours and shooting your entire family, dog, cat and pet rabbit Snuggles dead.

Asking him for something as exotic as some lettuce or ketchup could result in a pistol-whipping on the spot.

Lets just say customer relations wasn't the man's forte.

I will now describe the conversation that took place between us and said vendor.

Ian Tarr - Can I have an egg burger please?

Vendor - Well, I've got an egg, I've got a burger, but I've not got an egg burger.

Ian Tarr - Are you serious?

Vicious Vendor - Does a bear shit in the woods? Next please.

Stuart - Can I have a burger with some bacon on it?

Vendor - Well I've got some bacon, that doesn't necessarily mean I'm going to cook it.

Sandy Ample Charms - Can I have a large chip and fish please.

Vendor - I've got half a sausage left. Take it our leave it.

The disappointment of Friday night didn't sink in until the following Tuesday evening and the sight of Jim Smith's broad smile on Sky Television. The Oxford boss was giving a pre-match interview and confidently predicting his side would finish off the job tonight if they managed to take the chances they'd so carelessly missed at St James Park.

The Kassam stadium housed over 10,000 fans, an interested media, and of course Sky Sports.

As if Exeter's mountain wasn't big enough to climb, the Grecians had to face the nation for the second time in five days. Yet another game on TV. Yet another monkey on the back.

If Devon's finest were to get to Wembley, they needed to do something they'd not managed In 14 previous attempts. Win on TV.

What followed was as dramatic as any Premiership match, as nerve-jangling as any thriller, and more twists then a curly-wurly. It also finally provided the answer to a 14-year-old question, my nine sceptical friends, two bemused parents and one long suffering wife had been asking for over a decade. Why do I support Exeter City?

If you were watching Sky Sports on the eighth day of May 2007, you certainly got full value for your television licence.

Paul Tisdale pulled another surprise by dropping BOTH strikers from the first leg and adopting yet another formation. Having been over-run in midfield five days pervious, City's manager went with a 4-4-1-1 formation and replaced Stansfield & Logan with Lee Phillips and Jon Challinor.

The Grecians had a monopoly on the opening exchanges. After 4 minutes, Lee Elam gave Billy Turley a taste of things to come by forcing the Oxford keeper into a smart save. Chris Todd followed suit minutes later. The 1000 strong Grecian faithful were unmistakable in the opening exchanges, roaring their lungs out, shouting with all their might, making sure the 11 men in blue could hear every song, every chant, every word of encouragement.

174

On ten minutes they lifted the roof. Billy Jones cross into United's area was put away by Lee Phillips. The joy lasted 1.5 seconds. A late linesman's flag ruled the goal out and the game remained scoreless. I sat at home, foam seething from my mouth, like a dog with rabies. The replay cleared showed Phillips was onside.

Things got worse before they got better.

With practically their first attack of the game, Oxford took the lead. Burgess broke up a City attack and played the ball to Odubade, who found space between Todd and Edwards to fire off a shot. His effort looked harmless enough, but a combination of an unlucky bobble and a chocolate wrist from the normally dependable Martin Rice, resulted in the ball rolling into the bottom left hand corner to the delight of the home crowd.

1-0 on the night. 2-0 on aggregate.

Game over?

Bollocks to that. It was at that point Exeter City, facing down the barrel of a gun, standing in front of its own Everest, spat in the face of adversity and produced a stunning fight back to defy all the logic that television cameras had pronounced upon them since their first armchair outing over ten years ago.

The Grecians raised their game to a new level and kept knocking on the Oxford door in hope of getting an equalising answer.

Seven minutes from half-time a long throw was cleared back to Matthew Gill who drove a missile into the United area with the outside of his boot. The marauding Phillips climbed highest to bury a downward header past Turley and into the net.

Oxford 1-1 Exeter.

Game on? You bet your sweet ass it was.

The possessed animal that was Exeter City FC continued where they let off in the second half. Challinor narrowly poked Carlisle's cross wide. Phillips again warmed the hands of Turley. City looked the only winners at this point.

On the sideline Jim Smith was a worried man. The casual carefree nonchalance of United's manager was replaced with red cheeks and a menacing scowl.

This wasn't supposed to happen. This wasn't in the script.

Neither was what happened on 70 minutes.

Having replaced Carlisle ten minutes earlier, Adam Stansfield pulled down a searching Edwards ball, cut inside Burgess and fired his shot beyond the grasping Turley into the bottom of the home sides net.

Oxford 1-2 Exeter. Aggregate score 2-2. Have some of that!

The Kassam stadium was in stunned silence (apart from 1000 visiting lunatics in the South Stand). This was turning into a living nightmare for the Londoners in their own backyard.

Yet it could, nah, should have been, oh so different.

Before Exeter had levelled. Before Stansfield had beaten Turley and sent the Grecian army into raptures, the home side missed yet another astonishing gilt-edged chance.

With Tisdale going for broke - taking off Phillips and Elam for Logan & Mackie, City were caught out by a ball that split Edwards and Todd in two and released Oxford top goal scorer Rob Duffy free on goal. The United striker had just come on and found himself in acres of space with only Martin Rice to beat. As Rice committed himself, Duffy seemingly only had to roll the ball into the net. 20 goals this season. United's top marksman, goalkeeper perplexed on the ground.

Incredibly Duffy tamely placed the ball into the waiting arms of Martin Rice to the astonishment of the home crowd and the total and utter disbelief of his manager.

The final ten minutes was end to end adventure. City survived two penalty appeals; United's jittery defence was continuously tested.

Then with seconds left, deep into injury time, Jamie Mackie had a chance to put every single Exeter City fan in the stadium, pubs, clubs and armchairs of the world, out of their misery with a last gasp effort.

Latching onto a ball from Challimor, the young Scotsman broke free in the area, evaded a despairing tackle and fired in a shot, which Turley dramatically clawed away. It proved to be the last action of normal time.

By now I'd been reduced to a 5' 10" lump of jelly on my living room sofa. It had been a nightmare on my ticker up to this point, now there was the realistic chance that I actually might have a full-scale heart attack at 37 years of age if I had to witness anymore of this unfolded drama.

How I cursed Jamie Mackie.

How I turned the air blue with ten full minutes of ear shattering profanity for having not converted that chance with virtually the last kick of the game. Even when City had finished the first half of extra-time, I was still bemoaning my luck and swearing long and hard into the night.

By the end of the game I'd have needed three straight months in confession.

Nerves played the overwhelming factor in extra-time. Having slugged it out like two heavyweights over the past 200 minutes, nobody was going to let anything slip in the last ten.

And so to penalties.

Tisdale picked five men. The fans held their breath. I went for a walk.

It had become too much for me, so I took a sharp intake of breath, swigged down my 15th whiskey and went out into the night to have a chat with the man above.

I'm not going to say much Lord. Just five short words

You owe us this one!

Oxford took the first spot kick.

Rob Duffy - sending Rice the wrong way. Small consolation for his earlier howler.

Billy Jones stepped up next. And missed.

Mr reliable, the man who only misses against Kiddminster, stuck the post with his effort to hand Oxford the advantage.

They took a stranglehold on proceedings with their next two penalties.

Despite Gill and Taylor finding the net with their efforts, Burgess and Johnson both hit the target for United.

3-2 ahead, up stepped Irish midfielder Barry Quinn to take Oxford's fourth spot kick to try putting a two goal cushion between both sides and heap the world on Jamie Mackie's shoulders.

This was one Irishman whose luck I hoped deserted him.

He struck his effort down the middle were Rice had stood his ground to brilliantly turn away the former Republic international's effort.

There was enormous pressure on Jamie Mackie as he stepped forward in front of the hostile home crowd in the facing north stand to level the tie up.

The 18 year old stuck a sweet effort to the right of Turley and into the net.

3-3. One penalty each left.

Up stepped Oxford goalkeeper Billy Turley.

As he stood waiting for the referee whistle he looked extremely relaxed, cocky even, as if his penalty was a forgone conclusion.

The post had other ideas.

With a confident pose, a nonchalant jog up, and the stroke of a right foot, Turley's effort struck the right hand post and rebounded out.

One penalty left. One penalty to send Exeter City to Wembley for the first time in their 104-year history.

Richard Logan had that chance to create history. We watched and waited. By now I was back in front of the TV and resuming the standard praying position of both knees on the ground and hands pointed to heaven.

Up stepped Logan. Turley dived to his right. The ball stayed out.

Sudden death.

By the time Chris Zebroski walked up to take the first penalty of sudden death I'd pulled almost every follicle of hair from my head. Any more of this and a visit to Zonky Downes Wigs of Wonder was imminent.

Deja-vu returned to haunt the young striker. Just as he'd missed a crucial chance at the end of the first leg, the on-loan Plymouth man was out of luck again- striking the post with his penalty.

Again City was a spot-kick away from Wembley.

By now the watching public had got as much entertainment as five back-to-back World Cups (ok, I'll oversold it) - but the drama had to come to an end at some point before midnight!

It all rested on the shoulders of Exeter's 28-year-old defender Steve Tully.

As he walked to face his destiny, he showed no signs of fear whatsoever.

No hint of last minute jitters

Not even a trace of nerves about the enormity of the impending penalty.

He placed the ball. Smiled. Drove it low and hard past a helpless Billy Turley.

Exeter City was going to Wembley.

Chapter Seventeen
THAT'S LIFE

'That's life, that's what all the people say,
You're ridin' high in April, shot down in May.'
- Frank Sinatra

PRIDE - the quality or state of being proud. Inordinate self-esteem. A reasonable or justifiable respect.
The delight or elation arising from some act, possession or relationship.
God bless the Oxford English Dictionary.
I'd been searching for the words to describe my feelings at 10.21pm on the eighth night of May 2007, but was at a loss.
At a loss at how I couldn't put down on paper the overwhelming feeling of ecstasy, the adrenalin pumping delirium, the fist clenching, lung bursting, emotionally charged feeling of pure pride I'd felt as Steve Tully hammered home his penalty and ran to embrace his team-mates, manager and 1,000 Exeter City supporters on a amazing night in a little part of Oxfordshire.
Exeter City was going to Wembley.
Going there after a 220 minute astonishing rollercoaster ride which saw the Grecians lose a home leg, go two goals behind, amazingly claw their way back into a forgone conclusion, almost win the tie in normal time, endure thirty more heart-stopping minutes of stalemate, and finally overcome Oxford United with the longest ten minute penalty shoot out in the history of any human being that calls themselves a proud supporter of Exeter City Football Club.
The celebrations were simply one of a kind.
Different from the championship title of 1990, when City stormed Division Four and everything in it. Similar to the elation of Old Trafford, but not quite the same.
This was a game where a small club in Devon had proved to the public, their fans and most importantly themselves, that they could shine in the face of adversity, overcome overwhelming odds and display an astonishing never-say-die attitude for the crest they so proudly now kissed.
Oh, and finally win a sodding match on TV!
The ghost had been laid to rest. The jinx was cast aside. At the 15th attempt, Exeter City Football Club had finally won a match in front of television cameras.
Scenes of utter joy and elation emanated from the South Stand.
Fans embraced, players hugged, a unison of clenched fists pointed towards the heavens as City scarves adorned the Oxfordshire skyline.
By this stage I'd gone. The tears had already soaked my skin and through scalded eyes I watched as my mobile lit up with text messages of support and celebration for this amazing triumph.
I sent back six simple words to every single person that text me that night.
THAT'S WHY I SUPPORT EXETER CITY.
My emotional state was perilous. Going between a state of euphoria to a river of tears and a need to tell the entire world why I love this little non-league club. I cried an ocean that night as did many a Grecian around the globe.
Oh what it must have been like to be in the Kassam Stadium.
How it must have felt to see City refuse to buckle, and fight their way back

into a tie they'd no right to At 8.15 Oxford United were already Wembley bound. Already making arrangements of where to stay, what to do, how they'd feel when they lifted the play-off trophy at the famously revamped stadium and take their place back in the football league.

Two hours later, and three lonely fans in yellow jerseys alone in the stand, heads bowed told its own story.

Crestfallen. Heartbroken. Devastated. Utterly Devastated.

There would be hours, days, and weeks, of being inconsolable for these men. A season that started so brightly ended with a shattering climax on their home turf.

The healing process would only begin three months later with the start of a new season and the promise of promotion. It's a grieving process that every fan goes through at some point in their life. An end of the world feeling that nothing but time can console or start a healing process.

Five minutes ago Oxford were two short penalty kicks from Wimble.

Now Jim Smiths team would visit Farley Celtic next year.

The margin of defeat so minimal.

Pure adrenalin kept me up till 4am that night. I, like almost every other Exeter fan had relived the entire drama again in the early hours with the repeat of the match on Sky. Some were still on the phone. Some were drunk. Most were both.

Some were only just getting in their doors back in Devon after possibly the most insanely delightful journey back to the South West of England they were ever likely to experience.

The popping of champagne corks sounded in my humble abode that night (well two bottles. One miniature bottle of Moet and some cheap tat I'd won in a 1987 Christmas raffle at the local bingo hall.)

For the first time in my entire employed life, I couldn't wait to go to work the next morning. Couldn't wait to wear my freshly ironed Exeter best and take the plaudits from my friends, who'd been as stunned as I was about the performance.

You couldn't pay me a million quid to wipe the Cheshire cat grin off my face as I clocked in that next morning. With just 2 hours sleep to my name, I should have resembled the walking dead. My carcass should have been akin to zombies, and my eyes as red as the shirt I wore. Every once in a while you'll get days like this in your life. Days when the clouds seem extra fluffy, the sun that bit more radiant. You take time to savour the whistle of a bird, the ruffling of the gentle breeze among the trees.

In short you become a sap. At one with nature and in love with life. All because eleven men you've never met, won a game of football on a Tuesday night in some part of Oxfordshire.

To the outside world it was a half-decent way of killing two hours on the goggle box, but even now, less than 9 hours after it finished, every Exeter City fan spanning the globe knew they'd witness a classic and with it a little bit of history.

You didn't need to tell the thousand City souls who travelled that night; they'd witnessed a game, which would be talked about for years to come sitting on a high stool and a cold pint. You didn't need to tell the watching Grecian faithful that this was a game to be replayed in the head and regaled to their offspring and future generations of family for decades to come.

When the dust finally settled on this epic, it became obvious that now only one team stood between Exeter City and a return to the football league. Morecambe FC would be that team.

Despite being the outsiders in their semi-final, Sammy McEllroy's men beat York City to book their first appearance at the newly revamped Wembley. When the pairings were both decided the smart money would have been on a late May Wimble final between Oxford & York. Now the two unfashionable underdogs would battle it out for the right of league status.

Despite finishing above City in the play-off zone, Sammy McEllroy's men would start as underdogs. The Grecians stunning performance at Oxford would see to that, but more to the point – Morecambe's woeful record against Devon's finest.

In eight attempts since they first clashed in the Conference- the Shrimps had failed every time to get the upper hand on City. A record of 4 wins and 4 draws put Paul Tisdale's men in the driving seat.

In their own semi-final Morecambe had surprisingly overcome a rather sedate York City 2-1 after a scoreless draw at Kit Kat Crescent. This gave way to a severe doze of optimism among the Grecian faithful. With all due respect to McEllroy's men but everyone at St James Park knew, if you were given a choice between Oxford, York and Morecambe to meet at Wembley, the Shrimps would win hands down every time.

A quiet confidence spread throughout the town.

The realism Exeter City would walk out at Wembley in seven days time still hadn't really sunk in when tickets went on sale. Amazingly despite the 90,000 capacity and the weekly attendance at St. James' Park, there was panic within the first hour of ticket sales. By mid-morning, over 7,000 tickets had been sold and the system had gone haywire. Frantic calls were made to staff at the ground and the panic button had been well and truly pressed.

Some bought single. Some bought bulk. Most prayed for a voice on the phone or a website to tell them they had a confirmed ticket.

At the end of the first day trading, Exeter City had sold almost 10,000 tickets to the Grecian faithful.

Now it didn't take a mathematical genius to work out over 6,000 City fans sprung up overnight to claim a ticket. You didn't need Nostradamus to work out the Grecians would see a dramatic upsurge in support now that they were a week away from gracing the Wembley turf. From not bothering with a Saturday afternoon at St. James' Park, to travelling three hours on a cramped bus on the Sabbath day to watch Exeter City play for possibly the first time ever.

This was to be expected. Whilst everyone of the newfound faithful would be hoping for a City victory, most were going for a day out in the capital and the spectacle of a newly revamped Wembley Stadium.

Five excruciatingly slow days followed. The clock in work seemed to go backwards as I counted down the hours to the biggest game in Exeter City's 104-year history. This of course, gave me time to play out the forthcoming ninety minutes in my head. Don't say you haven't done it. Every football fan approaching a game of this magnitude will dissect in their brain. What drama could possibly unfold on match day? The various ways your club can emerge victorious or collapse calamitously, will shuffle through you're brain at least 27 times in the days leading up to the showdown.

At regular intervals you will find yourself constructing the precise way your club will overcome the opposition in vain hope your imagination gets it absolutely spot on, on the day. My vision centered on a woeful game of football and a Billy Jones penalty with six seconds left. The crowd holds their breath, Billy strides up and with the force of a cannon, drives both ball and Morecambe goalkeeper into the back of the net. They centre off. Ref blows whistle. City win 1-0.

As the players embrace, and thousands of Grecians celebrate, Morecambe manager McEllroy can be clearly seen vomiting on the sidelines.

I'm a nice guy, but in my dreams I'm a vicious bastard!

It didn't matter to me how City would win once it was Chris Todd walking those famous Wembley steps to collect the Conference Play-Off Trophy. It was of no consequence to me if Lee Elam impersonated a high board diver and won Exeter the match with one of the most outrageously awful penalty decisions ever seen at a football game.

Bully, Cheat, Con. I didn't care once we won.

It may not have been in keeping with the spirit of the game and bordering on psychotic but I was past the point of rational thinking.

Don't agree? – Here's four words for you.

NICE GUYS FINISH LAST.

By the time Friday came I was pumped.

To keep this adrenalin-fuelled momentum going, I went to go see ROCKY BALBOA- the latest and last in the saga of Sly Stallone's loveable underdog.

Everybody loves Rocky. It's our universal love of the underdog. Rocky was a Philadelphia two-bit slugger living a futile life of discouragement, surviving on hard work and honour whilst scrapping a living in seedy halls against fifth rate boxers.

Enter Apollo Creed and the chance of a lifetime for the Italian Stallion. The rest is history. Rocky is now an icon of American culture, so I needed to be first in line when the final installment of this classic hit our cinema screens.

The film is a real winner. Rocky loses his one true love (poor Adrienne - I shed a tear for Talia Shire in the graveyard scene), runs a restaurant were he regales past stories of former glories, whilst dumbing down the food – 'it's all edible- approves Rocky (systematically clearing the entire restaurant.) Spurred on by a virtual boxing match, Rocky gets itchy feet and climbs back into the ring with the World Heavyweight Champion - 30 years his junior (nice to see the brain damage is still in check), where he puts up the fight of his life in a climactic finale, and leaves the arena to a standing ovation of thousands and the feel good ending of the century.

Halfway through the film, Rocky gives a speech to his disinterested son about how the world is a mean and nasty place.

'You, me, or nobody, is going to hit as hard as life, and it will beat you to your knees and keep you there permanently if you let it. It's about how hard you can get hit and keep moving forward, that's how winning's done.'

If you know what you want, go get it, but you've got to be willing to take the hits and not point fingers and saying you're not where you are because of him, her or anybody. That's what cowards do and you're better than that. YOU'RE BETTER THAN THAT!

I left the cinema and ran 15 miles on my treadmill that night.

The alarm clock rang at precisely 5.54am Sunday morning.

The 20th day, of the fifth month of the year 2007 would possibly be the biggest of my 37 years on this planet and the 104 in Exeter City's history.

By the time dusk descended on Wembley Stadium tonight, Exeter's fate would have been decided.

Rotherham or Rushden. Stockport or Salisbury. A four-year gap could be bridged shortly after 4 today, if Exeter City beat Morecambe in the 2006/07 Nationwide Conference final.

Being London, my navigational skills are put to the test. Despite the flight from Waterford to Luton taking only 55 minutes, it takes almost another two hours in London to finally arrive at our Travelodge - a mere 20 minutes from Wembley Stadium. Even on the Lords day of rest there's a multitude of people rushing around like headless chickens trying desperately to get from A to B.

My condition is not helped by the play-list of songs currently occupying my MP3 player. For some strange reason, I cannot forward past the '30-minute sex mix section'. I'd normally use far more romantic interludes, and have to endure 'Don't give up on us baby,' on repeat whilst I fight my way through Kings Cross tube station.

What the hell was David Soul thinking? This was one half of the toughest crime-fighting duo of the 70's. A tough non-nonsense street-wise cop who solved crime once a week in 60 minutes with the help of his partner Starsky, (or three times a day if you're watching Bravo.) A blonde Adonis, with an eye for the ladies, and an automatic for the assholes! Yet here he was all soft-rocked out, sitting on a stool and praying for another chance with a piece of skirt that wants to bin him.

Poor Starsky. The next time there's a hostage situation in my local bank, I won't be calling for Hutch anytime soon.

When I do manage to skip past Soul's singing, I endure 45 seconds of 'By the time I get to Phoenix,' -Glen Campbell's heartless ode to the woman he's pissed off on without even saying goodbye, before Dr Hook's, 'Sylvia's Mother,' fills me with thoughts of throwing myself underneath the 11.58 to Walthamstow.

Even in a different city, -miles away from the rural Devon countryside and the comforting surrounds of Exeter, - familiar faces greet me the moment I walk into the reception of Wembley Travelodge.

Between a flurry of red and white jerseys, City scarves and moving bodies with Grecian headwear attached, I spy my season-ticketed soul mates.

They're all there. Stuart, Bob (pre-violent swearing Wembley mode), Ian Tarr, Martin, Kiss-the-seat Pete, and his delectable wife Sandy Ample Charms. The name needs no explanation. Last but not least - Crazy Greg, who'd just landed a platinum Visa from Barclays and was intent on maxing it out within the next 24 hours.

There was an air of anticipation that stretched the length of road and the convoy of Exeter City coaches that adorned it. We watched and waved almost two dozen, as they roared past the Travelodge on the way to Wembley. Waved our flags, hats and scarves like it was V.E. day. Waved at the coaches as if they carried our all-conquering troops as they arrived back on home soil, having defeated the tyranny of Mussolini and Hitler.

For those few precious minutes there was an impromptu Exeter love-in, and everyone from the entire city seemed unified by our little football club. Fans hanging from windows. Horns blaring. A chorus of City songs, echoing into the cold sterile London skyline. It was exhilarating.

The walk to Wembley is savoured step by step. That enormous arch of

Wembley stadium that had dominated the left window of my train ride grew ever closer. As I look at the cold granite beneath my feet my heart rate increases and pounds louder against the fabric of my new Exeter City shirt. It's an hour to kick-off and the moment is drawing ever closer. We march our way through suburbia, dodge speeding traffic and pass at least three dozen signposts before turning a corner and are greeted by Wembley Stadium.

Wembley Stadium. Exeter City at Wembley Stadium.

It had finally sunk in.

I stood there and smiled. There have been highlights in my short lifetime. Earning my first pay cheque. The birth of my daughter. Ireland in a World Cup. I now had a new entry in the top ten, maybe even the top five.

The glorious realisation I was standing outside the home of English football, about to watch the club I loved so passionately, so dearly that I well up with pride every time someone mentions their name, had finally hit home.

Life felt beautiful.

The stadium is a sight to behold. Despite the littered construction works and bottleneck of fans that reduce us to a standstill, this newly revamped monolith is a striking landscape. Thousands gaze in wonder beneath the watchful eye of Sir Bobby Moore - his statue welcoming the hoards to the home of English football. Just 24 hours earlier, Wembley had played host to a sterile F.A. Cup Final not worthy of the stadium in which it was played. Now Exeter and Morecambe would become the first ever football teams to contest a play-off final at any level, in arguably the world's most famous stadium.

Inside, we are greeted by a sea of red. Over 30,000 Exeter City fans have travelled from every corner of Devon, England and beyond. Everybody's up on their feet, taking photos, posing for cameras, greeting fellow friends. There's so much beauty for the eye to behold. The giant upper tiers, the immaculate surface, the collage of colours all encapsulated beneath the giant arch above us. I struggle like many to come to terms with the enormity of Wembley. The view is simply stunning and not a bad seat in the house.

Alcohol would be needed to play a massive part over the next ninety minutes. I head straight for the beverage section and order three glasses of wine.

Red. Bitter. Not the best.

Before I'm back at my seat, both sides have emerged to a deafening roar and a flood of ticker tape and balloons are simultaneously launched into the air. Scarves are waved, flags swayed from side to side. Thousands of grown men and women in tears. Tears of sheer and utter joyful pride. This was Old Trafford times two. Now all we needed was Morecambe to score as many as United that day. None.

The teams lined up, picked out the family members in the crowd, smiled and waved. The eleven men entrusted to bring league football back to the City were called out;

Paul Jones, Billy Jones, Chris Todd, Rob Edwards, Steve Tully, Lee Elam, Matthew Gill, Andy Taylor, Wayne Carlisle, Jon Challinor & Lee Phillips.

Finally, down to business.

Exeter City started like a team possessed. A house on fire. Pick your clichÈ - Tisdale's men didn't mess about. Within 9 seconds Lee Elam had forced a corner when his goal-bound effort was blocked. Minutes later again Elam caused havoc, but accidentally handled to end the attack. City owned the ball and the possession stats in the first five minutes must have been almost ninety per cent. 90 seconds later Exeter put the most important statistic of all on the board.

A goal.

Rob Edwards took a quick free kick which Jon Challinor gave chase to. The influential midfielder raced into the area, beat a Morecambe defender, before placing a beautifully floated ball to the far post and the incoming Lee Phillips who rose into the air and smashed his header powerfully past Scott Davies in the Morecambe goal to finish of a flowing City move.

Exeter City 1-0 Morecambe. 7 minutes in 83 from league football.

Wembley went crazy.

30,000 fans danced to the same tune, all singing from the gospel of Grecian. Poor Morecambe. How could their small but respectable 9,000 fans even start to cope with this? An onslaught both in the stands and field of play.

The early pressure was relentless. Gill went close soon after as Exeter went for the jugular. McElroy's men finally started to get to grips with the game and with 15 minutes gone, Paul Jones was forced to make a smart save from a stinging Curtis drive. Jones had been entrusted with the number 1 jersey, after almost seven games on the bench, due to Martin Rice's deciding to go AWOL after Manager Tisdale's decision to drop him for the final. In the days leading up to the final it had been a massive talking point, but Jones didn't leave a single soul in Wembley down that afternoon. The change would be fully justified.

It was at this point something changed. Looking back, I still like to think (like I will until I draw my last breath) that the Grecians took their foot off the pedal. Took their eye off the ball and the golden prize that awaited them. But after 15 minutes of relentless pressure Morecambe took over the match and it became Paul Jones against eleven men for the next half hour.

On 20 minutes, City's young shot-stopper got down magnificently to palm away another rasping drive, having seen it late. Exeter retreated and several close comrades twitched nervously in row 140 of the East lower stand. Fate dictated to me that we'd still win. After all we'd snuck into the play-offs, came from two goals behind to beat Oxford, and Morecambe had never beaten us in eight attempts. Throw in the fact Torquay had been relegated, and I was clasping the Virgin Mary in my right hand and saying prayers every time Morecambe attacked, I still thought this was a done deal. I'd worked damn hard being a model Christian over the past week and even forked over ten Euros to the collection plate at mass last Sunday. Surely the man above wouldn't inflict the unspeakable pain of losing a Wembley final?

20 seconds later Chris Todd gave away a penalty.

Maybe the Lord and myself weren't on the same wavelength.

City's captain slid in but upended Danny Carlton and referee Matt Oliver had no hesitation in pointing to the spot.

I needed the Virgin Mary to have a word with him. Had the man above completely lost his marbles? Did he know how insane I was? Was he actually relishing the moment I'd climb to the roof of Wembley and throw myself off to certain death if Exeter lost today?

Moments later Wayne Curtis stepped up, saw his penalty and resulting rebound magnificently saved by the inspired Paul Jones. It remained 1-0 to the Grecians.

That's better God - now no more messing about, ok?

Thanks Virgin Mary - I knew you'd talk him round.

There's only a certain amount of miracles our creator can work in a lifetime. The miracle of loaves and fishes don't come every day. Walking on water takes some planning. Raising yourself from the dead is especially tricky. Asking the man for at least half a dozen in 90 minutes of a football match is really taking the piss. And inevitably I'd run fresh out of favours and with it the Morecambe equaliser duly arrived on 42 minutes.

Ironically it came from an uncharacteristic mistake from the normally reliable Billy Jones. The Grecian defender ran to challenge Garry Thompson but instead of driving the ball out of the stadium and Thompson into the stands, Jones made a complete hash of his clearance. Thompson strode on and placed a firm drive past the seemingly unbeatable Jones and drew Morecambe level.

I felt sick to my stomach.

Ditto 29,999 other fans decked in red & white.

Although the equaliser had been coming and completely warranted, I had prayed for the Grecians just to hang on until half-time. Just to get into the dressing room with the lead. That would have dispirited Morecambe. McElroy's men would have trudged off the field dismayed at not winning, let alone being level, after so many great chances and a missed penalty. Now there was a spring in their step and all the momentum seemed to be with the Lancashire club.

Doubts now crept into my mind. Mr Pessimistic reared his pain-in-the-arse head again and now the game was anyones. The omens, which had been so blatantly biased in our favour before the game, now seemed to matter little. On one level we all hoped Lee Phillips 7th minute goal would be the cushion to a straight forward 3-0 walkover but that has vanished along with Phillips's himself who'd been forced to retire nine minutes before half-time with a hamstring injury.

Another three glasses of wine were devoured during the interval, as I got ready for possibly the most important 45 minutes of my life.

City started the second period brightly. The Grecians in block 140 had regrouped, cast aside any negativity and launched back into song. Stuart sung himself hoarse, Bob swore for England whilst Pete was surprisingly impressed with the cushioning on his seat. Thoughts of ripping it up and bringing it back to the season-ticket section of the Doble Stand must surely have crossed his mind. Ian's fez amazingly stayed on his noggin despite the various attempt to launch himself into orbit every time City launched an attack, whilst Sandy Ample Charms breasts jiggled to and fro like sweet,.....(back to the game Brian!) Challinor had the first shot in anger. Receiving an Andy Taylor pass, the midfielder tried a speculative effort that didn't trouble Davies. Adam Stansfield -who'd replaced the unfortunate Phillips- ran at the Morecambe defence at every chance possible- his pace clearly worrying both defence and goalkeeper. The latter was almost caught out when Stansfield charged down a routine Davies clearance, but couldn't control the ball and return it with interest into the net.

On 53 minutes a subdued Wayne Carlisle was replaced by Richard Logan whilst four minutes later the terribly frustrating Lee Elam (half the time I want to hug him- the other half murder him) was replaced by Jamie Mackie. Challinor who'd been playing a forwards role of late dropped back into midfield whilst Logan positioned himself for the freedom of Exeter City if he notched the winner.

Paul Tisdale now had his side set up 4-3-3. Again a bold move. Again a new

185

system. Conservatism is not in the Tisdale dictionary.

Mackie and Stansfield both had chances. Not clear-cut but enough to lift every interested Grecian bum out of their seats. The giant scoreboard would replay every tackle, every foul, and every talking point throughout the game. We'd gaze up in expectancy at it seconds after the drama had unfolded in real-time. With 8 minutes to go we'd already got ourselves in the mindset that this wasn't going to be resolved anytime soon.

The ball was launched into the Exeter half...

Yes we'd decided it wasn't going to anything other than penalties.

Morecambe's Danny Carlton got hold of the ball...

There would be at least another 40 minutes of waiting and wondering.

Carlton advanced, beat Edwards and fired his effort from 25 yards.

FUCK!!

1.5 seconds later the ball nestled in the roof of Paul Jones net.

At the precise moment I was picking out our penalty takers, Morecambe's Danny Carlton drove home an unstoppable drive from 25 yards to give Sammy McElroy's men the lead.

It's not an exaggeration on my behalf to say my entire world fell apart.

I could do nothing but slump to my knees. The living nightmare we all secretly dreaded was playing out before our very eyes.

McElroy ran onto the pitch rejoicing - how I wanted to kill him (that view still hasn't changed!) And for the first time in my life, I did something I'd never done in my happy-go-lucky, half-glass full life philosophy of life.

I gave up hope.

Even though there were 8 minutes left and at least a couple of minute's injury time to play, I gave up- accepted our fate and put my head in my hands. On one level, I hoped the man above could see my despair, shine a light on Jamie Mackie to hit an injury-time double and rejoice in a 3-2 win, but any lingering hopes among a disbelieving Exeter faithful went with Mattie Gillis sending off in injury time for a head butt on Blackburn.

A mass exodus filed out of Wembley moments later.

Exeter City 1-2 Morecambe.

Players fell to the floor in disbelief. This wasn't supposed to happen. Not after Southport on the last day. Not after Oxford. Not after the penalty shoot-out. Tears flowed freely on the pitch and in the stands.

I raised my head to applaud our gallant heroes and tried to make out every individual player in City's colours but my eyes scalded so much from the salt-water tears, that most seemed a blur. How I needed a hug. How we all did.

Can it be possible to have the best and worst day of your life all in the same 24 hours?

I didn't raise my head to watch Morecambe receive the play-off trophy. There's only so much pain I can endure in one day.

But they'd deserved it. In time that helped ease the pain. How worse it would have been to completely dominate a game, miss chance after chance, and get beaten by an offside goal five minutes into injury time?

Despite the overwhelming passion to find the nearest train track and throw myself underneath it, I stayed till the end. So did row 140,and 41 & 42. The need for thousands of Grecians to rocket to the nearest pub and drown themselves in a vat of whiskey was understandable, but having followed City through thick and thin that season we stayed until both sides had left the pitch.

That night we drank for an entire nation. Our little party emptied the entire wine vault of the Wembley Travelodge and an obscene amount of money was handed over the counter.

There was good banter between the Morecambe fans staying there and us.

They gloated about league football. we sung of Farsley Celtic.

They praised Sammy McEllroy; I placed a hex on him.

'We're in the football league,' shouted the fat bastard in Blue.

'We're in the Premier!' retorted a defiant Pete.

Of course he was right; we're in the Premier; The Blue Square Premier League. The Conferences new sponsors gave us a novel twist on things.

I struggled into bed at 2.31am. A noise emanated from my bed. My Mp3 had been left on. I listened briefly to Paul Simon singing about how crazy he was after all these years and lapsed into a coma.

Monday morning in a Travelodge is a depressing experience. Along with my throat feeling dry and a headache that will take at least six months to get rid off, the sound of traffic outside my window reminds me its yet another work day. I'm due back on nightshift tonight.

No a hope my friends. Not a hope.

Downstairs a handful of my group had stirred and breakfast is being sorted out. Unfortunately I'm on a schedule so haven't time for yet another post mortem about what went wrong yesterday.

I make my way out the door, turn right and head for the train station. The start of a long arduous trip home. I won't see my sofa until 5 today.

Standing on the platform, reliving every second from Wembley hurts like hell. Thankfully the train arrives to break my painful concentration on yesterday. If I'm to avoid having a mental breakdown on British Rail I better occupy my mind with anything other than football.

I reach for my Mp3, shove on my headphones and press play.

Willie Nelson – 'Always On My Mind'

Sweet Jesus.

Elton John – 'Don't Go Breaking My Heart'. Even Kiki Dee is putting the boot in. I can't seem to find one single song that doesn't include heartbreak of some kind.

Christ, I'm sad.

Song 34 comes on.

I love Peter Gabriel and settle on 'Don't give up' - his inspirational ballad from a time football couldn't make me feel like it's the end of the world.

Despite the haunting beauty of the song, its lyrics still seem to hit home.

'No fight left, it seems
I am a man whose dreams have all deserted.'

When all hope seems lost, my entire emotional well being is saved by Kate Bush.
'Rest your head, you worry too much
It's gonna be alright
When times are getting tough, you can fall back on us
Don't give up. Please, don't give up.'

Kate Bush I love you. And how right that angelic beauty was. I could bury my head in the sand. Continuously torture myself about what might have been and lose the passion to watch football again, but what good would it do. As bad as Wembley, was I still had Exeter. I still had my club. Four years ago that seemed a long shot. Relegation, administration and two chairman arrested on fraud charges. There seemed no hope.

But the club didn't give up. Here I was coming home from having seen my club play for the first time at Wembley in a play-off final with 30,000 Exeter City fans roaring their hearts out for the Grecians and I was sad!

Four years ago the club were doomed. Now debt free they were entering into the most exciting period of their history, with a fledging manager who'd just taken us to the greatest football stadium on this earth.

Common sense kicked in. My team was still here. I still had my club to delight or despair in each Saturday afternoon. I still had that choice. Even when I've shuffled off this mortal soil, there will still be an Exeter City. Life goes on. Somehow at that point Peter Gabriel sums it all up

'Whatever may come and whatever may go,
that rivers flowing, that rivers flowing.'

I smile to myself.
See, I'm better already.

ACKNOWLEDGEMENTS

I've had so much fun writing this book. I started on St. Stephens Day last year with the laptop my wife bought me for Christmas.

"If you're starting another book I'll break both your legs Kennedy" - she said.

"Just jotting a few notes honey….just jotting a few notes"

Again I had passengers along on my train of Grecian goodwill and would like to praise them to the rafters.

Frank Sealey, Gary Moore and everyone in the EXEC Club at Exeter City. The moment I announced I was writing the book you offered to help out not only financially but in any way possible. I was always proud to call myself a fan of the club but even prouder to have you as friends. Thank you for all your work.

Dave Cameron for taking time out of his hectic schedule to proofread the book. You're an absolute star - by the way any mistakes folks blame him!

Audrey Riordan in Cork, for proofing the remaining chapters Dave couldn't look at due to an extremely tight publishing schedule. Unfortunately I was left to do chapters 11-14 so watch out folks!

Keith Stone for you're magnificent photograph's and the way you automatically volunteered your help.

Martin Weiler for all those wonderful photo's including the St Albans snaps which gave those who didn't travel a sense of what it was like to get the soaking of a lifetime.

Leigh Page Photography for the amazing picture which adorns the back page.

Stephen Eames at St Albans for his detailed account of that day in Clarence park.

Jeff Connor and the paragraph from - POINTLESS. Words reproduced by permission of Hodder Headline GL.

Phil Minto at Pinnacle for the photograph and his words of wisdom about the Premiership Image rights!

For everyone at Exeter City who've endeavoured to help out with this publication in any way shape or form.

The North Devon Grecians for inviting me at Christmas and allowing me to present the book at your annual bash.

The East Devon Grecians. The Supporter's Trust and the commercial team at ECFC.

To George Hudd for the last minute Old Trafford photo's.

To my family for putting up with TWO books being wrote at the same time, especially my wife.

Ger, Josh & everyone at GK Print.

And the man above - my co-writer at all times through life.

If you all get as much enjoyment out of reading the book as I did in writing it, I be one happy camper.

BRIAN KENNEDY

A NOTE ON THE AUTHOR

Brian Kennedy was born in Waterford in 1969. Somehow between now and then he's managed to write five books and stay married to his long suffering wife.

His first book - CONFESSIONS OF AN EXETER CITY NUT - was released in 2004 and gained national media coverage in papers such as The Sun, Star, Mirror, Examiner and Irish Independent as well as television appearances on ITV, RTE and TV3.

A radio documentary of his life won a national PPI radio award in 2005.

His second offering, POOR 'OL HARRY SACK - the story of the most unluckiest gambler in the entire northern hemisphere, was released in June of 2006 and sold extremely well - the fact Kennedy got a local lap-dancing club to sponsor the book helped again get national press!

In December of 2006 Kennedy released his third book - SINGING THE BLUES, his own quirky look back at the history of local club Waterford United. The book quickly sold almost 1,000 copies in it's first two months, went into a reprint and remains Brian's biggest seller to date.

ONE FLEW OVER THE CROSSBAR is being released in November 2007, but just a month later Brian's fifth book - BLUE,WHITE & DYNAMITE, a collection of short stories about his local club Waterford, will be released as well.

Married to Sandra, they have two children - daughter Leanne and 18 month old son Callum. He features regularly on local radio and writes for The Grecian - Exeter's City's award winning programme.

An avid Arsenal fan, he still credit's the 26th of May 1989 as possibly the greatest moment in his life - Michael Thomas' goal to win the title at Anfield, however Exeter's 0-0 draw against Rochdale in 1997 runs it very close!

Future projects include completing the trilogy of Exeter City books and spending some well earned rest in a local mental institution.

WITH THANKS TO THE ExEC CLUB FOR MAKING IT ALL POSSIBLE.